THE **COMPLETE IDIOT'S GUIDE** TO

Total Nutrition Cooking

by Larrian Gillespie

ALPHA

A member of Penguin Group (USA) Inc.

ALPHA BOOKS

Published by the Penguin Group

Penguin Group (USA) Inc., 375 Hudson Street, New York, New York 10014, U.S.A.

Penguin Group (Canada), 10 Alcorn Avenue, Toronto, Ontario, Canada M4V 3B2 (a division of Pearson Penguin Canada Inc.)

Penguin Books Ltd, 80 Strand, London WC2R 0RL, England

Penguin Ireland, 25 St Stephen's Green, Dublin 2, Ireland (a division of Penguin Books Ltd)

Penguin Group (Australia), 250 Camberwell Road, Camberwell, Victoria 3124, Australia (a division of Pearson Australia Group Pty Ltd)

Penguin Books India Pvt Ltd, 11 Community Centre, Panchsheel Park, New Delhi—10 017, India

Penguin Group (NZ), cnr Airborne and Rosedale Roads, Albany, Auckland 1310, New Zealand (a division of Pearson New Zealand Ltd)

Penguin Books (South Africa) (Pty) Ltd, 24 Sturdee Avenue, Rosebank, Johannesburg 2196, South Africa

Penguin Books Ltd, Registered Offices: 80 Strand, London WC2R 0RL, England

International Standard Book Number: 1-59257-549-8
Library of Congress Catalog Card Number: 2006927522

08   07   06   8   7   6   5   4   3   2   1

Interpretation of the printing code: The rightmost number of the first series of numbers is the year of the book's printing; the rightmost number of the second series of numbers is the number of the book's printing. For example, a printing code of 06-1 shows that the first printing occurred in 2006.

Printed in the United States of America

Note: This publication contains the opinions and ideas of its author. It is intended to provide helpful and informative material on the subject matter covered. It is sold with the understanding that the author and publisher are not engaged in rendering professional services in the book. If the reader requires personal assistance or advice, a competent professional should be consulted.

The author and publisher specifically disclaim any responsibility for any liability, loss, or risk, personal or otherwise, which is incurred as a consequence, directly or indirectly, of the use and application of any of the contents of this book.

Most Alpha books are available at special quantity discounts for bulk purchases for sales promotions, premiums, fundraising, or educational use. Special books, or book excerpts, can also be created to fit specific needs.

For details, write: Special Markets, Alpha Books, 375 Hudson Street, New York, NY 10014.

Publisher: *Marie Butler-Knight*
Editorial Director: *Mike Sanders*
Managing Editor: *Billy Fields*
Acquisitions Editor: *Tom Stevens*
Development Editor: *Nancy D. Lewis*
Production Editor: *Megan Douglass*

Copy Editor: *Nancy Wagner*
Book Designers: *Trina Wurst/Kurt Owens*
Cover Designer: *Bill Thomas*
Indexer: *Tonya Heard*
Layout: *Ayanna Lacey*
Proofreader: *John Etchison*

Contents at a Glance

Contents

What the recipe symbols mean:

🌑 LOW SALT

🌑 GOOD SOURCE OF FIBER

🌑 LOW GLYCEMIC

🌑 LOW FAT

🌑 QUICK AND EASY

🌑 MAKE AHEAD

🌑 ONE POT

13 Fowl Play 141

Part 5: Side Dishes, Sassy Sauces and Dips, and Dessert Show Stoppers 241

15 Side Shows   243

Appendixes

Introduction

If you've become cranky hearing conflicting information about nutrition, this book is for you! It provides a comprehensive guide to cooking and to your becoming nutritionally fit in an easy-to-read format. I've written this book from both my personal and professional experiences as a physician and home cook who advises people how to eat and prepare their meals with total nutrition as their guide.

How to Use This Book

To make the reading of this book easy for everyone, I've divided it into five areas of interest:

Part 1, "Pyramid Power," clears up any confusion about the 2005 Food Pyramid. You'll learn the fundamentals of nutrition and what makes up each food category. I'll show you the importance of complex carbohydrates and powerful protein. You will learn how to separate the good fats from the bad and why fiber can be a secret to filling you up with fewer calories. Each person has his or her own special needs, so I've included a chapter on how to tailor your diet to help prevent heart disease, diabetes, high blood pressure, and cancer. And if you have any concerns that cooking with total nutrition in mind requires the mathematical skills of an Einstein, I've provided you with a sample seven-day menu plan that shows how easy it is cook nutritionally tasty meals.

Part 2, "Bountiful Breakfasts and Luscious Lunches," starts you on your way to making power-packed breakfast meals. First, you'll learn how to cook a simple egg recipe; then I'll take your skills up a notch and teach you how to make a frittata or oven-baked omelet. Waffles and pancakes will be your new secret health food when you see how I've adapted familiar recipes and even added chocolate! Cereals can be a minefield of nutrition dangers, but I'll guide you through them with my helpful tips and recipes. And dairy has taken a new role in weight control, so I'll teach you how to improve on your standard smoothie without pouring on the fat. Finally, you don't need to consume a Dagwood sandwich to get your daily fiber requirements. These recipes will make it easy to learn how to stack nutrition in your favor.

Part 3, "Soup-er Starters and Appeteasers," will let you party like a star. I'll tickle your mouth with delicious starters that will sparkle with loads of nutritional gems. No more cheese whiz on a cracker for you! You can feed a crowd with these recipes, or adapt them for an intimate dinner for two. You make the call. Soups can fill you up with memories of Mom's touch or help you make some of your own. You'll learn how easy it is to let a slow cooker be your helper when preparing vegetable soups. And when it comes to salads, these recipes can be a main course or just a simple addition to a scrumptious meal.

Part 4, "Mealtime Stars," takes you through every moveable source of protein and shows you how to prepare simple main courses with volumes of flavor. If you like to grill, you'll find lots of advice on how to cut the fat and new techniques for keeping your nutrition from going up in smoke. You'll learn my secret for guaranteed moist fish every time and ways to return the ocean flavor to frozen fish. I'll show you how to marinate, make the perfect roast turkey without basting, and turn out a meal in only 10 minutes with my rapid stir-fry techniques. Once you try these recipes, your family and friends will be clamoring for invites to your tasty dinner table. Who knew cooking nutritionally could be so much fun?

Part 5, "Side Dishes, Sassy Sauces and Dips, and Dessert Show Stoppers," will show you pastas and homemade sauces that will send everyone looking for your secret family recipes. You'll discover how to use condiments to make quick and easy sauces to dress up simple grilled meat without smothering the dish in calories. New choices in pasta products can improve your nutritional profile without losing taste, and you'll discover how to make your own pasta sauces without tons of salt or fat. I've given vegetables a new twist with recipes that can double as main meals. And no book on nutritional cooking would be complete without scrumptious desserts that feature comfort foods, cookies, and, yes, chocolate!

The appendixes contain a glossary of terms, conversion factors, and my handpicked sources for the best products that can help you simplify your cooking needs while ramping up the flavor.

Extras

To help you get the most from this book, I've added little helper information boxes.

Food for Thought
These tips will make cooking fun and easier.

Nutri Speak
Here's where you'll find definitions that will demystify food jargon.

Nutri Notes ———————
These notes contain information on nutrition and food
trivia that will put a smile on your
face or make you sound like a
real foodie.

 Smoke Signals ———————
You should keep these
warnings in mind as they may
affect your health.

Acknowledgments

To my mother Dorothy who drove me to cook simply because she couldn't.

To my daughter Alexian who fortunately married a man who can cook.

To my love Harsh who shares my enjoyment of life and food.

To my agent Marilyn Allen who recommended me for this project.

To Laughing Bettin' Rhett Butler, Scarlet the Harlot, Harley, Sapphire, and Spritzer, for being part of my tasting zoo and never rejecting a single recipe.

Trademarks

All terms mentioned in this book that are known to be or are suspected of being trademarks or service marks have been appropriately capitalized. Alpha Books and Penguin Group (USA) Inc. cannot attest to the accuracy of this information. Use of a term in this book should not be regarded as affecting the validity of any trademark or service mark.

Part

Pyramid Power

If you're confused about nutritional advice or have tried every popular diet but still don't feel healthy, then the first part of the book will prove to you that nutritious eating is neither complicated nor punishing.

This part will reveal the power of the new 2005 USDA Food Pyramid and give you the inside skinny on protein, carbohydrates, fat, fiber, and salt. Think of it as a basic tune-up for your nutritional engine. Once you grasp these basics, you'll be ready to start cooking from a total nutrition standpoint.

Understanding the New USDA Food Pyramid Nutrition Queens

In This Chapter

- ◆ Reviewing the new USDA Food Pyramid
- ◆ Discovering the treasure chest of healthy foods
- ◆ Making sure to exercise

If you're going crazy trying to figure out how to eat healthy, you're not alone. Almost every week another study comes out warning us that food once declared as healthy is anything but and may be contaminated with chemicals that are poisoning our bodies rather than helping to turn them into lean, mean, powerful machines. Add to this the billions of dollars behind the diet industry hawking one drastic plan after another to flush fat from our bodies, and we've become the fattest, most nutritionally confused generation ever.

Simply put, diets don't work. But eating and cooking with total nutrition in mind can change all of that, easily. No, I'm not talking about eating cardboard or tasteless weird stuff found only in trendy food chains or picked from endangered forests. I'm going to show you how to really eat healthy by preparing foods that will keep blood sugar levels down, put enough fiber into your diet to keep things moving without too much fat or salt, and at the same time help you avoid the consumption of mass quantities of calories as you accomplish this feat.

How can you do this, you ask in amazement? My answer is simply by choosing nutrient-dense selections from Mother Nature's house that anyone can prepare with ease while satisfying even the most persnickety eater. Now I can see that look of disbelief on your face, but it's true. All you have to do is understand how to select the Nutrition Queens from the new USDA Food Pyramid—you know, that Egyptian triangle that now has a set of steps running up to the top. The Nutrition Queens are the best choices in each of the categories of the food pyramid. Variety and portions hold the key to any healthy diet.

The New USDA Food Pyramid

In 1992, the United States Department of Agriculture (USDA) created a visual way to present the basic food groups, but they left out the importance of exercise as part of a healthy diet (hence the stairs in the new 2005 version). Also in the revised, updated Food Pyramid, oils were given a new importance in our diet and earned a separate category.

Over the years, scientific research has shown that not all fats are bad for us, leading to a better understanding of the health benefits observed from various diet lifestyles, such as the one consumed by people in the Mediterranean area. So let's put on our Indiana Jones hats and gather the keys to the treasures in the 2005 USDA Food Pyramid groups that can help all of us lead a healthy, totally nutritious, and fun lifestyle:

Food for Thought

To learn more about the new USDA Food Pyramid, visit http://mypyramid.gov. You'll find a pyramid just for kids, and you can customize your own Food Pyramid.

Group 1: Breads, cereal, rice, and pasta

Group 2: Vegetables and beans

Group 3: Fruits

Group 4: Milk, yogurt, and cheese

Group 5: Meat, poultry, fish, eggs, seeds, and nuts

Group 6: Oils

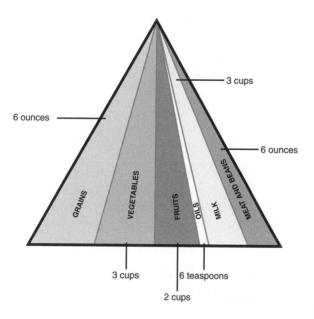

The new 2005 USDA Food Pyramid.

Let's examine these treasure chests of nutrition a little closer and see how they work.

Healthy *Whole Grains*

If ever there was a misunderstood food group, it's the mighty grains, the breads, cereal, rice, and pasta, rich in those starches and sugars called carbohydrates, which give us energy throughout the day. I know you've heard nothing but bad press about this category, but don't believe everything you read in a diet book. It's the processing and portion size that really matters.

In the "old days," breads were dense and made from whole grains rather than refined and processed flours which made them light and crushable as angel wings while stripping them of their complex nutritious elements, such as fiber, vitamins, and minerals. Portions also grew as we megasized everything from breakfast cereals to mac and cheese. USDA guidelines recommend 6 **one-ounce** servings per day.

Smoke Signals

Ounces are what's listed on your food labels. If you want to cook properly, you weigh items like pasta and rice, otherwise you end up serving too much. This is a very common problem.

This may sound like a lot, but just check out how teeny tiny a single serving of your favorites can be:

- ¼ large bagel
- 1 regular slice of bread
- 5 whole-wheat crackers
- 1 ounce DRY pasta
- ½ English muffin
- 1 ounce DRY oatmeal
- 1 small pancake
- 1 ounce uncooked rice
- 1 small tortilla
- 2 TB. unpopped popcorn
- ¼ cup cereal flakes

Now don't look so sad! Lots of carbohydrates contain nutrient-dense elements that can fill you up on less volume and with fewer calories and more health benefits than refined, highly processed versions. Just look at this list of *whole grains*:

- Barley
- Buckwheat
- Millet
- Oats
- Quinoa
- Rice, brown
- Rye
- Spelt
- Wheat, stone-ground

Nutri Speak

Whole grains or foods made from them contain all the essential parts and naturally occurring nutrients of the entire grain seed. If they are processed, the grain must provide the same rich nutrient balance as found in the whole grain.

Again, portion size does matter, but the grains listed above just happen to be higher in fiber than other varieties, and fiber not only fills you up, but can help lower your risk of heart disease and certain cancers, not to mention give you a boost in maintaining a healthy weight. So let's open the next nutritional treasure chest and see what we find.

Voluptuous Vegetables and Bountiful Beans

Fresh or flash-frozen vegetables are loaded with important vitamins and minerals, not to mention fiber, without the booby trap of a lot of calories or fat. USDA guidelines recommend 2 to 3 **cups** a day depending on activity, but this is one category where you really can't overdo it when selecting high-quality produce. Just look at what makes a **one-cup** serving:

- ◆ 2 cups raw greens, such as collards, spinach, lettuce, or romaine
- ◆ 2 medium carrots
- ◆ 1 large baked sweet potato
- ◆ 1 cup cooked squash, such as acorn, butternut, or zucchini
- ◆ 1 cup cooked beans, such as black beans, garbanzo, pinto, or kidney
- ◆ 1 ear corn
- ◆ 1 cup green peas
- ◆ 1 medium baked potato (not the megasize offered in the store)
- ◆ 1 cup raw broccoli or cauliflower florets
- ◆ 1 cup raw cucumbers
- ◆ 1 cup cabbage
- ◆ 2 large stalks celery
- ◆ 1 cup yellow or green beans
- ◆ 1 large sweet bell pepper
- ◆ 1 cup raw mushrooms
- ◆ 1 large tomato

Food for Thought
Choose rich, colorful vegetables because they contain higher levels of important nutrients and phytochemicals, such as vitamin A and vitamin C.

Looking for the best veggies and beans with the highest amount of vitamins, minerals, fiber, essential fatty acids, and phytonutrients? Then try these little nutrient-dense gems:

Asparagus	Collard Greens	Leeks	Squash
Avocado	Cucumber	Mushrooms	Swiss Chard
Bell Peppers	Eggplant	Mustard Greens	Tomatoes
Broccoli	Fennel bulb	Olives	Turnip Greens
Brussels Sprouts	Garlic	Onions	Beets
Cabbage	Green beans	Parsley	Carrots

Cauliflower	Green peas	Lettuce	Potatoes
Celery	Kale	Spinach	Yams
Black beans	Miso	Navy beans	Dried peas
Garbanzo beans	Pinto beans	Kidney beans	Soybeans
Lentils	Tempeh	Lima beans	Tofu

I bet I've listed many of your favorites. So let's open the next food treasure chest.

Fabulous Fruits

Think sweet and natural, and you've got Mother Nature's candy in your hand. Whole fruits with the peel offer a higher fiber count than juices, many of which are diluted with water and added sugar. The USDA recommends 2 **one cup** servings a day. Just one serving of fruit is:

- 1 small apple with the skin
- 1 large banana
- 32 seedless grapes
- 1 medium grapefruit
- 1 large orange
- 1 large peach
- 1 medium pear
- 3 medium plums
- 8 large strawberries
- 1 small wedge watermelon

These little nutrient-dense fruit gems can sparkle in anyone's shopping cart and will give you tons of benefit with fewer calories:

Apple	Grapefruit	Pineapple
Apricot	Grapes	Plum
Banana	Kiwi	Prune
Blueberries	Lemons/limes	Raisins
Cantaloupe	Orange	Raspberries
Cranberries	Papaya	Strawberries
Fig	Pear	Watermelon

See how easy this is becoming when you follow a healthy, nutritional selection of foods? Just tag along behind me to the next treasure chest.

Milk Matters

Nutrition experts wouldn't think of missing out on this category: milk, yogurt, and cheese, which can provide protein, vitamins, and minerals along with a highly digestible form of calcium, necessary for strong bones and teeth. Only foods that retain their calcium content are in this particular treasure chest, which eliminates butter, cream cheese, and cream. Reduced fat versions can help save unnecessary calories, but be sure there is some fat in order to absorb vitamin D, a necessary friend to calcium. USDA guidelines recommend 3 **one cup** servings a day. That means each serving can be:

♦ 1 cup reduced-fat milk

♦ 8 ounces plain yogurt

♦ 1¹/₂ ounces natural cheese

♦ 2 ounces processed cheese

♦ 2 cups cottage cheese

♦ ¹/₂ cup ricotta cheese

♦ 1¹/₂ cups low-fat ice cream

Nutri Speak

Even though two cups of cottage cheese is more than one cup, it is still considered a one-cup serving. Check out the website at http://mypyramid. gov and click on the serving samples for more examples.

Dairy products are an important source of calcium, which can help build strong bones and maintain a healthy weight. You don't need to consume full-fat versions to get most of the benefits. Reduced-fat versions will provide you with enough necessary fat to help you absorb vitamin D along with the calcium.

Okay, so now I can really see you smile, so let's hurry along to the next food treasure chest.

Svelte Meat

Meat, poultry, fish, eggs, seeds, and nuts—well, this is a big category because it's a major source of protein in your diet as well as the B vitamins, zinc, and iron. However, to avoid too much saturated fat, choose lean cuts. USDA guidelines recommend 5 to 6 **one ounce** servings. A serving is:

♦ 1 ounce of cooked meat, poultry, or fish

♦ ¹/₄ cup cooked beans (they count in both categories depending on whether or not you are a vegetarian)

- 1 egg

- 1 TB. peanut butter

- ¹/₂ ounce of nuts or seeds

- 2 TB. hummus

- 2 oz. tofu

- 1 oz. tempeh

Looking for the most nutrient-dense meat, fish, and nuts? Just choose from this sparkling selection:

Cod	Almonds	Eye of round	Calf's liver
Halibut	Cashews	Top round	Chicken
Salmon	Flaxseeds	Round tip	Lamb, loin
Scallops	Peanuts	Top sirloin	Turkey breast
Shrimp	Pumpkin seeds	Bottom round	Venison
Snapper	Sesame seeds	Top loin	Bison
Tuna, yellowfin	Walnuts	Tenderloin	Rabbit

Food for Thought

Iron is important for building a healthy blood profile. Best sources are animal proteins, such as liver, shellfish, beef, pork, lamb, and poultry.

If possible, select organic meats and wild rather than farm-raised fish, as the fat and skin of traditional sources may contain antibiotics, pesticides, or chemicals which can affect the hormone balance in your body. Sadly, contaminated food has become a reality of our world. For up-to-date information on health studies and nutrition, visit www.totalnutritioncooking.com.

Friendly Fats

The next treasure chest of nutrition, the oils group, became an official category with the new Food Pyramid, thanks to a better understanding of the differences between types of oils and fats. While you should keep solid, saturated fats to a minimum, fats high in monounsaturated fat can actually help lower cholesterol in the body … you know, that fatty acid in your blood that can clog up arteries and lead to a heart attack or stroke.

Hydrogenation, the process that turns liquid fats, such as vegetable oil, into partially solid versions that can be used to make margarine, may result in triggering inflammation in your body. These fats, called trans fats because they transform liquid fats into somewhat solid ones, inhibit the absorption of important omega fatty acids and can cause a deficiency in essential fatty acids in our bodies. And this is not a good thing!

Trans fats also hide in foods making them harder to detect. But as of 2006, food labels must show the amount of trans fats in a product, such as fried foods or baked goods like a cookie. You'll find the amount listed under the TOTAL FAT category. However, this is not foolproof, as tinkering with the serving size can reduce the amount to less than 0.5 grams, which does not have to be reported. So what fats can help us lead a totally nutrition-oriented lifestyle without oodles of trans fat? These can:

Food for Thought

For a complete understanding about nutrition, read *The Complete Idiot's Guide to Total Nutrition* by Joy Bauer. It's full of easy-to-follow nutrition advice and information on how to make healthy choices even when dining out.

- ◆ Olive oil
- ◆ Canola oil
- ◆ Peanut oil
- ◆ Soybean oil
- ◆ Sunflower oil
- ◆ Safflower oil

Olive, canola, and peanut oil have the highest levels of monounsaturated fats without the dangers of trans fats. These oils are also a major source of vitamin E, an important antioxidant that helps to combat inflammation that can cause heart disease, high blood pressure, and strokes. However, like all fats, one tablespoon contains 120 calories, making it easy to overconsume in this category. But don't worry! I'll give you some tricks for keeping your fat intake in line that won't hurt a bit. USDA guidelines recommend 5 to 6 teaspoons a day, which is no more than 2 tablespoons per person. But the amount of fat in foods varies. Just look at how many teaspoons of oil are in these common choices:

Food	Amount of Oil
¹/₂ medium avocado	3 tsp.
2 TB. vinaigrette salad dressing	2 tsp.
1 TB. mayonnaise-style dressing	2¹/₂ tsp.
4 large olives	¹/₂ tsp.

continues

continued

Food	Amount of Oil
1 TB. margarine without trans fats	2^1/$_2$ tsp.
1 TB. mayonnaise	2^1/$_2$ tsp.
2 TB. peanut butter	4 tsp.
1 oz. nuts	3 tsp.
1 oz. seeds	3 tsp.

Don't look so glum. I know it may seem tough, but when you start cooking with total nutrition in mind, you'll be enjoying the best fats with fewer calories. Now that's a healthy treasure!

Exhilarating Exercise

Keeping ourselves moving has become a challenge in today's world because we've replaced physical action with "digital" response. Basically, we spend too much time sitting and not enough raising our heart rates in a good way. Without physical exercise, we simply can't maintain a healthy weight. I've searched the scientific literature to find some way to disprove this concept, but the facts are clear: we need to exercise 30 minutes a day, not just lifting forks to our faces but working our entire bodies as well.

Food for Thought

For more information on exercise, visit The American College of Sports Medicine for guidelines on healthy exercise at www.acsm.org.

The key is making exercise consistent and enjoyable. So think about dancing, taking a walk around the neighborhood each night, gardening, or even playing sports as a key part of your goal when cooking with total nutrition in mind. That's why the new USDA Food Pyramid added steps up the side—to remind us that eating and exercising go hand in hand.

The Least You Need to Know

◆ Eating a variety of foods from the Six Food Groups can help you plan a nutritionally balanced diet without focusing on counting calories.

◆ Choose nutrient-dense foods for the biggest health bang for the buck. You'll save on calories while getting the best vitamins, minerals, fiber, carbs, and protein with the least amount of fat.

◆ Move! Plan a regular time of day for your 30 minutes of exercise, and be consistent. You'll stay focused, alert, and energetic.

Chapter 2

Tailoring Your Diet

In This Chapter

- Diet, exercise, and your health
- Keeping your blood sugar levels in check
- Maintaining variety and balance in your diet
- Portion control to keep satisfied

We all need motivation when it comes to change, and eating healthy is no exception. Too often we wait until something drastic happens in our lives to make a serious change in our habits. I don't want this to happen to you or someone you love, so let me encourage you to adopt a totally nutritious way of eating that will give you more energy, a certain lift in your step, and sparkle in your eyes while fueling your body with the best sources of key macronutrients.

Healthy Hearts

Keeping a healthy heart has as much to do with your lifestyle as it does with your genetics. Inflammation is the key to disease in the body, and obesity, smoking, lack of exercise, and poor nutrition contribute more than

50 percent to your chances of doing a face plant on the dining room floor from a heart attack or stroke. Just look at these statistics*:

♦ Heart disease is the leading cause of death for all Americans age 35 and older.

♦ Every 33 seconds someone in the United States dies from heart disease.

♦ Thirty-seven percent of all American deaths are due to heart disease.

♦ Heart disease and stroke account for 7 million hospitalizations every year.

♦ Heart disease causes disability in over 10 million Americans age 65 and older.

♦ 71,300,000 Americans have heart disease, high blood pressure, or strokes.

*Statistics are from the National Center for Health Statistics, 2003 report.

That sends shivers up my spine! But look at another common condition brought on by obesity and inadequate nutrition.

> **Smoke Signals**
>
> Soy protein is low in saturated fat and contains no cholesterol, which is good for your heart. However, the type of soy used in the United States is not the same as in Asia. Soy isoflavones can block thyroid function. If you have thyroid disease, do not use soy products.

Type 2 Diabetes

A change in our body's ability to handle glucose is a leading cause of inflammation that can result in damage to numerous vital parts. Instead of using the sugar in our blood to fuel the energy for our muscles to work, the body becomes "resistant" to the hormone messenger insulin and stores the extra sugar as body fat. This can lead to high blood pressure or high cholesterol levels in the blood, which in turn can cause a heart attack or stroke. Type 1 Diabetes is due to pancreatic damage and is inherited, while Type 2 is "late onset" and related to diet and obesity.

The shocking news is, Type 2 Diabetes is no longer a condition of the "over 40" crowd but is increasingly being diagnosed in our children, mainly due to improper nutritional choices and lack of exercise. Take a look at these statistics*:

♦ Diabetes is the sixth leading cause of death in the United States.

♦ 28 million people in the United States have diabetes.

♦ 1.3 million new cases are diagnosed each year.

♦ 210,000 people UNDER THE AGE OF 20 have diabetes. The figure may be much higher due to underreporting.

- Sixty-five percent of deaths among people with diabetes are due to heart disease and stroke.

- Diabetes is the leading cause of blindness among adults.

- Total cost of treating diabetes is $132,000,000,000 each year.

*Source is the American Diabetes Association, 2002 estimates.

Diabetes is the leading cause of non-traumatic amputations and kidney disease, not to mention a significant reason for miscarriage and tooth decay.

Nutri Notes

In 250 C.E., diabetes was diagnosed by tasting the urine of a sick person. Urine with high glucose and ketones present has a sweet, metallic taste.

High Blood Pressure

Carrying around those extra pounds from eating highly processed foods with loads of salt and the wrong fats can lead to another condition that can shorten your life. The condition I'm talking about is high blood pressure.

Your arteries serve as the network to carry blood throughout the body. As your heart pumps away, pressure is created within the walls of these arteries. Clog up those pathways with cholesterol plaques or damage their lining, and you get an increase in pressure, called hypertension. Now increase the volume of fluid that needs to pass along these traffic routes, and you've got the makings for a real pressure situation that can damage delicate organs in your body. High blood pressure has become an increasingly common finding in people with less than ideal nutrition and a leading cause of damage to their health. Consider these statistics*:

- 5 million premature deaths occur worldwide each year from high blood pressure.
- The incidence of hypertension increases with age, especially among women post menopause.
- Only 29 percent of those with high blood pressure have it under control.
- 50,000,000 Americans have high blood pressure.
- High blood pressure causes heart disease and strokes, the leading cause of death in the United States.

*Statistics are from American Heart Association, 2004.

Cancer

Nutrition also plays a critical role in another condition we've all heard about … cancer.

When cells in the body go a bit "mad," they change their normal reproductive pathways and become deranged, unruly little monsters that beat up on normal tissue in the body. In the early stages, potent chemicals in the body can sweep up cancer cells and destroy them, but if you don't keep those fighting soldiers in tip-top shape, they can be overwhelmed, allowing cancer terrorists to spread throughout the body. Just look at these statistics*:

One third of the 564,830 expected cancer deaths in 2006 will be related to poor nutrition, lack of exercise, and obesity, all of which can be prevented.

> **Nutri Notes**
>
> The American Cancer Society estimates that 10.1 million Americans with a history of cancer are alive in 2002. That's good news; here's some bad news. In 2006, they expect 170,000 deaths from smoking-related cancers alone. If you smoke, *stop!*

- 1,399,790 new cases of cancer will be diagnosed in 2006.
- $209,900,000,000 will be spent on the cost of treating cancer in the United States in 2006.

*Statistics are from The American Cancer Society, 2006.

Learning to eat with total nutrition in mind can be a potent weapon against a premature death. It can help you keep a healthy weight while boosting your immune system to protect vital organs. So what are some of the keys to cooking with total nutrition in mind?

Pulp Fiction

Fiber is a magic food which comes from the cell walls of plants and passes through the body like a giant vacuum cleaner, sweeping up cholesterol and slowing the release of sugar into the bloodstream. Fiber comes in two varieties: soluble and insoluble, depending on its ability to dissolve (or not) in water. Check out these great sources of fiber:

Soluble	Insoluble
Oats	Wheat bran
Brown rice	Corn bran

Soluble	Insoluble
Barley	Whole-wheat breads
Oat bran	Whole-wheat cereals
Dried beans	Fruits with the peel
Rye	Potatoes with skin
Seeds	Parsnips with skin
Carrots	Green beans
Corn	Broccoli
Cauliflower	
Fruits	

Some foods, such as fruits and vegetables, can provide both types of fiber, which makes them real nutritional gems. Insoluble fiber helps you keep a healthy bowel, which can decrease your risk for colon cancer. Fiber can give harmful bacteria or carcinogenic substances discarded from our foods the rush out of the body, making softer, more regular bowel movements.

Fiber can also help lower cholesterol, especially soluble fiber. Pectins in fruit and some vegetables bind with cholesterol preventing its absorption into the bloodstream. This helps to keep your arteries clean as a whistle so your blood pressure stays down.

Eating fiber-rich foods can have another benefit: they can fill you up with fewer calories. Soluble fiber tends to stick around in your stomach for a while, so you feel fuller

Nutri Notes

We also use pectin to make jelly beans, but you won't find your doctor writing a prescription for them to lower your cholesterol. Products high in sugar can stimulate insulin, which will increase your cholesterol.

longer. That means you won't miss the extra calories from high-fat, high-caloric foods that's you've eliminated from your diet. USDA guidelines recommend 25 to 35 grams of fiber a day. The recipes in this book are marked for good sources of fiber and will show you how easy it is to reach this goal when cooking with total nutrition in mind. One word of caution: *do not* exceed the recommended range, as too much fiber can block the absorption of necessary vitamins and minerals, especially calcium, zinc, magnesium, and iron.

Looking for some of the best fiber-rich foods? Try this selection:

Food	Grams Fiber
Bulgur wheat (1 cup)	16.00
Fiber 1 cereal (1/2 cup)	12.90
Garbanzo beans (1 cup)	10.56
100% bran (1/2 cup)	9.75
Barley (1 cup cooked)	8.80
All Bran (1/2 cup)	8.40
Pinto beans (1/2 cup cooked)	6.40
Raspberries (1 cup)	5.50
Bran flakes (1/4 cup)	5.00
Navy beans (1/2 cup cooked)	4.70
Pear (1 average size)	4.65
Kidney beans (1/2 cup cooked)	4.30
Blueberries (1 cup)	4.00
Green peas (1/2 cup cooked)	4.00
Broccoli (1/2 cup cooked)	3.60
Prunes (5 pieces)	3.00
Apple (1 medium)	3.00
Orange (1 medium)	3.00
Sweet potato (1 small)	3.00
Carrots (1/2 cup cooked)	2.50
Grapes (1 1/2 cups)	2.30
Spinach (1/2 cup cooked)	2.20
Banana (1 large)	2.00

Source: Now You're Cooking Program Database, 2006

You can see how many delicious foods contain oodles of fiber that can turn any recipe into a truly nutritious one. So let's tackle another way you can improve on your total nutrition.

Hold the Salt

If you've been feeling a little bloated lately, you may be carrying around extra water weight from ingesting too much salt. I know you think you're being careful by not making the salt shaker your sixth appendage, but salt is hidden in the majority of processed foods, such as soups, lunch meats, cheese, cereals, bread, and nuts. The USDA recommends that we limit our daily salt intake to no more than 2400 mg. That's about 1 teaspoon of table salt. Now consider how much salt is hidden in foods, and you can understand why you might be consuming much more salt than you thought.

Too much fluid in the body can increase your blood pressure, which can affect the kidneys and your heart. Some people are more "salt sensitive" than others, but the human body only needs $1/10$ teaspoon of salt each day to maintain a normal fluid balance. All of us could afford to cut back on our salt intake so I've provided recipes labeled low salt in this cookbook that contain no more than 140 mg. of sodium per serving. I guarantee you won't miss out on flavor!

Nutri Notes

Salt was once considered so precious it was traded as money and even taxed. Salt has also been valued for its medicinal qualities and ability to preserve foods such as meats.

Sea salt is hands down the best form of salt because it contains over 92 minerals that are necessary for good health. Commercially refined salt has only sodium and chloride present, along with iodine, sugar, and aluminum silicate. If you taste commercial grade salt, you get a bitter taste. However, natural sea salt is somewhat sweet. Cooks are enjoying the use of various types of sea salt, harvested from the coasts of Normandy, Ireland, and Hawaii. Interestingly, 1 teaspoon of sea salt contains only 1800 mg. of sodium. You'll find sea salt in specialty food stores or online. I've included my favorite sources in Appendix C.

Mix the Fats

Fats are important for hormone function, but they also contain 9 calories per gram, more than twice the calorie count per gram of proteins or carbs. Like many things, there are good fats and bad fats, but a new category of products may actually help to handcuff cholesterol.

Plant sterol spreads, such as Take Control, Benecol, or Smart Balance contain substances naturally found in small quantities in whole grains, vegetables, fruits, beans, nuts, and seeds. These elements, which look a lot like cholesterol, get in the way of real cholesterol, blocking its ability to be absorbed from your digestive track. Using products fortified with plant sterols and stanols can lower the bad cholesterol in your blood, LDL, by 20 points. But should everyone use them?

There's no question these products can be of benefit to many people fighting cholesterol issues, but using a supplement rather than consuming more of the natural product, such as whole grains, may not provide you with all the advantages. You'll find I have combined unsalted butter or monounsaturated oils with plant sterol spreads in many recipes to help you get the maximum benefit from each food.

Remember, fat from any source still provides a lot of calories, so you can't use plant sterol spreads in unlimited quantities. Mixing the fats, however, can give you the best of both worlds while improving your total nutrition. Look for recipes marked low fat in this book, as less than 30 percent of their calories are derived from fat and can easily help you stay slim, trim, and healthy.

Sweet Satisfaction

Sugar is an acquired taste, literally. We are not born with a requirement for sugar, and the USDA recommends no minimum amount. The average American consumes 150 pounds of sugar a year. So why are we so addicted to this sweet satisfaction?

Sugar triggers the release of the brain's natural pleasure chemicals, called beta endorphins, the same chemicals affected by morphine and heroin. That's why we get a "sugar high" when we eat it, but for some that's followed by withdrawal symptoms and a need for more sugar. Carbohydrates provide sugar or glucose for the body's energy source, but some of these carbs provide little else in nutrition for our bodies. Choosing complex carbohydrates, such as vegetables, whole grains, and fruits, provides not only fuel for your body but also lots of phytochemicals, vitamins, minerals, and fiber. Nutrient-dense carbs, as listed in the first chapter, are the best choice for sugar when cooking from a total nutrition perspective.

New research has focused on the rate a food can release sugar into the bloodstream, called the Glycemic Index. However, this approach does not take into consideration the amount of carbohydrates per serving. The Glycemic Load multiplies the Glycemic Index score times the number of carbohydrates in a serving to give a better understanding of how quickly that food will cause a rise in your blood sugar. I've labeled recipes in this book that are good for those watching their sugar response with a low glycemic symbol.

Food for Thought

For more information on the Glycemic Index and Glycemic Load of foods, visit www.glycemicindex.com.

Sugar substitutes have been controversial, but I feel they can be of benefit when you need a little sweetness but don't have room for the additional calories. Not all sugar substitutes are created equal when it comes to withstanding temperature levels.

Sucralose is a sweetener which you can use for baking as well as sweetening that cup of iced tea. Mixtures of sweeteners are commercially available as blends expanding our cooking repertoire even further. If you don't wish to use these substitutes, you can always use refined cane sugar. Just remember, one teaspoon adds 16 calories to any dish.

Portion Patrol

Now that you understand which foods are the best choices, you can eat *all* you want of them, right? Not a chance. The Fat Fairy will be visiting your doorstep faster than a bullet train if you think calories don't matter. Megasizing has become a national pastime, dramatically increasing the size of "standard" portions from twenty years ago. Don't believe me? Then take my Portion Distortion quiz at www.totalnutritioncooking.com/Portionquiz.htm. It's quite an eye opener!

I know many diets out there tell you calories are not important, but it's the carbs … or the protein … or when you eat specific foods and in what combination that will make you lose weight. You would need the metabolism and the exercise of a hummingbird to pull that one off! So let me share with you a few secrets to keeping control of your portion sizes:

◆ Get a food scale. I can attest to this one from personal experience. I thought I knew how much a serving of breakfast cereal was until I weighed my standard amount. I was shocked to discover I had three servings in my bowl. Pasta is another killer. A standard serving is really small and pales in comparison to a restaurant's portion, which could easily feed a family of four! Look for a scale that allows you to zero out the bowl. You'll not only save calories but money as well when you adjust your expectations for these products.

◆ Use smaller plates. Studies show that what our eyes take in tells our stomachs how much to expect. If the plate looks full, we're convinced we've been fed enough. I know it sounds like a stupid trick, but who says our stomach is that smart anyway? So serve dinner on luncheon plates and breakfast on a salad plate. Put a scoop of ice cream in a teacup rather than a larger bowl. Works for me!

◆ Think of your plate as a clock. Divide it into quarters, and put two servings of vegetables, one serving of protein, and one serving of whole grain on the plate. You'll always find time to eat right with this approach.

Food for Thought

For more information on mini meals, pick up a copy of *The Menopause Diet Mini Meal Cookbook* by Larrian Gillespie or visit www.menopausediet.com.

♦ Consider eating five or six times a day. Research shows that consuming equal meals around 250 to 300 calories at a time keeps your blood sugar levels smooth and steady. Just think of them as mini meals that you can have every 3 to 4 hours. Not only will this keep your body fueled all day long, but it can also rev up your metabolism to burn more fat.

♦ Read labels. Serving sizes can be manipulated to meet government standards for nutrition claims. Check and see if the portion size makes sense.

Cooking with total nutrition in mind can do a lot more than save on your grocery bill. Instead of waiting in an emergency room or your doctor's office to undergo tests, you'll have more time to do what makes you happy—being with your family and friends.

The Least You Need to Know

♦ Diet and exercise can prevent nearly half of the causes for premature death.

♦ Focus on keeping your blood sugar levels in control while keeping salt and fats to a minimum.

♦ Choose a variety of foods in each category to get the maximum health benefits from your diet. Balance your diet with a mix of nutrient-dense foods and newer, enhanced products to give yourself a healthy profile.

♦ Portions *do* matter, so learn how to eat without feeling a need to stuff yourself. You'll be satisfied and consume fewer calories when selecting lean protein, good fats, and high-fiber vegetables.

Chapter 3

Sample Seven-Day Meal Plan

In This Chapter

- ◆ Using the recipes in this book
- ◆ Unlimited combinations
- ◆ Ready, set, get cooking!

Now that you understand the basics of cooking with total nutrition in mind, let me show you how to use this book to suit your particular nutritional needs. I have identified recipes for you that meet the following requirements and have marked them with these symbols:

⬤ This recipe has 30 percent or less of its calories coming from fat per serving.

⬤ This recipe will provide 2.5 gm. or more of fiber per serving.

⬤ This recipe has approximately 140 mg. or less of sodium per serving.

⬤ This recipe contains a moderate glycemic load of carbohydrates to help control blood sugar.

⬤ This recipe will take 30 minutes or less to prepare and cook.

⬤ Make this recipe ahead, and reheat or complete it later.

⬤ Make this recipe in one pot or a slow cooker.

If you need to restrict your sodium consumption, just select the recipes marked with the ⬤ symbol. If you want to follow a low-fat profile, look for the ⬤ symbol. It's really that simple.

Unlimited Combinations

The Complete Idiot's Guide to Total Nutrition Cooking allows you unlimited combinations of great foods just by swapping one ingredient in the same category for another. Say you don't like broccoli but adore zucchini. Terrific! Just substitute your favorite nutrient-dense vegetable for another. If you need help, all you have to do is refer to the lists in Chapter 1. I've also given you more information in each recipe chapter along with some recipe variations.

Ready, Set, Get Cooking!

Now for some really practical advice. You don't have to make each and every meal nutritionally perfect. Your daily needs vary as well as your energy requirements, so look for an *average weekly balance* rather than daily when planning your meals. Just keep these guidelines in mind:

- ◆ Keep sodium consumption to less than 2400 mg. a day on average.
- ◆ Keep the calories from fat to no more than 30 percent and saturated fat to around 10 to no more than 15 grams a day on average.
- ◆ Try to consume 25 to 35 grams of fiber a day on average.

Food for Thought

If you want to create your own recipes, try "Now You're Cooking" software which I used to design all these recipes. You can find more information at www.totalnutritioncooking.com.

Cooking with total nutrition in mind is not a boot camp approach. It's about spending time with your family nurturing them with the best food you can prepare to help them live a healthy, balanced life.

Take a look at this Seven-Day Menu Plan I have put together from recipes in this book. Each day varies in the amount of calories, fat percentage, sodium, and fiber, but when you average the week out, you get a terrific healthy week of balanced nutrition. So wrap that apron around your waist, and get cooking!

Day 1

Breakfast:

Pear Almond Buttermilk Waffles, 2 servings (page 48)
2 TB. plant sterol spread

Snack:

Red, White, and Blue Cottage Cheese (page 52)

Lunch:

Grandma's Chicken and Rice Soup (page 93)
Down Under Berry Kiwi Salad (page 111)

Snack:

Peaches and Cream Sparkler (page 52)

Dinner:

Artichokes with Garlic Sauce (page 244)
Broiled Lemon Sole (page 120)
Devil's Own Angel Food Cake (page 292)

1437.19 calories
113.57 g. protein
154.78 g. carbohydrate
30.22 g. total fat
11.2 g. saturated fat
19.6% calories from fat
134.57 mg. cholesterol
1853.05 mg. sodium
24.03 g. fiber

Day 2

Breakfast:

Chocolate Peanut Butter Smoothie (page 51)

Snack:

Apple Cheese Stick (page 54)

Lunch:

Tuna Bean Salad Sandwich (page 72)

Snack:

Honey Bunny's Carrot Salad, 2 servings (page 107)

Dinner:

Curry Dip (page 264)
$^1/_2$ cup carrots
$^1/_2$ cup celery
Grilled Citrus Chicken (page 152)
Sound of Music Blueberry Cream (page 310)

1449.31 calories
104.72 g. protein
185.18 g. carbohydrate
39.12 g. total fat
13.13 g. saturated fat
25% calories from fat
212.97 mg. cholesterol
1729.32 mg. sodium
31.91 g. fiber

Day 3

Breakfast:

Peachy Wheat Germ Crunch (page 61)
1 slice Oroweat Honey Fiber Bread
1 TB. plant sterol spread

Snack:

$^1/_2$ avocado

Lunch:

Pecos Bill Tomato Chili Salad (page 108)
Whole-Wheat Low-Carb Tortilla

Snack:

Zucchini Mint Soup (page 102)

Dinner:

Fettuccine with Broccoli and Carrots (page 270)
Eggplant Towers (page 247)
Almond Chocolate Pudding (page 300)

1304.95 calories
57.15 g. protein
165.71 g. carbohydrate
52.36 g. total fat
10.37 g. saturated fat
36% calories from fat
84.73 mg. cholesterol
1262.63 mg. sodium
34.02 g. fiber

Day 4

Breakfast:

Sunrise Frittata with Tomatoes, Zucchini, and Onions, 2 servings (page 36)
1 slice Oroweat Honey Fiber Bread
1 TB plant sterol spread

Snack:

Sweet Shrimp and Pineapple Salad (page 112)

Lunch:

Turkey Wrap (page 166)
Snickering Doodles Cookies, 2 (page 302)

Snack:

Hot Ginger Pear Soup (page 97)

Dinner:

Saigon Beef BBQ (page 186)
Sesame Lemon Broccoli (page 253)
Roasted Summer Fruit (page 311)

1415.1 calories
89.83 g. protein
176.17 g. carbohydrate
42.69 g. total fat
12.55 g. saturated fat
27% calories from fat
195.44 mg. cholesterol
1570.43 mg. sodium
41.3 g. fiber

Day 5

Breakfast:

Kellogg's Special K Low-Carb Lifestyle with Blueberries (page 60)
1 cup 2 percent milk

Snack:

Roasted Asparagus, cold (page 253)

Lunch:

Fruit and Yogurt Mélange (page 53)

Snack:

Portobello Tomato Basil Sandwich (page 65)

Dinner:

Tilapia with Zucchini, Fennel, and Onion (page 139)
Wild Rice with Tangerine and Pine Nuts (page 286)
Chili Coffee Mocha Custard (page 305)

1379.8 calories
90.06 g. protein
164.7 g. carbohydrate
41.44 g. total fat
13.19 g. saturated fat
27% calories from fat
104.83 mg. cholesterol
920.82 mg. sodium
25.91 g. fiber

Day 6

Breakfast:

Connemara Steel Cut Oatmeal with Cinnamon and Raisins (page 57)
$1/2$ cup 2 percent milk

Snack:

1 apple with skin
1 rye crisp cracker slice

Lunch:

Tomato Salad with Cottage Cheese (page 114)

Snack:

1 oz. pistachios

Dinner:

Penne with Shrimp, Asparagus, and Walnuts (page 274)
Earl Grey Orange Granita with Mint (page 307)

1449.42 calories
99.37 g. protein
164.94 g. carbohydrate
56.57 g. total fat
8.58 g. saturated fat
35% calories from fat
139.88 mg. cholesterol
1013.7 mg. sodium
37.77 g. fiber

Day 7

Breakfast:

Simply Simple Eggs and Canadian Bacon (page 35)
1 slice Oroweat Honey Fiber Bread
1 TB. plant sterol spread

Snack:

Sourdough Tomato and Ricotta Cheese Sandwich (page 53)

Lunch:

Crab in Spicy Orange Dressing (page 105)
Apple Date Pecan Oat Bar (page 299)

Snack:

Fish Soft Taco (page 123)

Dinner:

Tangerine Chicken with Almonds and Raisins (page 158)
Aztec Zucchini Salad (page 107)
Poached Pears with Blackberry Balsamic Sauce (page 310)

1489.42 calories
122.02 g. protein
128.53 g. carbohydrate
57.49 g. total fat

16.56 g. saturated fat
34% calories from fat
492.45 mg. cholesterol
1151.45 mg. sodium
28.67 g. fiber

Weekly Average

1417.88 calories
96.67 g. protein (27%)
162.85 g. carbohydrate (45%)
45.69 g. total fat (29%)
12.22 g. saturated fat (7%)
186.05 mg. cholesterol
1357.34 mg. sodium
31.94 g. fiber

The Least You Need to Know

♦ Look for recipes marked with symbols that match your particular nutritional needs.

♦ Variety is great, so feel free to exchange foods from a similar category for each other in any recipe.

♦ Concentrate on a weekly, not daily, average of nutrients when planning your meals.

Part 2

Bountiful Breakfasts and Luscious Lunches

Breakfast is the most important meal of the day because it provides the fuel to keep your body running efficiently. The recipes in this part will make your mornings a favorite part of the day.

First, together we tackle the versatile egg, a little powerhouse of nutrition in a shell. Next, you'll learn how to make waffles and pancakes that can pack a powerful fiber punch without sacrificing flavor. Dairy can help you lose weight, so check out the smoothies that are quick and easy to make. Cereals can be loaded with "bad" calories, but I'll show you how to read the labels to select a brand that will boost your energy but not your fat. Finally, take the work out of fixing family lunches with these great sandwich recipes.

Chapter 4

Rise and Shine

In This Chapter

- ◆ Be an eggspert
- ◆ Coddle yourself
- ◆ Avoid *Sam and Ella*

If you're looking for a great source of protein that's low in calories, don't scratch eggs off your nutritional shopping list. Yes, I know they've gotten a bad rep, but some of that is due to the misunderstanding that cholesterol in food was 100 percent responsible for your laboratory results. Thanks to more research, scientists have shown that saturated fat, genetics, and lifestyle play the leading role in determining your blood cholesterol reading, so there's no reason to avoid eggs on a heart-healthy diet.

An egg is composed of a yolk and a white part called albumen. This clear liquid contains more than half the egg's total protein, niacin, potassium, sodium, magnesium, and riboflavin count without any fat. It also serves as a shock absorber for the yolk, should the egg get kicked from the nest.

The egg yolk, on the other hand, contains biotin, vitamin A, E, and D. In fact, an egg yolk is one of the only natural food sources of vitamin D. It's true that the egg yolk contains fat, but it's mostly the good unsaturated kind. The yolk is also the source of lutein, an important antioxidant that can help prevent macular degeneration, an eye disease that results in blindness. It seems another component of the mighty egg yolk, lecithin, helps to improve our body's ability to absorb lutein better than from other sources, such as spinach.

An egg is an inexpensive way to provide your body with high-quality nutrients in one tiny package. Studies have shown that consuming about 2 whole eggs a day can help to protect against eye diseases, breast cancer, and even melanoma, a skin cancer, without raising cholesterol. Eggs are chock-full of choline, a B vitamin that can lower the levels of homocysteine, an amino acid that damages blood vessels, so coddle yourself and include my egg-ceptional recipes in your weekly diet.

Before you get out the skillet, let me advise you on some important safety tips when dealing with eggs. In 1985, the Centers for Disease Control discovered salmonella, a bacterium that causes diarrhea, vomiting, fever, and headache, not just on the outer shell of an egg but inside as well. However, salmonella is everywhere ... on a sponge and even on your fingertips. So why all the fuss? There's no way to discover if an egg is already a hot bed for bacterial breeding. So here's the way to crack down on food safety:

- ◆ Always buy fresh eggs. This means check the sell-by date on the carton.
- ◆ Keep eggs refrigerated until use in order to slow down the growth rate of this nasty bug. If a recipe calls for room temperature eggs, leave them out no more than 30 minutes before cooking.
- ◆ Never mix eggs with a fork or kitchen tool that has been in contact with raw food, such as poultry.
- ◆ Always wash everything, including your hands, when dealing with raw foods before handling something that won't be cooked.
- ◆ Don't invite *Sam and Ella* to your house by serving undercooked eggs. Stick with scrambled, hard-boiled, or poached eggs for maximum safety.

Perfect Hard-Boiled Eggs

4 whole eggs   Pinch of salt

1. Place eggs in a small saucepan and cover with water. Add a pinch of salt. Bring to a boil over medium-high heat. Turn heat to low and boil gently for 2 minutes.

2. Remove the pan to the counter and cover. Set a timer for 11 minutes.

3. Drain eggs. Put ice cubes in a bowl of water and plunge eggs into ice water for 2 minutes. Drain and peel.

Makes 4 servings
Prep time: none
Cook time: 13 minutes
Each serving has:
71.52 calories
6 g. protein
0.59 g. carbohydrate
4.81 g. total fat
1.49 g. saturated fat
204 mg. cholesterol
60.48 mg. sodium
0 g. fiber

Food for Thought

If you accidentally drop an egg on the floor, sprinkle it with lots of salt, and cleanup will be a snap. The salt gives the egg a granular texture and can be picked up with a towel rather than remain slippery.

Simply Simple Eggs and Canadian Bacon

2 eggs   2 slices Canadian Bacon

1 TB. unsalted butter   Pepper, freshly ground

1. Heat a 6-inch nonstick skillet on low heat, and put 1 tablespoon unsalted butter into the pan to melt.

2. Add 2 pieces of Canadian bacon to the pan, and heat for 30 seconds, then turn over.

3. Crack one egg on top of each piece of bacon, and season lightly with fresh pepper. Place a lid on top of the pan, and lower the heat to simmer. Check the pan after 1 minute, and continue cooking until egg yolk and white are cooked.

Makes 2 servings
Prep time: none
Cook time: 2 minutes
Each serving has:
142.4 calories
9.46 g. protein
0.94 g. carbohydrate
10.91 g. total fat
5.19 g. saturated fat
229.5 mg. cholesterol
177.3 mg. sodium
0 g. fiber

Poached Eggs with Almost Homemade Béarnaise Sauce

Makes 2 servings
Prep time: 5 minutes
Cook time: 5 minutes
Each serving has:
190.2 calories
8.85 g. protein
14.99 g. carbohydrate
10.83 g. total fat
2.44 g. saturated fat
209 mg. cholesterol
461.9 mg. sodium
1.86 g. fiber

2 eggs
1 TB. white wine vinegar
$^{1}/_{8}$ tsp sea salt

2 slices whole-wheat bread, toasted
2 TB. Almost Homemade Béarnaise Sauce (see Chapter 17)

1. Fill a 10-inch skillet with 3 inches of water. Place it on the stove and cover. Turn the heat to high.

2. Crack each egg into a small cup.

3. When water comes to a boil, add vinegar and salt. Gently pour each egg into water and cover. Turn off the heat. Set a timer for 3 minutes for medium-firm eggs.

4. Remove egg with a slotted spoon, and place on slice of toasted whole-wheat bread. Top with 1 tablespoon Almost Homemade Béarnaisé Sauce and enjoy.

Sunrise Frittata with Tomatoes, Zucchini, and Onions

Makes 4 servings
Prep time: 5 minutes
Cook time: 8 minutes
Each serving has:
99.78 calories
9.75 g. protein
2.54 g. carbohydrate
5.56 g. total fat
0.89 g. saturated fat
0.63 mg. cholesterol
141 mg. sodium
0.6 g. fiber

1 TB. olive oil
$^{1}/_{2}$ cup zucchini, finely diced
1 tomato, small and finely diced

$^{1}/_{4}$ cup green onions, diced
2 egg whites
1 cup egg substitute

1. Heat a 6-inch nonstick skillet on medium heat. Add olive oil, and sauté zucchini, tomato, and green onions until soft.

2. Mix egg whites with egg substitute, pour over vegetables, and cover. Reduce the heat to moderately low and cook until set, about 5 minutes. Shake pan occasionally to prevent sticking.

3. Slide frittata onto a plate, and divide into 4 portions to serve.

Tweetie Omelets with Salmon and Capers

1 TB. unsalted butter	1 tsp. capers
2 eggs	4 oz. smoked salmon or lox
2 egg whites	1 tsp. chives, diced

Makes 2 servings
Prep time: 1 minute
Cook time: 4 minutes
Each serving has:
205.9 calories
19.97 g. protein
1.03 g. carbohydrate
13.03 g. total fat
5.6 g. saturated fat
232.6 mg. cholesterol
1293 mg. sodium
0.05 g. fiber

1. Heat a 6-inch nonstick skillet on medium heat, and add 1 tablespoon unsalted butter to melt.

2. Lightly beat 2 medium eggs and 2 egg whites together; then pour into the pan.

3. Let set for 15 seconds or until edges start to cook. Take a rubber spatula and lightly draw outer edge of egg to the middle, allowing more uncooked egg to come in contact with the heated surface. Do this a few more times; then add capers and pieces of smoked salmon or lox to the far side of the pan away from you and allow mixture to cook to desired firmness.

4. To serve, grab the handle sideways and slide filled portion of omelet onto a plate, tipping the pan to fold unfilled side of omelet over salmon filling. Top with chives. Cut in half and serve.

Smoky Eggs

Makes 2 servings
Prep time: 5 minutes
Cook time: 4 minutes
Each serving has:
157.9 calories
9.83 g. protein
3.22 g. carbohydrate
11.61 g. total fat
2.41 g. saturated fat
204 mg. cholesterol
116.2 mg. sodium
0.44 g. fiber

1 TB. olive oil

¹/₄ cup onion, diced

1 clove garlic, crushed

2 eggs

2 egg whites

¹/₄ tsp. chipotle pepper in adobo sauce

1 TB. fresh cilantro, chopped

1. Pour olive oil into a 6-inch nonstick skillet and heat over low heat. Add diced onion and garlic, and cook until soft. Stir to prevent garlic from burning.

2. In a bowl, combine eggs with egg whites, and beat to blend. Add chipotle pepper sauce to egg mixture and blend.

3. Pour pepper/egg mixture into the pan with garlic and onions, and cook, drawing a rubber spatula continuously through egg mixture. Gather cooked eggs to one side of the pan, and keep sweeping egg mixture until it is cooked and still moist.

4. Top with freshly chopped cilantro and serve.

Wild Bird Nest Scramble

2 whole-wheat hamburger
buns

1 TB. unsalted butter

2 eggs

2 egg whites

¹/₄ cup cheddar cheese,
shredded

1 TB. salmon eggs

Makes 2 servings
Prep time: 4 minutes
Cook time: 3 minutes
Each serving has:
382.1 calories
22.19 g. protein
23.39 g. carbohydrate
22.83 g. total fat
11.77 g. saturated fat
276.7 mg. cholesterol
510.8 mg. sodium
3.24 g. fiber

1. Cut out the center in each half of 2 whole-wheat hamburger buns with a biscuit cutter, and toast buns.

2. In a 6-inch nonstick skillet, melt one tablespoon unsalted butter.

3. Combine eggs and egg whites in a bowl, and beat to blend. Pour into the heated pan and cook, drawing a rubber spatula continuously through eggs. Gather cooked eggs to one side of the pan, and keep sweeping egg mixture until it is cooked and still moist.

4. Put 2 cut-out toasted rolls on a plate, and fill centers with scrambled egg mixture. Top with shredded cheddar cheese, and add a dollop of salmon eggs on top of the "nest."

Variation: Consider adding some fresh spinach leaves to the base of the "nest" for even more nutritional benefits. The heat from the eggs will wilt the spinach naturally.

 Nutri Notes _____

The French knew 625 ways to prepare eggs by the time of the French Revolution. French brides break an egg on the threshold of their new home for good luck and healthy babies.

Chapter 5

Flip-Over Specials

In This Chapter

- ◆ Whole grain choices
- ◆ Punch up the fiber
- ◆ Sweet additions

Your family will wake up to the benefits of breakfast when you make these flip-over specials from whole grain flours. Ounce for ounce, whole grains can turn a morning meal into a powerhouse of nutritional energy while keeping a close tab on the calorie count. No more high-fat, sugary choices will deprive your family of essential vitamins and nutrients when you try my simple substitutions to your family's favorite recipes.

Breakfast is an ideal time to sneak in some fiber, which can help prevent constipation, lower your risk of heart disease, and may even protect you against colon and breast cancer. Fiber is sadly lacking in most store-bought breakfast offerings, which feature highly processed flours instead of whole-some stone-ground versions. Soluble fiber, found in nuts and fruits, can even help slow down the rise in blood sugar from good carbohydrates by calming down your stomach's digestion.

Looking for something sweet to top these healthy choices? Consider unpeeled apples or pears or berries fresh from the store. You'll not only be serving your family little gems of flavor but also helping meet their 5 servings of fruit or vegetables a day. And if you're rushed during the week, make each of these recipes ahead and freeze them for a fast, convenient breakfast that won't bust the calorie bank. See how easy it is to cook with total nutrition in mind?

Raspberry Buttermilk Pancakes

Makes 12 servings
Prep time: 5 minutes
Cook time: 10 minutes
Each serving has:
89.76 calories
6.01 g. protein
10.76 g. carbohydrate
2.84 g. total fat
1.44 g. saturated fat
6.25 mg. cholesterol
156.1 mg. sodium
2.28 g. fiber

$^1/_2$ cup all-purpose flour

1 cup soy flour

1 tsp. sugar substitute, such as Splenda

$^3/_4$ tsp. baking powder

$^3/_4$ tsp. baking soda

1$^1/_2$ cups buttermilk

2 eggs

2 TB. unsalted butter, melted

2 cups raspberries, fresh or frozen

Nonstick cooking spray

1. Heat the oven to 200°F. Heat griddle on medium-high heat.

2. Combine flours in one bowl with baking powder, sugar substitute, and baking soda. In another bowl, whisk together buttermilk, eggs, and butter. Pour this mixture into dry ingredients, stirring to form a smooth batter. Fold in raspberries.

3. Spray griddle with nonstick cooking spray. Pour $^1/_4$ cup batter per pancake onto the hot griddle. Cook for 2 minutes or until bubbles appear on surface and edges are dry. Lift edge to check for golden brown underneath. Flip with spatula, and cook for 1 to 2 more minutes. Place on a plate covered loosely with foil to keep warm in the oven for about 20 minutes.

 Nutri Notes _____

If you don't have buttermilk available, just mix 1 cup milk with 1 tablespoon white vinegar, and let it sit for 5 minutes. It makes a great substitute.

Pumpkin Banana Pancakes

³/₄ cup oat bran flour

¹/₄ cup whole-wheat flour

¹/₂ cup all-purpose flour

1 TB. baking powder

16 oz. canned pumpkin

¹/₄ cup banana, mashed

1 egg

¹/₄ cup 2% milk

Nonstick cooking spray

Makes 12 servings
Prep time: 5 minutes
Cook time: 10 minutes
Each serving has:
68.44 calories
3.06 g. protein
14.48 g. carbohydrate
1.14 g. total fat
0.34 g. saturated fat
17.39 mg. cholesterol
132.3 mg. sodium
2.56 g. fiber

1. Heat the oven to 200°F. Heat griddle on medium-high heat.

2. Combine flours in one bowl with baking powder. In another bowl, whisk together pumpkin, banana, egg, and milk. Pour this mixture into dry ingredients, stirring to form a smooth batter.

3. Spray griddle with nonstick cooking spray. Pour ¹/₄ cup batter per pancake onto the hot griddle. Cook for 2 minutes or until bubbles appear on surface and edges are dry. Lift edge to check for golden brown underneath. Flip with spatula, and cook for 1 to 2 more minutes. Place on a plate covered loosely with foil to keep warm in the oven for about 20 minutes.

Smoke Signals

Be sure you use only pure canned pumpkin. The sweetened version is labeled pumpkin pie and will add unwanted calories and sugar to this healthy recipe.

Oat Pancakes with Almonds, Raisins, and Cherries

Makes 12 servings
Prep time: 5 minutes
Cook time: 10 minutes
Each serving has:
195.6 calories
6.95 g. protein
27.95 g. carbohydrate
6.75 g. total fat
2.68 g. saturated fat
43.34 mg. cholesterol
202.2 mg. sodium
3.13 g. fiber

1 cup rolled oats

³/₄ cup instant oatmeal with raisins and spices

¹/₂ cup all-purpose flour

¹/₄ cup whole-wheat flour

1 tsp. baking powder

¹/₂ tsp. baking soda

1 cup 2% milk

2 eggs

3 TB. unsalted butter, melted

2 tsp. sugar substitute, such as Splenda

Nonstick cooking spray

¹/₄ cup almond slices

¹/₂ cup cherries, unsweetened in a jar, drained

1. Heat the oven to 200°F. Heat griddle on medium-high heat.

2. In a bowl, mix *rolled oats*, instant oatmeal with raisins and spices, flours, baking powder, and baking soda. In another bowl, whisk together milk, eggs, butter, and sugar substitute. Pour this mixture into dry mixture, and stir to form a smooth batter.

3. Spray griddle with nonstick cooking spray. Pour ¹/₄ cup batter per pancake onto the medium-hot griddle. Cook for 2 minutes or until bubbles appear on surface and edges are dry. Lift edge to check for golden brown underneath. Flip with spatula, and cook for 1 to 2 more minutes. Place on a plate covered loosely with foil to keep warm in the oven.

4. Top with almond slices and cherries.

Whole-Wheat Silver Dollar Pancake Mix with Cinnamon Pecan Apples

1^1/$_2$ cups whole-wheat flour

1 cup all-purpose flour

1 tsp. cinnamon

2 TB. baking powder

1 tsp. sea salt

2 tsp. sugar substitute, such as Splenda

2 eggs

2^1/$_4$ cups 2% milk

^{1}/$_4$ cup canola oil

Nonstick cooking spray

^{1}/$_4$ cup apple, unpeeled and coarsely diced

^{1}/$_4$ cup pecan pieces

Makes 24 servings
Prep time: 5 minutes
Cook time: 15 minutes
Each serving has:
91.97 calories
2.95 g. protein
11.33 g. carbohydrate
3.2 g. total fat
0.67 g. saturated fat
18.72 mg. cholesterol
237.2 mg. sodium
1.26 g. fiber

1. Heat the oven to 200°F. Heat griddle on medium-high heat.

2. In a bowl, mix flours, cinnamon, baking powder, salt, and sugar substitute. In another bowl, whisk together eggs, milk, and oil. Pour this mixture into dry mixture, and stir to form a smooth batter.

3. Spray griddle with nonstick cooking spray. Pour ^{1}/$_8$ cup batter onto the hot griddle, forming silver dollar–size pancakes. Cook for 2 minutes or until bubbles appear on surface and edges are dry. Lift edge to check for golden brown underneath. Flip with spatula, and cook for 1 to 2 more minutes. Place on a plate covered loosely with foil to keep warm in the oven for about 20 minutes.

4. Top with coarsely diced apples and pecans.

Lemon Whole-Wheat Waffles with Blackberries

Makes 10 servings
Prep time: 5 minutes
Cook time: 10 minutes
Each serving has:
174.4 calories
5.7 g. protein
22.99 g. carbohydrate
7.18 g. total fat
3.96 g. saturated fat
57.75 mg. cholesterol
171.8 mg. sodium
3.67 g. fiber

1 cup whole-wheat flour

³/4 cup all-purpose flour

1¹/2 tsp. baking powder

¹/2 tsp. baking soda

1 cup reduced-calorie yogurt, lemon flavored

³/4 cup 2% milk

2 eggs

4 TB. unsalted butter, melted

1 tsp. sugar substitute, such as Splenda

2 tsp. lemon zest, finely chopped

Nonstick cooking spray

2¹/2 cup blackberries, fresh or frozen

1. Preheat oven to 200°F to keep waffles warm as they bake. Preheat waffle iron.

2. In a bowl, mix flours, baking powder, sugar substitute, and baking soda. In another bowl, whisk together yogurt, milk, eggs, butter, and 1 teaspoon lemon zest. Pour this mixture into dry mixture, and stir to form a smooth batter.

3. Spray waffle iron with nonstick spray, and pour ¹/3 cup of batter on the hot iron. Close the lid, and bake for 2 to 3 minutes or until waffles are golden brown and don't stick to the griddle. Place them directly on the rack in the oven to keep them crisp while preparing the remaining waffles.

4. Top with blackberries and remaining lemon peel.

Mocha Waffles

³/₄ cup oat bran flour

¹/₄ cup whole-wheat flour

¹/₂ cup all-purpose flour

³/₄ cup unsweetened, non-alkalized cocoa powder

¹/₂ cup sugar substitute, such as Splenda

1¹/₂ tsp. baking powder

¹/₂ tsp. baking soda

2 TB. instant coffee powder

2 oz. dark unsweetened chocolate, melted

3 TB. unsalted butter, melted

1 cup reduced-fat sour cream

3 eggs

Nonstick cooking spray

Makes 10 servings
Prep time: 10 minutes
Cook time: 10 minutes
Each serving has:
221.6 calories
7.83 g. protein
21.33 g. carbohydrate
17.02 g. total fat
9.74 g. saturated fat
79.83 mg. cholesterol
167.2 mg. sodium
3.76 g. fiber

1. Preheat oven to 200°F. Preheat waffle iron.

2. In a medium-size bowl, mix flours, *cocoa powder*, sugar substitute, baking powder, and baking soda. In another small bowl, dissolve instant coffee powder in ¹/₄ cup hot water and add to chocolate and butter. In another bowl, mix sour cream and eggs.

3. Pour all wet ingredients into flour mixture, and stir until a smooth batter is formed.

4. Lightly spray the waffle iron with nonstick spray, and spoon about ¹/₃ cup into the hot iron. Close the lid, and bake for 1 to 2 minutes or until edges are set and do not stick to the griddle. They will not be crisp in this recipe. Transfer to an ovenproof platter, and keep warm in the oven for about 20 minutes.

Nutri Speak _____

There are two types of **cocoa powder:** Regular (American) and Dutch (called European process). The Dutch version has been treated with alkali, such as baking soda, to neutralize its acidity. Both versions of cocoa powder have much less fat and fewer calories than baking chocolate because the cocoa butter has been removed.

Pear Almond Buttermilk Waffles

Makes 16 servings
Prep time: 15 minutes
Cook time: 10 minutes
Each serving has:
79.89 calories
3.69 g. protein
12.01 g. carbohydrate
1.95 g. total fat
0.31 g. saturated fat
1.07 mg. cholesterol
227.7 mg. sodium
0.8 g. fiber

1¹/₂ cup all-purpose flour

¹/₂ cup almonds, ground

1 tsp. baking powder

1 tsp. baking soda

¹/₂ tsp. sea salt

1 tsp. sugar substitute, such as Splenda

2 cups buttermilk

¹/₂ tsp. almond extract

¹/₂ cup ripe pears, peeled and coarsely chopped

4 egg whites

Nonstick cooking spray

1. Preheat oven to 200°F. Preheat waffle iron.

2. Combine flour, ground almonds, baking powder, baking soda, salt, and sugar substitute. Whisk together buttermilk and almond extract. Pour this into flour mixture, and add chopped pear.

3. In another bowl, beat egg whites until stiff peaks form. Using a rubber spatula, gently fold whites into batter.

4. Spray waffle iron with nonstick spray, and pour ¹/₃ cup of batter on the hot iron. Close the lid, and bake for 2 to 3 minutes or until waffles are golden brown and don't stick to the griddle. Place them directly on the rack in the oven to keep them crisp while preparing the remaining waffles.

Smoke Signals

When beating egg whites, never use a plastic bowl as it may have residual fat, which will prevent the egg whites from forming stiff peaks. Glass or steel bowls are better choices for performing this task. Be certain no egg yolk gets into the mix as it contains fat and will prevent proper beating of the whites. As a precaution, wipe your bowl and beaters with a small amount of vinegar or lemon juice.

Chapter 6

So Smooth

In This Chapter

- ◆ Dairy does it
- ◆ Fiber fruities
- ◆ Protein power

Dairy has been churning things up when it comes to helping you keep a tab on a healthy lifestyle. Not only is dairy rich in calcium and vitamin D, which build strong bones, but it also contains high amounts of leucine and conjugated linoleic acid, which are amino acids that can shrink your belly fat.

But not all dairy products get a gold star when we consider their type of fat. Just drink 3 glasses of whole milk a day, and you get the same amount of saturated fat as 13 strips of bacon! So steer clear of most full-fat versions, and select low-fat or reduced-fat products if you want to reduce your risk of diabetes and heart disease.

Dairy products make a perfect companion to high-fiber fruits. This combo can even help lower your risk of colon, stomach, and cervical cancer while keeping a check on your blood sugar levels. Just one cup of reduced-fat yogurt can provide almost 25 percent of your daily calcium needs while helping to boost your immune function and lower blood pressure. So I've provided lots of fruitful suggestions for quick breakfast smoothies that will start your day off right.

And if you're looking for a great source of protein, just say cheese. Whey protein, found in dairy, is a naturally complete protein as it contains all the essential amino acids your body needs to build strong muscles. It even earns the top spot as the best natural source for branched chain amino acids which your muscles require during exercise to keep going. And if you want to keep that full set of Chiclets in your mouth healthy, eating mozzarella, Swiss, Cheddar, or Monterey Jack can prevent cavities and help stimulate new enamel on your teeth. Cheese can block tooth-decaying acids produced by bacteria found in many sugar-loaded carbohydrates children seem to inhale, so keep the doctor away with an apple and cheese stick a day.

Bodice Ripper Smoothies

Makes 1 serving
Prep time: 1 minute
Cook time: none
Each serving has:
493 calories
43.45 g. protein
56.03 g. carbohydrate
11.48 g. total fat
5.85 g. saturated fat
58.89 mg. cholesterol
393.4 mg. sodium
3.6 g. fiber

1 cup plain low-fat yogurt

1 cup milk

2 TB. whey protein powder

2 TB. wheat germ

¹/₂ banana

2 TB. unsweetened apple-sauce

Ice cubes, if desired

1. Place yogurt, milk, protein powder, wheat germ, banana, and applesauce into a blender. Add ice cubes if you want a frozen or slushy version. Blend until smooth.

Variation: substitute berries of any kind for banana or applesauce for a different flavor and still get lots of good fiber.

 Nutri Notes —————

The average U.S. cow produces 53 pounds of milk per day, or 6.2 gallons. The milk bottle was invented in 1884 and plastic containers appeared in 1964.

Chocolate Peanut Butter Smoothie

¹/₄ cup yogurt

³/₄ cup milk

1 TB. peanut butter

1 TB. chocolate powder, unsweetened

1 tsp. sugar substitute, such as Splenda

1. Place yogurt, milk, peanut butter, chocolate powder, and sugar substitute into a blender. Add ice cubes if you want a frozen or slushy version. Blend until smooth.

Variation: For a real taste treat, add half a banana for more fiber and a potassium boost.

Makes 1 serving
Prep time: 1 minute
Cook time: none
Each serving has:
270.5 calories
15.46 g. protein
24.85 g. carbohydrate
12.97 g. total fat
4.62 g. saturated fat
17.21 mg. cholesterol
154.2 mg. sodium
2.61 g. fiber

Food for Thought _____

You can reduce the fat in peanut butter by storing the jar upside down in the cupboard, then tossing the oil that separates.

Peaches and Cream Sparkler

Makes 2 servings
Prep time: 1 minute
Cook time: none
Each serving has:
112.8 calories
10.2 g. protein
15.04 g. carbohydrate
2.15 g. total fat
1.18 g. saturated fat
7.1 mg. cholesterol
134.6 mg. sodium
2.11 g. fiber

$^1/_2$ cup 2% milk

1 cup peaches

1 TB. soy powder

12 oz. lemon-lime soda, no calorie

2 tsp. almonds, sliced

1. Place milk, peaches, soy powder, soda, and almonds into a blender. Add ice cubes if you want a frozen or slushy version. Blend until smooth.

Variation: try using pears instead of peaches, and add just a drop of almond extract for another breakfast sparkler.

Smoke Signals

Whey protein powder is a safer choice than soy powder for those with a thyroid problem, as it doesn't contain isoflavones that can block your thyroid function, resulting in fluid retention, fatigue, and weight gain.

Red, White, and Blue Cottage Cheese

Makes 1 serving
Prep time: 1 minute
Cook time: none
Each serving has:
268.8 calories
32.23 g. protein
22.32 g. carbohydrate
5.73 g. total fat
2.86 g. saturated fat
18.98 mg. cholesterol
920.9 mg. sodium
4.46 g. fiber

1 cup 2% cottage cheese

$^1/_4$ cup blueberries

$^1/_4$ cup raspberries

1/4 cup strawberry slices

1 tsp almonds, sliced

1. Place *cottage cheese* in a bowl. Top with blueberries, raspberries, strawberries, and almonds.

Nutri Speak

Cottage cheese is also known as pot cheese or farmer's cheese. It comes in small, medium, or large curds, which are drained but not pressed, so some whey remains.

Fruit and Yogurt Mélange

8 oz. carton whole-milk yogurt

8 grapes, halved

¹/₄ tsp. ground cumin

1 tsp. sugar substitute, such as Splenda

1 oz. walnuts, finely chopped

¹/₂ banana, sliced

¹/₄ tsp. sea salt

¹/₄ tsp. paprika

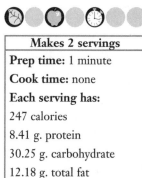

Makes 2 servings
Prep time: 1 minute
Cook time: none
Each serving has:
247 calories
8.41 g. protein
30.25 g. carbohydrate
12.18 g. total fat
3.07 g. saturated fat
14.4 mg. cholesterol
348.8 mg. sodium
3.09 g. fiber

1. Place yogurt in a bowl, and mix in grapes, cumin, sugar substitute, walnuts, and banana with salt to taste. Sprinkle with paprika and serve.

Variation: use dry-roasted peanuts or pecans instead of the walnuts for a different flavor.

Sourdough Tomato and Ricotta Cheese Sandwich

1 slice sourdough bread

2 oz. ricotta cheese

3 fresh basil leaves

2 slices tomato

Makes 1 serving
Prep time: 3 minutes
Cook time: 2 minutes
Each serving has:
128.4 calories
8.14 g. protein
12.67 g. carbohydrate
5.08 g. total fat
2.91 g. saturated fat
17.46 mg. cholesterol
166.8 mg. sodium
0.9 g. fiber

1. Toast bread, and top with ricotta cheese, basil leaves, and tomato slices.

 Nutri Notes _____

It takes 10 pounds of milk to make 1 pound of cheese. Americans eat the equivalent of 10 acres of pizza topped with cheese every day.

Apple Cheese Stick

Makes 1 serving
Prep time: 1 minute
Cook time: none
Each serving has:
145.8 calories
7.12 g. protein
19.85 g. carbohydrate
4.96 g. total fat
2.94 g. saturated fat
16.39 mg. cholesterol
132.1 mg. sodium
3.38 g. fiber

1 apple   1 stick mozzarella string cheese

1. Cut apple (with skin on) into wedges, remove seeds, and core portion.

2. Remove the plastic covering stick of mozzarella or string cheese.

Variation: Open a package of calcium-enriched diet chocolate powder, and dip apple pieces into it as you enjoy the cheese.

Food for Thought _____

Keep a fresh package of string cheese in your purse daily as a quick, nutritious snack, so you won't be tempted to munch on high-carb foods, like potato chips or pretzels, which can raise your blood sugar and leave you hungry in an hour.

Chapter **7**

Cereal Killers

In This Chapter

♦ Look for stone-ground
♦ Don't process
♦ Pack some fiber and protein

Choosing a breakfast cereal today is like navigating a nutritional minefield. Labels screaming Heart Healthy or packaging designed with fruity berries dancing on the box could misdirect you when it comes to selecting an overall nutritious cereal for your family. Many cereals are stripped of their natural benefits, then sweetened with sugars and laced with hydrogenated oils to extend their shelf life.

These "Frankencereals" can elevate your blood sugar and clog your arteries faster than you can say "It's alive!" So let me steer you clear of this problem area in your grocery store by giving you these simple guidelines.

Look for "whole" grains. It's not just the fiber in a cereal that matters. Other precious nutrients need to be present, too, like selenium, vitamin E, magnesium, and copper, which can protect your body against cancer, heart disease, and diabetes. Food labels don't always make it clear which cereals are whole grain, such as oatmeal, cream of rye, and Wheatena. Cream of wheat, cream of rice, and grits don't have any whole grains in them due to processing, even though they feature "good for a healthy heart" banners. The banners only mean they are low in fat and cholesterol. Unlike bread, most multigrain hot cereals are all or mostly all whole grain. Just to show you how far cereal makers will go, advertisers are now promoting "cereal bars" as a healthy choice. In reality, these are nothing more than jam on a white piece of bread because they lack whole grains and fiber.

Watch the sugar content of any cereal. When companies (and not Mom) do the sweetening, you never know what you are getting. You want to look for a cereal that provides no more than 20 percent of its calories per serving from sugar. Most flavored brands sag under a 30 to 40 percent sugar high, so be a smart total nutritional cook and add your own fruit and sweetener.

If you want to strive for the 20 to 35 grams of fiber a day, cereals and grains can rapidly fill that requirement. Fiber comes in both soluble and insoluble form, both of which are necessary to control cholesterol levels. So the more fiber in a cereal, the better. Look for labels showing at least 4 grams.

Protein is another important factor. The more fiber that remains in a cereal, the more protein is retained because there is less processing of the grain. This means your stomach will take longer to digest the grain as it's more nutritionally dense. So choose cereals that have whole grain as their first ingredient, a fiber and protein content each of at least 4gm per serving, and no more than 1 percent of their calories from sugar, and you'll be eating with total nutrition in mind.

Connemara Steel Cut Oatmeal with Cinnamon and Raisins

1 cup soy milk

¹/₂ cup water

¹/₂ cup Irish steel-cut oats

1 tsp. ground cinnamon

1 tsp. salt substitute

¹/₄ cup raisins

¹/₄ tsp. almond extract

1 tsp. sugar substitute, such as Splenda Brown Sugar

Makes 2 servings
Prep time: 2 minutes
Cook time: 25 minutes
Each serving has:
260.58 calories
9.05 g. protein
46.76 g. carbohydrate
5.63 g. total fat
0.31 g. saturated fat
0 mg. cholesterol
17.23 mg. sodium
6.96 g. fiber

1. Place milk, water, Irish oats, cinnamon, and salt substitute in a saucepan and bring to a boil. Reduce the heat, cover, and simmer for 20 minutes until soft but still liquid. Remove from the heat and let stand. Mixture will thicken as it stands.

2. Blend in raisins and almond extract. Sweeten with a sugar substitute to taste.

Nutri Speak

Steel cut oats are sold as Irish oatmeal and contain 50 percent more protein than bulgur wheat and twice as much as brown rice. Steel cut oats have a high soluble-fiber content, which can lower cholesterol.

Quinoa Cooked Cereal with Cherries and Pecans

Makes 2 servings
Prep time: 5 minutes
Cook time: 30 minutes
Each serving has:
340.55 calories
11.97 g. protein
40.52 g. carbohydrate
15.75 g. total fat
2.8 g. saturated fat
9.47 mg. cholesterol
84.8 mg. sodium
4.27 g. fiber

$^1/_2$ cup quinoa

1 cup 2% milk

1 cup water

$^1/_4$ cup cherries

1 tsp. salt substitute

$^1/_4$ cup pecan nuts

1 tsp. sugar substitute, such as Splenda

1. Thoroughly rinse dry grain quinoa with water until water runs clear.

2. Dry the quinoa in a pan on medium heat. Once dry, increase the heat to high and toast quinoa for 5 minutes, stirring often to prevent burning.

3. Combine quinoa with milk, water, cherries, and salt substitute, and bring to a boil. Cover and then simmer for 15 minutes or until tender. Grains will be transparent and puffy.

4. Top with pecan pieces and sugar substitute.

Quaker Mother's Oat Bran Cereal with Cinnamon Apple Surprise

1 cup Quaker Mother's Oat Bran Cereal

1¹/₄ cups water

¹/₂ cup apple, diced with skin

1 tsp. salt substitute (or to taste)

¹/₄ tsp. ground nutmeg

¹/₂ tsp. ground cinnamon

¹/₂ cup almonds, sliced

1 tsp. sugar substitute, such as Splenda

Makes 2 servings
Prep time: 5 minutes
Cook time: 20 minutes
Each serving has:
305.8 calories
11.97 g. protein
10.36 g. carbohydrate
15.48 g. total fat
1.42 g. saturated fat
0 mg. cholesterol
12.42 mg. sodium
9.92 g. fiber

1. Measure out *oat bran* cereal into a saucepan. Add water, diced apples, salt substitute, nutmeg, and cinnamon. Bring to a boil, then cover, reduce heat, and simmer for 15 minutes.

2. Top with almond slices, and sweeten with sugar substitute as desired.

Nutri Speak

Oat bran is a plant food high in soluble fiber. It also goes by Avena farina, common groats, haws, and oatmeal.

Kashi Go Lean Morning Wakeup Bowl

Makes 2 servings

Prep time: 2 minutes

Cook time: none

Each serving has:

141.52 calories

10.7 g. protein

23.64 g. carbohydrate

3.19 g. total fat

0.27 g. saturated fat

0 mg. cholesterol

63.65 mg. sodium

8.24 g. fiber

1½ cups Kashi Go Lean Cereal

1 cup soy milk

½ cup blueberries

1 tsp. sugar substitute, such as Splenda

1. Carefully measure out cereal into two bowls. Add milk and berries. Sweeten with sugar substitute to taste.

Nutri Notes

Indians in the Northwest Territories smoked blueberries to preserve them through winter. Blueberries are ranked number one in antioxidant activity when compared to 40 other fruits and vegetables. One half cup of blueberries has only 42 calories and no fat. Blueberries are also a good source of dietary fiber.

Kellogg's Special K Low-Carb Lifestyle with Blueberries

Makes 2 servings

Prep time: 2 minutes

Cook time: none

Each serving has:

161.7 calories

13.61 g. protein

21.34 g. carbohydrate

5.48 g. total fat

1.27 g. saturated fat

0 mg. cholesterol

126.9 mg. sodium

7.57 g. fiber

1½ cups Kellogg's Special K Low-Carb Lifestyle Cereal

1 cup soy milk

½ cup blueberries

1 tsp. sugar substitute, such as Splenda

1. Portion cereal into 2 bowls and add soy milk and blueberries. Sweeten with sugar substitute as desired.

Smoke Signals

There is no USDA definition for "low carb" claims on food packaging. Always check fiber, sugar, and carbohydrate content per serving to find the best cereal for your health.

Shredded Wheat and Bran Munchie

2 cups low-fat yogurt

1 cup strawberry slices

2¹/₂ cup Kraft Shredded Wheat and Bran Cereal

1 tsp. sugar substitute, such as Splenda

Makes 2 servings
Prep time: 2 minutes
Cook time: none
Each serving has:
390.7 calories
20.34 g. protein
74.34 g. carbohydrate
4.92 g. total fat
2.46 g. saturated fat
14.95 mg. cholesterol
177.2 mg. sodium
10.32 g. fiber

1. Mix together yogurt, strawberries, shredded wheat, and sugar substitute for a crunchy, quick breakfast for two.

Food for Thought

Bran is an excellent cereal, rich in fiber and slow to raise your blood sugar. It also keeps you satisfied for a longer period of time. Add it to burgers or as a topping to dairy for extra benefits.

Peachy Wheat Germ Crunch

¹/₂ cup regular QUAKER, KRETSCHMER Wheat Germ

1 cup plain yogurt

1 cup peaches, fresh or frozen without syrup

1 tsp. sugar substitute, such as Splenda

Makes 2 servings
Prep time: 2 minutes
Cook time: none
Each serving has:
178.07 calories
13.81 g. protein
28.64g. carbohydrate
2.3 g. total fat
0.55 g. saturated fat
2.21 mg. cholesterol
94.91 mg. sodium
4.1 g. fiber

1. Pour *wheat germ* cereal into two bowls. Top with yogurt and peaches. Sweeten with sugar substitute as desired.

Nutri Speak

Wheat germ is the vitamin-rich seedling plant within the wheat grain. It is removed during processing of cereals, taking the fiber, fats, minerals, and protein with it. It is commonly sold toasted.

8

Savory Sandwiches

In This Chapter

- ◆ Choose whole grain bread
- ◆ Watch the fat
- ◆ Spice it up

Bread is indeed the staff of life, but not if you choose highly processed varieties that float in your hands and provide only chemicals instead of nutrient-dense, wholesome grains. Just pick up a loaf of processed bread and weigh the difference in your hands. Whole grains are dense, heavier products because the entire wheat kernel (germ, bran, and endosperm) are still intact, while commercially processed breads are lighter than marshmallows and can easily be crushed. So don't be fooled by "stealth health" advertising lingo claiming "100% whole wheat" when you're really feeding your family a glob of dough. Select dense breads with the first ingredient as whole wheat, and you'll be picking up the benefits of a higher-fiber product, too.

When making sandwiches, fat has a way of appearing in mass quantities, which can send your nutritional plans on a detour. With my help, you can make your own tasty spreads that lower the fat but not the flavor. Mustards can add even more variety to your nonfat options. Try using Dijon, hickory, or even Key Lime varieties when building your Dagwood special, and I'll guarantee you won't miss the fat. And don't forget about the moistness factor. Lettuce and tomatoes contain phytochemicals that help prevent cancer, so don't be a "Sandwich Scrooge" and be stingy with these nutritional jewels.

Salt is hidden in many processed meats, making them a less than ideal choice for a total nutritional cook. I'll show you the better ones and even how simple it is to make your own deli products. Herbs can punch up the flavor, so experiment with basil, chervil, and greens such as spinach and arugula if you want to make a sandwich sparkle. The possibilities are endless when you cook with total nutrition in mind.

Peanut Butter Nutty Cereal Crunch

Makes 4 servings
Prep time: 2 minutes
Cook time: 2 minutes
Each serving has:
484.9 calories
20.91 g. protein
32.25 g. carbohydrate
34.36 g. total fat
6.79 g. saturated fat
0 mg. cholesterol
149.4 mg. sodium
7.05 g. fiber

1 cup chunky style peanut butter, without added salt

1 cup Kellogg's Special K low-carb lifestyle cereal

4 slices raisin bread

1. In a bowl, mix peanut butter and cereal, smashing down flakes to incorporate.

2. Toast raisin bread.

3. Place two slices of toasted raisin bread on a plate and spread the peanut butter/cereal mixture evenly between them. Top with remaining two slices of toasted bread. Cut in half to serve.

Portobello Tomato Basil Sandwich

2 large Portobello mush-
rooms (4 inches wide)

2 slices medium tomato

5 leaves basil

1 oz. Alpine Lace reduced-fat
Swiss cheese

1. Clean mushrooms, removing brown gills and stems.

2. Fill one mushroom cap with tomato slices, basil leaves, and top
   with cheese slice. Place in the toaster oven at 325°F for 5 minutes to melt cheese.

3. Top with remaining mushroom cap and serve.

Makes 1 serving
Prep time: 2 minutes
Cook time: 2 minutes
Each serving has:
146.2 calories
13.17 g. protein
12.07 g. carbohydrate
6.47 g. total fat
3.56 g. saturated fat
20 mg. cholesterol
128.8 mg. sodium
3.22 g. fiber

Food for Thought

Portobello mushrooms have a very meaty flavor that comes
out when grilled or toasted. Store them in a brown paper
bag in the refrigerator for a week, but do not rinse them, or you'll
end up with a soggy, moldy mess. These mushrooms are an excellent source of niacin, a B vitamin which helps to lower cholesterol.

Avocado and Swiss Whole-Wheat Sandwich

Makes 1 serving
Prep time: 2 minutes
Cook time: none
Each serving has:
366.4 calories
18.2 g. protein
24.96 g. carbohydrate
23.88 g. total fat
5.69 g. saturated fat
20 mg. cholesterol
511.4 mg. sodium
9.63 g. fiber

2 slices Oroweat Carb Counting 100% Whole-Wheat Bread

1 TB. reduced-fat mayonnaise

¼ cup spinach leaves

2 slices avocado

1 oz. Alpine Lace reduced-fat Swiss cheese

1. Onto each slice of bread, spread reduced-fat mayonnaise, and then add spinach leaves.

2. Top with slices of avocado and cheese. Place one slice of bread on top of the other and serve.

Nutri Notes _____

The Aztecs believed the avocado was such a potent aphrodisiac that they forbade virginal women from stepping outside the house when the fruit was being harvested.

Chicken Artichoke Curry Salad Sandwich

2 slices whole-wheat bread

1 TB. Kraft 97% fat-free mayonnaise

1 TB. nonfat yogurt

1 tsp. curry powder

3 small artichoke hearts, canned in water, drained, and chopped coarsely

1 stalk celery, diced

3 oz. chicken breast, cooked and shredded

Makes 1 serving
Prep time: 5 minutes
Cook time: none
Each serving has:
329.1 calories
33.81 g. protein
36.2 g. carbohydrate
10.51 g. total fat
1.53 g. saturated fat
72.6 mg. cholesterol
549.5 mg. sodium
5.99 g. fiber

1. Place two slices of bread on a plate.

2. In a bowl, combine mayonnaise, yogurt, and curry powder. Add artichoke hearts and celery, then shredded fresh chicken breast. Spread on one slice of bread. Top with the other slice of bread and slice to serve.

Food for Thought

The easiest way to make a moist chicken breast is to poach it. Bring a saucepan of water to a boil; then drop in the skinless chicken breast, cover, and turn off the heat. The breast will be cooked yet still tender within 15 minutes. Cool, and then shred. Extra chicken breasts can be cooked at the same time with no extra cooking time and stored in a plastic bag in the refrigerator for future meals.

Tarragon Chicken, Raisin, and Almond Sandwich

Makes 1 serving
Prep time: 2 minutes
Cook time: none
Each serving has:
324.9 calories
31.62 g. protein
32.38 g. carbohydrate
12 g. total fat
1.41 g. saturated fat
72.6 mg. cholesterol
407.4 mg. sodium
2.43 g. fiber

2 slices sourdough bread

1 TB. Kraft 97% fat-free mayonnaise

1 TB. nonfat yogurt

1/8 tsp. fresh tarragon leaves, finely chopped

1 TB. raisins

1 TB. almonds, sliced

3 oz. chicken breast, cooked and shredded

1 slice tomato

1 leaf romaine lettuce

1. Place two slices of bread on a plate.

2. In a bowl, combine mayonnaise, yogurt, tarragon, raisins, and almonds. Toss in shredded chicken breast, and mix thoroughly.

3. Place mixture on slice of bread and top with tomato and lettuce. Cover with remaining piece of bread. Slice and serve.

Southwest Chicken Salad Tortilla

Makes 4 servings
Prep time: 5 minutes
Cook time: 1 minute
Each serving has:
291.3 calories
33.19 g. protein
35.11 g. carbohydrate
9.96 g. total fat
0.91 g. saturated fat
59.81 mg. cholesterol
399.6 mg. sodium
12.71 g. fiber

1/4 cup Kraft 97% fat-free mayonnaise

1/4 cup nonfat yogurt

1 tsp. fresh lime juice

1/2 tsp. ground cumin

1/2 cup black beans, drained

1/4 cup red onion, diced coarsely

2 cups chicken breast, cooked and diced

1/2 cup red bell pepper, coarsely chopped

4 low carb whole-wheat tortillas

1. In a bowl, combine mayonnaise, yogurt, lime juice, and cumin.

2. Add beans, red onion, chicken breast, and bell pepper, and combine with mayonnaise mixture.

3. Divide mix evenly into four portions. Warm each *tortilla* in the microwave for 10 seconds in a plastic bag on high. This will make tortilla supple. Place one serving of mixture from one edge to within 4 inches of opposite edge in the middle of tortilla. Now fold those 4 inches over mixture, overlapping about 1/4 of mixture. Fold one of the long sides over the flap and tuck edge under

filling to make it secure. Make a small diagonal fold on remaining edge of tortilla to help seal the bottom. Now bring final edge over and let it set for about a minute before eating.

Nutri Speak _____

Tortilla is a Mexican unleavened wheat flour or corn masa bread. However, in Spain, tortilla means a potato dish cooked with peppers, olives, and eggs. A whole-wheat tortilla provides 8 grams of fiber, 2 grams of fat, and 11 grams carbohydrates, resulting in a net carb count of 3 grams.

Open-Face Melted BLT

1 slice whole-wheat bread	1 slice tomato
1 TB. stone-ground mustard	1 slice Canadian bacon
1 TB. nonfat yogurt	1 oz. Alpine Lace reduced-fat Swiss cheese
1 leaf romaine lettuce	
2 TB. cannellini beans, mashed	

1. Place bread on a plate. In a bowl, combine mustard and yogurt; then spread on bread.

2. Build sandwich by placing lettuce leaf filled with mashed beans on top of bread; then place tomato, bacon, and cheese.

3. Place in a toaster oven and toast until cheese is melted.

Makes 1 serving
Prep time: 2 minutes
Cook time: 2 minutes
Each serving has:
238 calories
17.6 g. protein
24.78 g. carbohydrate
7.81 g. total fat
3.86 g. saturated fat
30.31 mg. cholesterol
570.4 mg. sodium
3.25 g. fiber

Food for Thought _____

Cannellini beans are an excellent replacement for fat in any meal. An easy way to prepare them is with a stick or immersion blender in the can. Purée them into a nice spreadable consistency. Use within 4 days when stored in the refrigerator.

Pineapple Ham Kaiser

Makes 1 serving
Prep time: 3 minutes
Cook time: none
Each serving has:
399.9 calories
26.45 g. protein
43.41 g. carbohydrate
13.45 g. total fat
4.92 g. saturated fat
46.32 mg. cholesterol
1466 mg. sodium
2.87 g. fiber

1 whole-wheat Kaiser roll

1 TB. Dijon mustard

¹/₂ cup pineapple rings, drained

2 slices lean ham

1 tsp. sunflower seeds

1 oz. Alpine Lace reduced-fat Swiss cheese

1 leaf romaine lettuce

1. Split whole-wheat Kaiser roll, and spread with mustard.

2. Place drained pineapple rings on one half of roll, and top with ham, sunflower seeds, cheese, and lettuce. Place second half of roll on top and serve.

Food for Thought

Seeds are an inexpensive way to bump up the fiber content of a sandwich or salad. Just one ounce provides 3 grams of fiber. Sunflower seeds also provide a significant amount of vitamin E, magnesium, and selenium, powerful antioxidants important to your diet.

Turkey Avocado with Honey Mustard Sandwich

2 slices sourdough bread

1 TB. honey mustard

1 cup alfalfa sprouts

3 oz. non-processed turkey breast slices

2 slices avocado

1 leaf romaine lettuce

Makes 1 serving
Prep time: 2 minutes
Cook time: 2 minutes
Each serving has:
407.2 calories
27.67 g. protein
44.74 g. carbohydrate
13.72 g. total fat
1.83 g. saturated fat
30.37 mg. cholesterol
933.4 mg. sodium
6.21 g. fiber

1. Toast sourdough bread.

2. Spread honey mustard on both slices; then top one slice with sprouts, turkey, avocado, and lettuce. Cover with remaining slice of bread and serve.

Food for Thought

Alfalfa sprouts pack a punch when it comes to iron, protein, fiber, and many essential vitamins. They are a very nutrient-dense food with few calories and no fat; so use them in unlimited quantities.

Turkey Club Sandwich

2 slices Oroweat Honey Fiber Whole Grain Bread

1 TB. nonfat yogurt

1 TB. Dijon mustard

1 TB. Kraft 97% fat-free mayonnaise

3 oz. turkey breast slices

1 slice tomato

1 cup spinach leaves

1 oz. Alpine Lace reduced-fat, reduced-sodium provolone cheese

Makes 1 serving
Prep time: 5 minutes
Cook time: none
Each serving has:
393.2 calories
37.3 g. protein
43.58 g. carbohydrate
11.78 g. total fat
3.4 g. saturated fat
45.69 mg. cholesterol
1405 mg. sodium
9.83 g. fiber

1. Place two slices of bread on a plate.

2. In a bowl, mix mayonnaise, yogurt, and mustard; then spread on both slices of bread.

3. Assemble sandwich by adding turkey, tomato, spinach leaves, and cheese. Top with remaining slice of bread.

Tuna Bean Salad Sandwich

Makes 2 servings
Prep time: 2 minutes
Cook time: none
Each serving has:
407.5 calories
32.57 g. protein
63.91 g. carbohydrate
3.39 g. total fat
0.84 g. saturated fat
23.81 mg. cholesterol
393.9 mg. sodium
13.17 g. fiber

1 large whole-wheat pita

4 oz. tuna packed in water, drained

1 slice white or yellow onion, finely chopped

15 oz. cannellini beans, mashed

1 clove garlic, mashed

1 leaf romaine lettuce

1. Cut pita in half, and split open.

2. In a bowl, combine tuna, onion, beans, and garlic.

3. Place one-half leaf of lettuce inside pita half, and fill with half tuna mixture. Repeat with remaining pita half.

Smoke Signals

Although high in omega fatty acids, tuna has been shown to contain low levels of mercury and should be consumed no more than once a week. Avoid it entirely if you are pregnant or nursing. Substitute chicken or salmon in this recipe for an equally tasty dish.

Salmon Lemon Basil Pitas

3 small whole wheat pitas

1 can (7 oz.) salmon packed in water, drained (or leftover cooked salmon)

1 medium celery stalk, finely diced

3 fresh leaves basil, torn into pieces

2 TB. fresh lemon juice

1 clove garlic, minced

3 leaves romaine lettuce, diced

3 slices tomato, diced

Makes 3 servings
Prep time: 5 minutes
Cook time: none
Each serving has:
190.21 calories
18.28 g. protein
17.69 g. carbohydrate
5.42 g. total fat
1.3 g. saturated fat
41.62 mg. cholesterol
220.75 mg. sodium
2.82 g. fiber

1. Cut pitas open at upper third.

2. In a bowl, combine salmon, celery, basil, lemon juice, and garlic.

3. Place one lettuce leaf inside each pita, then diced tomato followed by one third tuna mixture.

Food for Thought

Romaine lettuce is the best choice for any sandwich as it is the highest in fiber, potassium, folic acid, and water of all lettuces. Romaine lettuce will keep in the refrigerator for 5 to 7 days if kept away from apples, bananas, and pears, which give off a gas that will cause the lettuce to turn brown.

Sunflower Crab Sandwich

Makes 6 servings

Prep time: 5 minutes

Cook time: none

Each serving has:

320.3 calories

32.32 g. protein

28.62 g. carbohydrate

8.87 g. total fat

1.22 g. saturated fat

100.9 mg. cholesterol

534.7 mg. sodium

5.8 g. fiber

6 slices whole-wheat bread

1 can (24 oz.) cooked crab, drained

1 cup cannellini beans

2 TB. honey mustard

1 tsp. fresh thyme leaves

2 stalks green onions, finely sliced

$1/2$ cup sunflower seeds

1. Place three slices of bread on a plate.

2. In a bowl, combine crab, beans, mustard, thyme, onions, and seeds.

3. Spread evenly between three slices of bread, and top with remaining slices. Divide into six sections and serve.

Nutri Notes

Imitation crab is made from Pollock fish paste treated with sugar, sorbitol, and tons of chemicals, including dyes. Its only resemblance to crab is the form the processor shapes it into. Avoid this "Frankenfish" if you want to eat with total nutrition in mind.

Philly Cheese Steak

4 mixed grain hotdog buns

1 plum tomato, coarsely diced

2 jalapeño peppers, coarsely diced

5 strips bell pepper, coarsely diced

1 TB. red wine vinegar

¹/₄ cup water

1 TB. onion, coarsely chopped

1 cup broccoli florets, finely chopped

8 oz. Boar's Head top round reduced-sodium roast beef, coarsely chopped

¹/₄ cup Alpine Lace reduced-fat Swiss cheese, shredded

Makes 4 servings
Prep time: 5 minutes
Cook time: 5 minutes
Each serving has:
255.6 calories
23.37 g. protein
22.22 g. carbohydrate
8.89 g. total fat
3.96 g. saturated fat
40.67 mg. cholesterol
304.1 mg. sodium
2.67 g. fiber

1. Split open hotdog buns.

2. In a pan, combine tomato, peppers, vinegar, water, onion, and broccoli, and sauté over medium heat until just soft but not limp.

3. Add chopped beef and cheese, and combine until melted. Divide evenly between buns and serve.

Part 3

Soup-er Starters and Appeteasers

The French may know a secret or two when it comes to putting a smile on your face with an appetizer. In this part I will show you how to get your digestive juices started with food that is not only a great source of nutrition but also makes your mouth sing with pleasure.

Soups are comfort foods and always bring back memories of cozy winter meals in the kitchen. I'll show you how to make rich, flavorful soups that can fill your house with the aroma of home cooking all day long without making you a slave in the kitchen. Cooking was never easier!

Looking for stunning salad recipes? You'll find these gems requested over and over by your family and friends. Salads are so versatile you can make them as a side or a main dish full of powerful antioxidants and vitamins. There will be no more rabbit food compositions when you cook with total nutrition in mind.

Chapter 9

Appetizers to Amuse Your Mouth

In This Chapter

◆ Grill and chill out

◆ Take the dip into nutritious eating

◆ Enjoy the original mini meal

Nothing is better at revving up your metabolism than a great starter or appetizer. It's the "teaser" that can start your digestive juices flowing and help your body extract the maximum nutrients from your main meal. Just smelling food can trigger a response in your tummy that turns on its grinding action, called the peristaltic wave. This churning mechanism lubricates your digestive engine. It starts important enzymes or juices flowing that break up the proteins, fats, and carbohydrates in your food. No wonder appetizers are called "starters"!

Dips will make ordinary vegetables put a smile on anyone's face if you concentrate on mouth-appeal. Use reduced-fat products, but not necessarily nonfat versions, for a better mouth feel. This will cut back on calories and saturated fat without sacrificing flavor. Vegetables that crunch in your mouth contribute important enzymes and fiber, which can lower your risk of certain cancers, so don't be stingy with veggies when fixing an appetizer. These recipes show you how easy it is to wow even the most jaded party person or persnickety family member.

Appetizers are the original portion control mini meal. You can even make a nutritious meal out of a few starters and skip the idea of a main course. Just think of them as small bites that carry big flavor. Concentrate on appetizers that pack fiber into your diet, which will keep you satisfied with fewer calories. Use only stone-ground whole grain crackers or breads to slow down the rise in blood sugar from starchy foods. You'll be munching your way to a nutritious lifestyle in no time with these favorites of mine.

Nutri Speak

The word **appetizer** comes from the French word for "aperitif," a traditional glass of wine or cocktail to whet the appetite.

Asparagus Prosciutto Wrap

1 lb. asparagus (about 18 spears)

½ lb. prosciutto ham, sliced paper thin

1 TB. olive oil

Makes 6 servings
Prep time: 5 minutes
Cook time: 7 minutes
Each serving has:
130.6 calories
13.72 g. protein
4.77 g. carbohydrate
7.73 g. total fat
3.01 g. saturated fat
0 g. cholesterol
801.5 g. sodium
1.59 g. fiber

1. Heat the oven to 500°F. Hold asparagus spears at both ends, and snap off tough bottom of asparagus stalks by bending in half. Discard ends and save tender tips. Wrap piece of prosciutto around each spear, spiraling upwards from stalk end.

2. Line a flat pan with nonstick aluminum foil, and coat with olive oil. Arrange wrapped spears in the pan, and place in the oven for 5 minutes. Turn spears and roast for 2 more minutes or until prosciutto is crisp.

Variation: If prosciutto is not available, you can substitute lean ham slices.

Black Bean and Blue Cheese Potato Slices

1 TB. black beans

1 TB. garlic, minced

1 TB. canola oil

2 TB. rice wine vinegar

$^1/_4$ cup tomatoes, coarsely diced

$^1/_4$ cup blue cheese, crumbled

$^1/_4$ cup spring onions, chopped

1 cup baby potatoes, whole

Makes 24 servings
Prep time: 10 minutes
Cook time: 12 minutes
Each serving has:
20.66 calories
0.75 g. protein
1.55 g. carbohydrate
1.31 g. total fat
0.51 g. saturated fat
1.85 mg. cholesterol
35.13 mg. sodium
0.19 g. fiber

1. Combine beans and garlic in a bowl. Smash coarsely with a fork.

2. Mix in oil and vinegar; then stir in tomato, cheese, and spring onions. Cover and let stand 2 hours.

3. Boil potatoes in lightly salted water until tender, about 12 minutes. Cool. Slice boiled baby potatoes into $^3/_8$-inch slices. Spoon 1 teaspoon of bean mixture onto each slice.

Cashew Goat Cheese Phyllo Rolls

$^1/_2$ cup roasted cashews, unsalted and chopped

1 cup goat cheese

8 sheets phyllo, defrosted in fridge overnight

$^1/_4$ cup unsalted butter, melted

Nonstick cooking spray

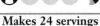

Makes 24 servings
Prep time: 20 minutes
Cook time: 15 minutes
Each serving has:
62.51 calories
2.37 g. protein
1.48 g. carbohydrates
5.37 g. total fat
2.91 g. saturated fat
9.71 mg. cholesterol
42.7 mg. sodium
0.13 g. fiber

1. Mix cashews and cheese together in a bowl. Set aside.

2. Remove sheet of *phyllo*, and keep remaining 7 sheets covered with a damp towel to prevent drying. Brush sheet of phyllo lightly with melted butter. Spoon $^1/_8$ mixture along long edge, leaving a $^1/_2$-inch margin. Fold phyllo over mixture, then fold the edges over like a burrito. Continue rolling phyllo into a cylinder. Don't worry about any tears in the dough. Just brush with some additional butter and the edges will stick back together. Brush finished edge with melted butter to seal. Repeat with 7 remaining sheets until mixture is used. Place plastic wrap inside a 10×15-inch baking dish, layering more plastic wrap between layers. Cover and refrigerate until ready to serve.

3. Preheat oven to 425°F.

4. Place phyllo rolls on a baking sheet sprayed with nonstick cooking spray. Bake for 15 minutes or until golden brown. Remove from the pan with a wide spatula and cool on a rack. Slice into 3 equal parts per roll.

Nutri Speak

Phyllo means "leaf" in Greek, but the dough was created in Istanbul, Turkey, during the Ottoman Empire. Today phyllo dough is found in the freezer section of your grocery store. Just remember to defrost it for at least 8 hours, then let it come to room temperature before using, or you'll end up with broken sheets.

Gruyère Apple Spread

Makes 16 servings
Prep time: 5 minutes
Cook time: none
Each serving has:
38.13 calories
4 g. protein
0.58 g. carbohydrate
3.36 g. total fat
1.88 g. saturated fat
9.78 mg. cholesterol
31.49 mg. sodium
0.11 g. fiber

3 oz. cream cheese

2 oz. low-fat Gruyère cheese

2 tsp. 2% milk

1 tsp. stone-ground or French mustard

¼ cup apple, diced with skin

1 TB. pecans, chopped

1 TB. chives, snipped

1. In a small bowl, beat cream cheese. Shred cheese and mix with milk and mustard until well blended. Stir in apple, pecans, and chives. Cover and refrigerate 1 hour.

2. Serve on rye or stone-ground whole-wheat crackers or as a dip for vegetables.

Hot Artichoke Dip

1 cup artichoke hearts, frozen or canned

5 oz. Parmesan cheese, grated

8 oz. low-fat cheese, such as neufatchel

8 oz. sour cream

¹/₂ tsp. French mustard

Makes 18 servings
Prep time: 10 minutes
Cook time: 40 minutes
Each serving has:
89.88 calories
5.19 g. protein
2.07 g. carbohydrate
6.88 g. total fat
4.32 g. saturated fat
20.46 mg. cholesterol
208.58 mg. sodium
0.43 g. fiber

1. Defrost artichoke hearts if frozen or drain one can. Place Parmesan cheese, low-fat cheese, sour cream, and mustard in a food processor, and pulse to chop artichoke hearts. Then puree until well mixed. Place in an ovenproof bowl large enough to accommodate the mixture; cover and refrigerate until 1 hour before serving. This prevents the mixture from separating.

2. Heat oven to 325°F. Place the uncovered dish in the oven and bake for 40 minutes until top is lightly browned and mixture is hot in the center. Let cool 15 minutes before serving.

3. Serve with fresh, raw vegetables for dipping.

Food for Thought _____

To make individual servings, use mushroom caps filled with 1 tsp. of the hot dip for better portion control.

Mexican Fiesta Salsa

Makes 6 servings
Prep time: 10 minutes
Cook time: none
Each serving has:
21.31 calories
0.95 g. protein
4.62 g. carbohydrate
0.27 g. total fat
0.04 g. saturated fat
0 mg. cholesterol
400.12 mg. sodium
1.24 g. fiber

$^1/_4$ cup onion, diced

$^1/_4$ cup fresh cilantro, chopped

2 cups tomatoes, diced

$^1/_4$ cup jalapeño chili, finely chopped

1 tsp. sea salt

3 cups cucumber, sliced into $^1/_4$-inch thick rounds

1. Place onion, cilantro, tomatoes, and jalapeno chili in a bowl. Season with sea salt and toss.

2. Serve with cucumber slices.

Prosciutto Wrapped Stuffed Chocolate Dates

Makes 24 servings
Prep time: 10 minutes
Cook time: 2 minutes
Each serving has:
70.53 calories
3.01 g. protein
6.72 g. carbohydrate
4.33 g. total fat
1.16 g. saturated fat
1.13 mg. cholesterol
84.38 mg. sodium
0.83 g. fiber

1 cup Medjool dates, about 24, pitted

$^1/_4$ cup apple, peeled and finely diced

$^1/_4$ cup goat cheese

1 TB. dark and unsweetened chocolate, grated

3 oz. prosciutto ham, about 8 slices

24 walnut halves

1. Open dates and remove any seeds.

2. Mix apples, cheese, and chocolate together. Fill each date with a small amount of cheese mixture, and press one walnut half inside and close. Wrap $^1/_3$ piece prosciutto ham around each date and secure with a toothpick.

3. Heat a griddle on high. Then reduce heat, and place prosciutto-wrapped dates on the griddle, turning often until prosciutto is crisp. Serve immediately.

Variation: Omit ham and add 1 teaspoon of hot pepper jelly to cheese mixture with the chocolate.

Pumpkin Pie Hummus

2 TB. tahini

2 TB. fresh lemon juice

1 tsp. pumpkin pie spice

1 tsp. peanut oil

³/₄ tsp. sea salt

1 can (15 oz.) pumpkin

1 TB. pumpkin seeds

Makes 10 servings
Prep time: 5 minutes
Cook time: none
Each serving has:
39.45 calories
1.07 g. protein
4.67 g. carbohydrate
2.29 g. total fat
0.35 g. saturated fat
0 mg. cholesterol
182.77 mg. sodium
1.55 g. fiber

1. Place *tahini*, lemon juice, pumpkin pie spice, peanut oil, salt, and pumpkin into the food processor or blender, and purée until smooth.

2. Turn into a serving dish and fold in pumpkin seeds.

3. Serve with whole grain crackers, pita wedges, or crisp vegetables.

Nutri Speak

Tahini is a thick ground paste made from sesame seeds that is used to flavor mashed beans or hummus. The name is derived from the Turkish word for sesame flour or oil (tahin) and the Arabic word for grind (tahana).

Shrimp in a Blanket

Makes 48 servings
Prep time: 10 minutes
Cook time: 20 minutes
Each serving has:
44.63 calories
3.34 g. protein
1.96 g. carbohydrate
2.42 g. total fat
0.84 g. saturated fat
12.85 mg. cholesterol
537 mg. sodium
0.01 g. dietary fiber

³/₄ lb. bacon, thinly sliced

2 lbs. raw shrimp (medium-size, 24 count per pound)

10 oz. teriyaki sauce

toothpicks

1. Cut bacon slices in half, removing any obvious fatty sections. Wrap bacon around each shrimp. Secure with toothpicks.

2. Place in a 9×13-inch baking dish. Pour teriyaki sauce over shrimp. Cover and refrigerate 1 hour.

3. Bake uncovered at 400°F 20 to 25 minutes or until bacon is crisp. Drain and serve.

Smoke Signals

If you are allergic to shellfish, you may be unable to process a protein called tropomyosin. Avoid clams, oysters, lobster, crayfish, mussels, and snails.

Smoky Cilantro Lime Shrimp

Makes 4 servings
Prep time: 20 minutes
Cook time: 4 minutes
144.3 calories
3.82 g. protein
1.85 g. carbohydrate
13.9 g. total fat
1.89 g. saturated fat
27.36 mg. cholesterol
621.6 mg. sodium
0.25 g. fiber

2 tsp. lime zest

¹/₄ cup fresh lime juice

¹/₄ cup fresh cilantro coarsely chopped

1 tsp. sea salt

2 TB. sugar substitute, such as Splenda

¹/₂ tsp. chipotle chili powder

¹/₄ cup olive oil

¹/₂ lb. raw shrimp (medium-size, 24 count per pound)

Wood skewers, soaked in water, about 1 hour

1. Combine lime peel, lime juice, cilantro, salt, sugar substitute, and chipotle powder in a small bowl. Whisk in olive oil slowly to blend. Marinate shrimp in sauce for 15 minutes.

2. Place shrimp on water-soaked wood skewers, and grill quickly until just opaque. Brush with any remaining marinade just before serving.

Sweet Potato Crispy Won Tons

1¹/₂ lbs. sweet potatoes

¹/₂ cup ricotta cheese

3 TB. Parmesan, ground

¹/₈ tsp. nutmeg

¹/₄ tsp. sea salt

³/₈ tsp. dried ground sage

24 small won ton wrappers

Small dish with water

Nonstick cooking spray

Makes 24 servings
Prep time: 10 minutes
Cook time: 1 hour
Each serving has:
56.7 calories
1.68 g. protein
10.89 g. carbohydrate
0.69 g. total fat
0.4 g. saturated fat
2.54 mg. cholesterol
70.71 mg. sodium
0.95 g. fiber

1. Preheat oven to 375°F.

2. Poke holes in sweet potatoes, and place them in a pan. Roast for 45 minutes or until soft, turning once for even baking. Let cool.

3. Scoop flesh from sweet potatoes to equal one cup, and combine with ricotta cheese, Parmesan, nutmeg, salt, and sage.

4. Spoon 2 teaspoons mixture into center of each won ton wrapper. Lightly wet edges with water, and bring opposite edges together to form a triangle. Press edges to seal. Store in the refrigerator for up to one day at this point until ready to bake covered with plastic wrap.

5. Place won tons onto a baking sheet lightly coated with cooking spray, and bake for 17 minutes or until crisp.

Nutri Notes

Look for sweet potatoes that are small to medium size with few bruises. Do not store them in the refrigerator because they will rot.

Tiered Yogurt Cheese Spread

Makes 32 servings
Prep time: 1 day
Cook time: none
Each serving has:
43.28 calories
1.79 protein
3 g. carbohydrate
2.8 g. total fat
1.15 g. saturated fat
5.83 mg. cholesterol
59.88 mg. sodium
0.34 g. fiber

Food for Thought

Skim milk and plain nonfat yogurt are lowest in saturated fat and cholesterol. If separation of the whey occurs, just stir the yogurt to blend the whey back into the mixture.

6 cups low-fat yogurt

2 TB. garlic, sliced

2 TB. fresh basil, chopped

1 TB. fresh rosemary, chopped

1 TB. fresh thyme, chopped

1 TB. fresh sage, chopped

1 TB. shallot, minced

3 TB. olive oil

1 tsp. lemon zest

1/2 tsp. sea salt

1/4 tsp. pepper flakes

1/2 cup artichoke hearts, drained or defrosted and diced

1/2 cup red bell pepper, diced

1. Drain yogurt overnight in the refrigerator in a colander lined with 4 layers of cheesecloth or in a yogurt strainer. Discard liquid and spoon yogurt cheese into a medium-size bowl; cover and refrigerate for 3 more hours or until quite firm.

2. Combine garlic, basil, rosemary, thyme, sage, shallot, olive oil, lemon rind, salt, and pepper flakes in a small bowl. Chop artichokes and peppers, and combine in another bowl.

3. Place one quarter yogurt cheese into a glass container; then spread half herbal mixture on top. Repeat with another layer of yogurt cheese; then place half the artichoke and peppers mixture on top. Repeat with another layer of cheese and herbal mixture, ending with a layer of peppers and artichokes on top. Cover and refrigerate for 12 hours or up to 1 week.

4. Serve at room temperature with rye krisp crackers or vegetable sticks.

Warm Olives in Citrus

2 tsp. cumin seeds

1¹/₂ cups green olives, in oil

¹/₂ tsp. dried thyme

1 tsp. black pepper

1 tsp. orange zest

1 tsp. lime zest

1 TB. orange juice

Makes 12 servings
Prep time: 5 minutes
Cook time: 3 minutes
Each serving has:
34.87 calories
0.47 g. protein
0.63 g. carbohydrate
3.65 g. total fat
0.46 g. saturated fat
0 mg. cholesterol
709.8 mg. sodium
0.48 g. fiber

1. Toast cumin seeds until fragrant in a large, dry skillet over high heat. Remove the pan from the heat, and add olives, thyme, and pepper. Place over medium heat for about 3 minutes or until warmed through.

2. Transfer to a bowl, and sprinkle orange and lime zest over them. Squeeze small amount of orange juice over olives and serve.

White Bean Dip with Garlic, Lemon, and Basil

4 cups canned navy beans

¹/₃ cup fresh basil, chopped

¹/₄ cup fresh lemon juice

1 TB. olive oil

2 cloves garlic, smashed

Water as necessary

Salt and pepper to taste

Makes 24 servings
Prep time: 5 minutes
Cook time: none
Each serving has:
57.84 calories
3.46 g. protein
9.84 g. carbohydrate
0.79 g. total fat
0.13 g. saturated fat
0 mg. cholesterol
196 mg. sodium
2.65 g. fiber

1. Drain *navy beans*. Combine beans, basil, lemon juice, olive oil, and garlic in a food processor. Process until smooth, adding water as necessary until a dipping consistency is achieved. Season with salt and pepper to taste.

2. Refrigerate for 1 hour before serving with raw vegetables.

Nutri Speak

Navy beans, also known as Yankee beans, are white, round beans used by the Navy since the mid-1800s. They are popular in pork and bean recipes.

Chapter 10

Soups to Warm Your Soul

In This Chapter

◆ Economize with meat soups

◆ Volumize with vegetables

◆ Bulk up on beans

Soup is one of my favorite dishes because you simply can't make a bad one. Trust me on this point. All you have to do is soften some onions, add left-over vegetables, throw in a few cups of water, and play around with the seasoning. That's it! If you need to stretch your food dollars, soups can make even Old Scrooge smile. It's a wonderful way to use leftover poultry or inexpensive cuts of meat without breaking the bank. Add any protein, such as fish, fowl, or tofu, and you've got a nutritious meal in a bowl.

In this chapter, I'll show you how to pump up the volume of any basic soup by adding chunky pieces of vegetables. Cut them any way you want, toss them in, and ignore them. They'll do all the work for you by supplying lots of vitamins and fiber to your meal. Don't overcook the vegetables, as it will break down the fiber. Simply cook until a knife can just pierce the outer layer.

Wimpy soups are a thing of the past. You can make any soup a "total manly" soup by adding vegetables, grains, beans, or even pasta. Barley is a nutritious powerhouse, as it contains twice the amount of fatty acids as wheat and is rich in selenium and fiber. It can even help to lower cholesterol. Want to cut the fat in your soup? Put it in the refrigerator until cold. The saturated fat will become solid on the top, making it easy to remove it from the dish.

Beans are another great healthy food, as they contain insoluble fiber that can lower cholesterol while helping you to control your weight. Ounce for ounce, beans provide complex carbohydrates that are slow to raise your blood sugar and possess half the calories of fat. They can even help you reach your daily recommended intake of calcium. My favorites are chickpeas or garbanzo beans, black beans, and navy beans, but I've never met a bean I didn't like. Use them to your advantage when preparing any of these delicious recipes. And don't ignore the liquid portion of any soup.

Think of broth as a liquid foundation. Choose a richly flavored base as a companion to your medley of vegetables, and you'll be cooking like Grandma in no time.

Very Berry Soup

Makes 4 servings
Prep time: 5 minutes
Cook time: 30 minutes
Each serving has:
274.5 calories
7.34 g. protein
61.64 g. carbohydrate
1.83 g. total fat
0.33 g. saturated fat
0 mg. cholesterol
18.95 mg. sodium
14.49 g. fiber

1 cup pearl barley

6 cups water

1 cup fresh or frozen raspberries

1/2 cup raisins

1 cup fresh or frozen cherries

2 tsp. sugar substitute, such as Splenda

1 tsp. ground cinnamon

1. Using a pressure cooker, place barley and 2 cups water in the pan. Close the lid, lock into place, and set on a high flame. When the cooker reaches full pressure, slightly reduce the heat and cook for 10 minutes. Transfer the pressure cooker to the sink and run cold water over it until the pressure valve lowers and allows you to open the cooker.

2. Replace the cooker on the stove over medium heat and add remaining water, raspberries, raisins, and cherries. Cook for 30 minutes or until thickened. Add sugar substitute to desired sweetness; then place in the refrigerator until well chilled.

3. Sprinkle with cinnamon upon serving.

Variation: If you don't have a pressure cooker, you can cook the barley in boiling water for 30 minutes. Be sure to use twice the amount of water to the measurement of barley.

Food for Thought

Cinnamon can help lower your blood sugar and cholesterol, so don't hesitate to use lots of it whenever possible.

Cajun Shrimp Soup

1 TB. olive oil

1/2 cup green bell pepper, sliced

1/4 cup green onions, coarsely chopped

1/2 tsp. garlic, minced

3 cups tomato juice

1 bottle (8 oz.) clam juice

1 TB. Old Bay Seasoning (more if preferred)

1 bay leaf

Sea salt to taste

1/4 cup long grain rice, uncooked

1 lb. raw, peeled shrimp (medium-size, 24 count per pound)

Hot sauce to taste

Makes 6 servings
Prep time: 10 minutes
Cook time: 20 minutes
Each serving has:
92.29 calories
8.61 g. protein
8.5 g. carbohydrate
3 g. total fat
0.44 g. saturated fat
54.72 mg. cholesterol
292 mg. sodium
1.33 g. fiber

1. Pour olive oil into a large pot over medium heat. Sauté peppers, onions, and garlic until tender. Stir in tomato juice and clam juice, and season with *Old Bay Seasoning*, bay leaf, and salt. Bring to a boil, and stir in rice. Reduce heat and cover. Simmer 15 minutes, until rice is tender.

2. Stir in shrimp, turn off the heat and let shrimp poach in soup for 5 minutes or until shrimp are opaque. Remove bay leaf, and season with hot sauce.

Grandma's Chicken and Rice Soup

30 oz. low-sodium chicken broth

2 tsp. garlic, finely chopped

1/2 tsp. tarragon

1 chicken breast (9 oz.), frozen or cooked

1 lb. tomatoes, coarsely diced

1 cup wild rice, cooked in bag

1 cup zucchini, chopped

1/2 tsp. black pepper

Makes 6 servings
Prep time: 5 minutes
Cook time: 15 minutes
Each serving has:
144.4 calories
17.71 g. protein
13.62 g. carbohydrate
2.18 g. total fat
0.58 g. saturated fat
25.85 mg. cholesterol
89.9 mg. sodium
1.58 g. fiber

1. In a Dutch oven or large saucepan, add broth, garlic, tarragon, and bring to a boil. Add chicken, tomatoes, rice, zucchini, and pepper.

2. Return to a boil, then reduce the heat and cover. Simmer for 5 minutes or until heated through.

Chicken Butternut Squash Soup

Makes 6 servings
Prep time: 10 minutes
Cook time: 35 minutes
Each serving has:
229.69 calories
19.43 g. protein
22.86 g. carbohydrate
5.61 g. total fat
1.27 g. saturated fat
41.03 mg. cholesterol
104.4 mg. sodium
0.57 g. fiber

Food for Thought

Butternut squash is loaded with vitamin C, potassium, fiber, and beta carotene. It tastes similar to pumpkin and can be stored for 3 months in a dry place.

2 lbs. butternut squash

1 TB. olive oil

1 tsp. garlic, minced

1 cup onion, coarsely sliced

2 TB. celery, coarsely diced

32 oz. low-sodium chicken broth

1 TB. sugar substitute, such as Splenda Brown Sugar blend

$1/4$ tsp. ground nutmeg

$1/4$ tsp. ground ginger

$1/8$ tsp. cayenne

2 lbs. roasted chicken breast, thinly sliced

1. Peel butternut squash, and cut down the middle into two sections. Use a spoon to scoop out seeds and any fibers. Put $1/2$ cup water into an 8×8-inch glass pan. Place squash face down into the pan, and cover with plastic wrap. Microwave on high for 20 minutes.

2. Combine olive oil, garlic, onion, and celery in a 3-quart microwave safe casserole. Cover tightly with a lid or plastic wrap, turned back slightly on one side. Microwave on high until vegetables are tender, 3 to 5 minutes.

3. Pour broth into a 4-cup glass measure and microwave on high 5 minutes.

4. Spoon flesh from squash into food processor bowl, and add cooked vegetables. Process into a smooth mixture. Add sugar substitute, nutmeg, ginger, and cayenne. Process quickly to blend.

5. Return mixture to a casserole, and stir in warmed chicken broth and cooked, thinly sliced chicken. Cover again, and microwave on high until heated through, 8 to 10 minutes. Let stand, covered, 3 to 5 minutes.

Chicken Little Chowder

$^1/_2$ cup carrots, coarsely chopped

1 cup 2% milk

1 cup low-sodium chicken broth

$^1/_2$ tsp. white pepper

1 cup onion, coarsely chopped

2 tsp. garlic, minced

$^1/_2$ lb. chicken breast, cut into 1-inch pieces

$^1/_4$ cup potato flakes

1 tsp. lemon juice

Makes 4 servings
Prep time: 10 minutes
Cook time: 6 hours
Each serving has:
160.6 calories
19.18 g. protein
13.01 g. carbohydrate
3.4 g. total fat
1.6 g. saturated fat
40.04 mg. cholesterol
145.5 mg. sodium
1.95 g. fiber

1. Combine carrots, milk, chicken broth, pepper, onion, garlic, and chicken in a slow cooker. Cover and cook on low for 5 to 6 hours or until chicken is thoroughly cooked. Add potato flakes and stir well to combine.

2. Cook mixture on high, uncovered, for 5 to 10 minutes or until chowder has thickened and dried potato flakes have dissolved.

3. Stir in lemon juice and serve.

Cream of Cauliflower Soup

1 TB. peanut oil

1 cup onion, coarsely chopped

$3^1/_2$ cups low-sodium vegetable broth

$^1/_2$ cup carrots, coarsely sliced

1 lb. cauliflower

1 cup half-and-half

$^1/_8$ tsp. ground nutmeg

$^1/_4$ tsp. fresh thyme, chopped

$^1/_4$ tsp. sea salt

$^1/_4$ tsp. black pepper

1 TB. fresh parsley, chopped

Makes 6 servings
Prep time: 10 minutes
Cook time: 10 minutes
Each serving has:
158.3 calories
4.95 g. protein
17.37 g. carbohydrate
8.4 g. total fat
3.36 g. saturated fat
16.29 mg. cholesterol
618.5 mg. sodium
3.09 g. fiber

1. Pour peanut oil into a 4 quart pan over medium heat. Add onion and cook, stirring often, until soft and translucent. Slice carrots and separate cauliflower into small florets. Stir in homemade Low-Sodium Vegetable Broth (later in this chapter) and increase heat to high. Bring to a boil, then add carrots and cauliflower to broth. Reduce the heat, cover and gently boil until vegetables are tender when pierced (about 7 minutes.)

2. Transfer mixture to a food processor after cooling about 10 minutes. DO NOT OVERFILL as mixture will expand when processed. Purée in 3 batches until smooth. Return to the pan and add half-and-half and nutmeg. Gently cook over medium heat until steaming hot again. Season with salt and pepper, and garnish with parsley.

Cranky Crab Soup with Spinach

Makes 6 servings
Prep time: 10 minutes
Cook time: 15 minutes
Each serving has:
257.4 calories
32.14 g. protein
23.63 g. carbohydrate
3.76 g. total fat
0.87 g. saturated fat
82.58 mg. cholesterol
2113 mg. sodium
4.46 g. fiber

3¹/₂ cups low-sodium vegetable broth

2¹/₂ cups water

1 cup carrots, halved and thinly sliced

1 cup zucchini, quartered and thinly sliced

¹/₄ cup green onion, thinly sliced

1 cup spinach leaves

2 lbs. thawed crabmeat

¹/₂ cup potato flakes

1 tsp. white pepper

1 tsp. sea salt

1. In a large saucepan bring broth and water to boil. Add carrots and simmer, covered, for 5 to 7 minutes. Add zucchini, onions, and spinach, and simmer for 2 to 3 minutes longer.

2. Rinse crab under cool running water. Break into portions; then add to soup. Heat for 5 to 6 minutes or until crab is heated through.

3. Stir in potato flakes, and season to taste with salt and pepper.

Hot Ginger Pear Soup

3 lbs. Bartlett pears, firmly ripe

2 tsp. sugar substitute, such as Splenda

1 TB. cinnamon stick

1 tsp. cloves, whole

1 tsp. freshly grated or ground ginger

4 cups water

1 tsp. vanilla flavoring or 1 bean, split

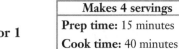

Makes 4 servings
Prep time: 15 minutes
Cook time: 40 minutes
Each serving has:
211.6 calories
1.47 g. protein
53.57 g. carbohydrate
1.55 g. total fat
0.12 g. saturated fat
0 mg. cholesterol
9.38 mg. sodium
9.33 g. fiber

1. Peel, halve, and core pears. Place in a 4-quart pan. Add sugar substitute, cinnamon stick, cloves, ginger, and 3 cups water. If using vanilla bean, add now, otherwise, reserve vanilla flavoring until soup is made. Bring mixture to a boil over high heat, cover, reduce heat, and simmer for 30 minutes.

2. Remove pears and ginger from cooking liquid using a slotted spoon and transfer to a food processor or blender. Purée until smooth. Set aside.

3. Boil reserved cooking liquid over high heat until reduced to 1½ cups (about 10 minutes). Remove from heat, and discard cinnamon and cloves. Lift out vanilla bean, pat dry, and place in a small amount of vodka for future use.

4. Stir purée into reduced liquid. If using vanilla flavoring, add it now. Add enough water to make 6 cups if necessary. Return to medium heat, stirring often until hot. Garnish with mint sprigs.

Homemade Low-Sodium Vegetable Broth

Makes 8 servings
Prep time: 15 minutes
Cook time: 8 hours
Each serving has:
111.4 calories
2.93 g. protein
25.73 g. carbohydrate
0.53 g. total fat
0.08 g. saturated fat
0 mg. cholesterol
50.37 mg. sodium
3.9 g. fiber

1 cup onion, peeled and quartered

$^1/_4$ cup carrots, coarsely chopped

$^1/_2$ cup parsnips, coarsely chopped

$^1/_2$ cup potato, peeled and coarsely chopped

$^1/_2$ cup mushrooms, coarsely chopped

3 cloves garlic, crushed

2 cups leeks, coarsely chopped

1 cup celery, coarsely chopped

8 cups water

8 peppercorns

4 whole cloves

1 TB. fresh parsley, chopped

2 bay leaves

1. Into a cold pan, put onions and $^1/_4$ cup water. Sauté until water is evaporated. Continue stirring onions slowly until caramelized, about 15 minutes, adding water as needed. In a slow cooker, combine carrots, parsnips, potato, mushrooms, garlic, leeks, celery, water, peppercorns, cloves, parsley, and bay leaves with the caramelized onions. Cover and cook for 8 hours. Strain out all vegetables and seasoning. Cool broth; then refrigerate for up to 5 days or freeze in portions.

Food for Thought _____

Parsnips are a high-glycemic vegetable used to sweeten dishes in the absence of sugar or honey. The flavor compounds are located in the skin, so don't peel them. They are a good source of potassium, which can help to lower blood pressure.

Sweet Red Pepper Soup

1 cup red onion, coarsely sliced

3 tsp. garlic, mashed

1 TB. unsalted butter

1¹/₂ cups red bell pepper, coarsely chopped

1¹/₂ cups tomatoes, chopped

¹/₂ tsp. anise seed

¹/₂ tsp. herbs de Provence

¹/₂ tsp. paprika

15 oz. low-sodium chicken broth

¹/₄ cup reduced-fat sour cream

Makes 4 servings
Prep time: 10 minutes
Cook time: 20 minutes
Each serving has:
107.9 calories
5.21 g. protein
9.98 g. carbohydrate
5.79 g. total fat
3.2 g. saturated fat
14.36 mg. cholesterol
44.91 mg. sodium
2.14 g. fiber

1. Chop onion, tomato, and peppers.

2. In a medium saucepan cook onion and garlic in hot butter until tender but not brown. Add peppers; cover and cook over medium heat for 8 to 10 minutes or until peppers are soft, stirring occasionally.

3. Add tomato, anise seed, *herbs de Provence*, and paprika. Add broth. Bring to a boil; remove from heat. Cool slightly.

4. Pour soup into a blender container or food processor bowl. Cover and blend until smooth; return to saucepan. Stir in sour cream and heat through, but do not boil.

5. To serve, spoon into soup bowls. Top each serving with about 1 tablespoon of Lemon Sour Cream (see recipe in Chapter 19) and draw a knife through to swirl.

Nutri Speak

Herbs de Provence is a mixture of lavender, basil, fennel seed, sage, rosemary, thyme, marjoram, and summer savory herbs. The mixture is traditionally packed in tiny clay pots and can be found in grocery stores or ordered from a specialty company.

Three Bean Chili Soup

Makes 8 servings
Prep time: 5 minutes
Cook time: 8 hours
Each serving has:
357.6 calories
19.51 g. protein
66.77 g. carbohydrate
2.49 g. total fat
0.45 g. saturated fat
0 mg. cholesterol
1261 mg. sodium
13.46 g. fiber

30 oz. garbanzo beans, drained and rinsed

30 oz. red kidney beans, drained and rinsed

30 oz. white northern beans, drained and rinsed

30 oz. low-sodium beef broth

1 cup tomatoes, coarsely diced

$^1/_4$ cup jalapeño peppers, finely diced

1 cup onion, coarsely chopped

4 tsp. chili powder

1 tsp. garlic, minced

$^1/_4$ tsp. black pepper

$^1/_4$ tsp. red chili pepper flakes

1. In a 4-quart slow cooker, combine garbanzo beans, kidney beans, white beans, broth, tomatoes, peppers, onion, chili powder, garlic, black pepper, and red pepper flakes.

2. Cover and cook on low-heat setting for 6 to 8 hours.

Tito Taco Soup

Makes 8 servings
Prep time: 10 minutes
Cook time: 6 hours
Each serving has:
372.2 calories
24.47 g. protein
47.04 g. carbohydrate
9.4 g. total fat
4.26 g. saturated fat
38 mg. cholesterol
403.6 mg. sodium
10.42 g. fiber

1 lb. 15% fat ground beef

15 oz. black beans

15 oz. garbanzo beans

1 can (14.5 oz.) stewed tomatoes with chilies

1 package taco seasoning mix

1 cup water

1. In a large skillet, cook ground beef until brown; then drain off fat. Transfer to a crock pot and stir in black beans, garbanzo beans, tomatoes, seasoning mix, and water.

2. Cover and cook on low heat setting for 6 to 8 hours or on high heat for 3 to 4 hours.

Turkey Gobble Soup

12 oz. turkey breast, raw, cut into one-inch cubes

1 TB. peanut oil

1/2 cup onion, coarsely chopped

1/2 cup red bell pepper, coarsely chopped

1/2 tsp. garlic, minced

30 oz. low-sodium chicken broth

1/3 cup quick-cooking barley

1 cup broccoli rabe

1 tsp. fresh tarragon

1 tsp. white pepper

1/2 tsp. sea salt

Makes 4 servings
Prep time: 10 minutes
Cook time: 20 minutes
Each serving has:
260.2 calories
30.67 g. protein
17.95 g. carbohydrate
7.3 g. total fat
1.67 g. saturated fat
36.65 mg. cholesterol
1604 mg. sodium
4.72 g. fiber

1. In a Dutch oven, cook and stir turkey breast pieces in hot peanut oil over medium heat for 5 minutes. Remove turkey from the pan.

2. Add onion, pepper, and garlic to the Dutch oven, stirring frequently to prevent garlic from burning. Cook for 3 minutes. Add turkey.

3. Add broth, barley, broccoli rabe, and tarragon, and bring to a boil. Cover and simmer for 10 to 12 minutes or until barley is tender. Season with pepper and salt as needed.

Nutri Notes

Broccoli rabe, or rapini, is related to the turnip, not broccoli. It is grown for its pungent shoots and is prized in Italian cuisine for its bittersweet flavor. To remove the bitterness, merely plunge the rapini into boiling water for 1 minute, then drain. Garlic is an ideal cooking companion.

Zucchini Mint Soup

Makes 4 servings
Prep time: 10 minutes
Cook time: 30 minutes
Each serving has:
103.4 calories
4.72 g. protein
4.26 g. carbohydrate
7.81 g. total fat
1.21 g. saturated fat
0.87 mg. cholesterol
43.37 mg. sodium
0.97 g. fiber

2 TB. olive oil

$^1/_2$ cup onion, coarsely chopped

1 tsp. garlic cloves, mashed

1 cup zucchini, thinly sliced into chunks

$^1/_4$ cup cucumber, coarsely diced

15 oz. low-sodium chicken stock

2 TB. mint leaves, thinly sliced

1 cup water

$^1/_4$ cup tomato, coarsely diced

1. Heat oil in a saucepan over medium heat, and add onion and garlic. Cook until onion is translucent, being careful not to burn garlic. Add zucchini and cucumber, and cook for 3 minutes until zucchini is bright green.

2. Add stock and 1 cup water. Bring to a boil; then reduce and simmer for 12 minutes or until veggies are tender. Pour mixture, after cooling slightly, into a blender or food processor and purée. Return mixture to the pan, and add mint leaves. Season with salt as necessary.

3. Serve in a bowl topped with a few diced tomatoes. Add mint sprig for decoration.

Chapter 11

Seductive Salads

In This Chapter

- ◆ Flavors Shine
- ◆ Raw Power
- ◆ Pepper and Oil Secrets

Salads are a wonderful way to let flavors shine while providing your family with a good source of nutrients. Just think of your salad as a canvas: start with the basic lettuce; add some colorful root vegetables and chunks of protein; and finish with a splash of dressing topped with a sprinkle of seeds or nuts. Now you have a masterpiece that could replace your multivitamin.

Salads have been relegated to a side dish, but they are really an important mini meal that can boost your metabolism. As an added bonus, they can be nutrient dense, which means you get the most nutritious elements for the least calories.

Let's face it. Cooking techniques, such as boiling, can result in valuable nutrients being washed down the drain. Food can lose up to 85 percent of its nutritional value depending on preparation, making it a "dead food." Eating a fresh salad can keep your diet in balance. Don't forget that fruit can add fiber and vital nutrients to your diet. Berries, such as blueberries and cranberries, can even help prevent tooth decay by blocking cavity promoting bacteria from adhering to those pearly whites.

Salads make a nutritious meal if you don't bury them in dressing. Remember, it's not dressing *with* salad if you want to keep the calories and saturated fat in line. If you see dressing in the bottom of the bowl, you've added too much! Avoid any commercial dressing that has a high saturated fat level or uses the word "hydrogenated" on the label if you want to keep a good cholesterol profile.

Not all oils are created equal. Choose ones high in the good fats, called monoun-saturated fatty acids, such as extra virgin olive oil, canola (rapeseed) oil, or peanut oil. Prepare your own dressings whenever possible to keep a tight control on fat. Eat like the French, and mix some vinegar, olive oil, and mustard together for a healthy salad dressing you can have any time, even in a restaurant. Balsamic vinegar can kick it up a notch if you want something different from red or white vinegar dressings. If you are eating out, ask for the dressing on the side, and dip your fork into the dressing before taking a bite. You'll enjoy the flavor but not the calories of an overdressed salad. For that extra punch, fresh ground peppercorns can add amazing flavor without calories to any salad. Experiment with different varieties, such as Tellicherry black peppercorns or Muntok white peppercorns, for a richer, aromatic flavor. Your mouth will simply giggle with every bite.

Imperial Dragon Wrap Salad

Makes 4 servings
Prep time: 10 minutes
Cook time: 10 minutes
Each serving has:
230.7 calories
16.02 g. protein
10.12 g. carbohydrates
15.14 g. total fat
2.74 g. saturated fat
44.71 mg. cholesterol
319.5 mg. sodium
2.74 g. fiber

1 tsp. peanut oil
$^1/_2$ lb. ground turkey breast
1 TB. green curry paste
1 TB. garlic, crushed
1 TB. low-sodium soy sauce
1 TB. sugar substitute, such as Splenda
1 TB. fresh basil, chopped

1 cup tomato, coarsely diced
$^1/_2$ cup bean sprouts
4 leaves lettuce, such as romaine or butter leaf
$^1/_2$ cup dry-roasted peanuts
$^1/_2$ cup fresh cilantro, chopped

1. In a medium pan, heat peanut oil over low heat. Add turkey, curry, garlic, soy sauce, and sugar substitute. Cook until done.

2. In a bowl, toss turkey mixture with basil, tomatoes, and sprouts.

3. Place lettuce leaf on a plate, fill with turkey mixture, and top with chopped peanuts and cilantro. Wrap like a taco and enjoy.

Crab in Spicy Orange Dressing

1 cup fennel, sliced

1 TB. olive oil

3 TB. fresh lemon juice

Salt and pepper to taste

2 cups orange juice

1 tsp. chili powder

1 TB. unsalted butter

12³/₄ oz. canned or fresh crabmeat

1¹/₂ tsp. ground cumin

¹/₄ tsp. cayenne pepper

Makes 6 servings
Prep time: 15 minutes
Cook time: 20 minutes
Each serving has:
147.2 calories
13.5 g. protein
11.26 g. carbohydrates
5.52 g. total fat
1.71 g. saturated fat
58.76 mg. cholesterol
216.4 mg. sodium
0.97 g. fiber

1. Trim top and bottom of fennel bulb; then quarter lengthwise and slice quarters into ¹/₈-inch slices. Place in a mixing bowl and toss with olive oil, 2 tablespoons lemon juice, and season to taste with salt and pepper.

2. Just before serving make the sauce. In a small saucepan bring orange juice, remaining lemon juice, and cayenne pepper to a simmer over medium-high heat. Reduce to ¹/₃ cup (about 15 to 17 minutes). Remove from the heat and whisk in butter.

3. Drain crab and check for any shell fragments. Mix with ground cumin and cayenne pepper.

4. To serve, mound fennel strips on the plate, press down in the middle, and arrange crab meat mixture on top. Drizzle dressing around base of fennel and over crab.

5. Stack basil leaves, cut in julienne strips, and sprinkle on top of crab.

Nutri Notes

To julienne basil, merely stack the leaves, and then roll them up like a cigar. Using a knife, cut crosswise into ribbons.

Grilled Chicken Salad

Makes 2 servings	

Prep time: 10 minutes

Cook time: 7 minutes

Each serving has:

145.1 calories

22.34 g. protein

9.78 g. carbohydrates

1.94 g. total fat

0.42 g. saturated fat

49.33 mg. cholesterol

974.4 mg. sodium

1.33 g. fiber

Nutri Notes

Shallots are an excellent source of potassium, vitamin C, and folate, and are low in fat, cholesterol, and sodium. You can find them in the onion section of your grocery store.

6 oz. chicken breast, boneless and skinless

2 tsp. garlic, chopped

1 tsp. fresh cilantro, chopped

3 TB. reduced-sodium soy sauce

1 tsp. sugar substitute, such as Splenda

$^{1}/_{2}$ tsp. black pepper

$^{1}/_{2}$ tsp. turmeric

2 TB. reduced-sodium soy sauce

2 TB. fresh lime juice

2 tsp. sugar substitute, such as Splenda

$^{1}/_{4}$ cup shallots, finely chopped

$^{1}/_{2}$ tsp. chili powder

2 leaves romaine lettuce

1 tsp. sesame seeds

1. In a plastic bag, marinate chicken breast in mixture of garlic, cilantro, 1 tablespoon soy sauce, 1 teaspoon sugar substitute, pepper, and turmeric for one hour.

2. In another bowl, mix 2 tablespoons soy sauce, lime juice, 1 teaspoon sugar substitute, shallots, and chili powder. This will be your dressing.

3. Preheat a grill or griddle on high. Remove chicken from marinade, and grill until cooked, about 5 minutes. When cool, slice on an angle into 8 pieces. Place chicken pieces in dressing and coat thoroughly.

4. Place large leaf of lettuce in an oval bowl. Top with 4 slices of chicken, and sprinkle with some sesame seeds.

Honey Bunny's Carrot Salad

1 cup pineapple, packed in water

1¹/₂ cups carrots

1 tsp. honey

1 tsp. fresh lemon juice

¹/₂ tsp. sea salt

¹/₄ tsp. ground nutmeg

¹/₄ cup reduced-fat sour cream

Makes 4 servings
Prep time: 5 minutes
Cook time: none
Each serving has:
80.15 calories
1.47 g. protein
14.62 g. carbohydrates
2.39 g. total fat
1.25 g. saturated fat
5.82 mg. cholesterol
332.9 mg. sodium
2.13 g. fiber

1. Drain pineapple. Grate carrots.

2. Mix honey, lemon juice, salt, and nutmeg. Blend in sour cream. Add carrots and pineapple. Serve chilled.

Nutri Notes _____

Carrots contain minerals, such as iron, magnesium, and selenium, which may cause arcing in a microwave. They can even be used to make random lasers.

Aztec Zucchini Salad

¹/₂ cup tomato

1¹/₂ TB. fresh lemon juice

3 TB. peanut oil

Salt and pepper to taste

¹/₃ cup fresh spearmint leaves

¹/₄ cup fresh parsley

1 lb. zucchini

Makes 4 servings
Prep time: 10 minutes
Cook time: none
Each serving has:
120.05 calories
1.87 g. protein
5.64 g. carbohydrates
10.8 g. total fat
1.85 g. saturated fat
0 mg. cholesterol
11.67 mg. sodium
2.15 g. fiber

1. Place tomato cut into ¹/₄-inch dices into a small bowl.

2. Make dressing by whisking lemon juice, peanut oil, and salt and pepper to taste in a bowl.

3. In a food processor, chop mint and parsley. Remove the chopping blade, replace it with a shredding one, and shred zucchini over herbs. Transfer mixture to a large bowl, and drizzle ³/₄ of dressing over zucchini mix. Drain tomatoes, and toss with remaining dressing mix.

4. Divide zucchini between 4 plates. Add tomatoes, and garnish with spearmint leaves.

Pecos Bill Tomato Chili Salad

Makes 4 servings
Prep time: 30 minutes
Cook time: none
Each serving has:
88.76 calories
4.51 g. protein
8.36 g. carbohydrates
4.81 g. total fat
3.11 g. saturated fat
11.68 mg. cholesterol
602.3 mg. sodium
2.15 g. fiber

8 oz. poblano peppers, sliced, seeded and chopped

1 cup tomatoes, coarsely diced

¹/₂ cup red onions, thinly sliced

1 tsp. minced garlic

1 tsp. dried oregano

3 TB. fresh cilantro, chopped

3 TB. fresh lime juice

¹/₂ tsp. sea salt

1 cup butter leaf lettuce

¹/₄ cup cotija cheese

1. Toss peppers with tomatoes, onion, garlic, oregano, cilantro, lime juice, and salt. Cover and let rest 30 minutes.

2. Line platter with lettuce, and spoon salad on top. Sprinkle with *cotija cheese.*

Nutri Speak

Cotija cheese is a sharp, crumbly Mexican goat cheese known as the "Parmesan of Mexico." You can substitute any sharp, firm feta cheese for it in any recipe.

Salmon and Three Bean Salad with Walnuts

1 can (14.75 oz.) salmon

1 cup fresh green beans, cut on the diagonal into 2-inch pieces

1 cup canned cannellini beans

1 cup canned pinto beans

$^1/_2$ cup cucumber, thinly sliced

$^1/_2$ cup cherry tomatoes, cut into halves

$^1/_2$ cup green onions, coarsely sliced

1 garlic clove, crushed

$^1/_4$ cup walnut oil

3 TB. cider vinegar

3 TB. red wine vinegar

1 tsp. mustard

1 TB. walnut pieces

Makes 4 servings
Prep time: 7 minutes
Cook time: none
Each serving has:
444.3 calories
30.92 g. protein
32.77 g. carbohydrates
22.02 g. total fat
3.13 g. saturated fat
57.5 mg. cholesterol
282.5 mg. sodium
8.73 g. fiber

1. Drain salmon, removing any bones, and set aside.

2. Cook green beans in lightly salted boiling water for 4 minutes. Immediately plunge into ice water bath. Drain.

3. In a large bowl, mix salmon, green beans, cannellini beans, pinto beans, cucumber, tomatoes, and onions.

4. Mix dressing by combining garlic, walnut oil, cider vinegar, red wine vinegar, and mustard in a jar. Close the lid tightly, and shake until mixed. Pour over salad just before serving, and mix well. Top with walnut pieces.

Wrap It Up Ginger Pork

Makes 6 servings
Prep time: 15 minutes
Cook time: 20 minutes
Each serving has:
198.6 calories
23.55 g. protein
8.12 g. carbohydrates
7.9 g. total fat
2.72 g. saturated fat
62.75 mg. cholesterol
244.1 mg. sodium
2.05 g. fiber

1 lb. pork tenderloin

2 tsp. fresh ginger, finely grated

1 cup onion, thinly sliced

1 cup red bell pepper, cubed

1 cup green onion, sliced on the diagonal

2 cloves garlic, crushed

1 jalapeño or serrano pepper, finely chopped

2 TB. reduced-sodium soy sauce

2 TB. fresh lime juice

1 tsp. sugar substitute, such as Splenda

12 leaves romaine lettuce

1. Preheat the oven to 500°F. Place pork tenderloin on a piece of foil on a roasting pan. Place in the middle of the oven, and roast for 20 minutes. Remove and let rest 10 minutes before slicing into thin strips. Place in a large bowl.

2. Add ginger, onion, red bell pepper, and green onions to the pork. Set aside.

3. Combine garlic, pepper, soy sauce, lime juice, and sugar substitute in a small bowl, and pour over pork. Mix well.

4. Serve pork in a bowl with lettuce leaves. Have each person take a lettuce leaf and fill with pork mixture. Then fold and eat like a sandwich.

Smoke Signals

Sear roasting at 500°F allows lean meat to remain juicy. Always clean your oven before *and* after cooking at this temperature to prevent your smoke alarm from becoming a kitchen timer.

Down Under Berry Kiwi Salad with Poppy Seed Dressing

3 TB. sugar substitute, such as Splenda

3 TB. reduced-fat mayonnaise

2 TB. 2% milk

1 TB. poppy seeds

1 TB. white wine vinegar

6 leaves romaine, chopped

¹/₂ cup fresh strawberry slices

¹/₂ cup kiwi fruit, diced

1 cup blueberries

2 TB. almonds, slivered

Makes 6 servings
Prep time: 10 minutes
Cook time: none
Each serving has:
83.1 calories
2.09 g. protein
10.22 g. carbohydrates
4.5 g. total fat
0.61 g. saturated fat
3.02 mg. cholesterol
69.48 mg. sodium
2.73 g. fiber

1. Combine sugar substitute, mayonnaise, milk, poppy seeds, and vinegar, and whisk until smooth.

2. Place lettuce in a large bowl, and add strawberries, kiwi, blueberries, and almonds. Toss to mix well, and then divide between 6 plates. Drizzle dressing over each serving.

Sweet Shrimp and Pineapple Salad

Makes 2 servings
Prep time: 5 minutes
Cook time: none
Each serving has:
108.4 calories
7.71 g. protein
20.43 g. carbohydrates
0.8 g. total fat
0.12 g. saturated fat
36.48 mg. cholesterol
343.2 mg. sodium
3.65 g. fiber

8 cooked, frozen peeled shrimp (medium-size, 24 count per pound)

8 romaine lettuce leaves torn into pieces

1 cup red bell pepper, sliced into strips

1 cup pineapple, packed in water, drained

1 TB. reduced-sodium soy sauce

2 TB. fresh lemon juice

1 tsp. sugar substitute, such as Splenda

1 red chili pepper, finely chopped

1 TB. chives, finely chopped

1. Defrost frozen, cooked shrimp.

2. Arrange lettuce segments on 2 plates, and top with red bell pepper strips.

3. Mix pineapple, soy sauce, lemon juice, sugar substitute, and chili pepper together with shrimp, and divide between the two plates. Top with chives and serve.

Nutri Notes _____

Shrimp got a bad rap when all fats were considered "equal." It's low in saturated fat and is a good source of iron, niacin, protein, and zinc.

Thai Beef Salad

5 TB. fresh lime juice

4 TB. fish sauce

1 tsp. sugar substitute, such as Splenda

¼ cup jalapeño peppers, finely diced

1 lb. top round steak

6 oz. bean sprouts

3 oz. fresh basil leaves

3 oz. fresh mint leaves

1 head butter leaf lettuce, torn into pieces

Makes 4 servings
Prep time: 30 minutes
Cook time: 4 minutes
Each serving has:
215 calories
29.57 g. protein
15.89 g. carbohydrates
4.84 g. total fat
1.57 g. saturated fat
69.17 mg. cholesterol
1549 mg. sodium
2.9 g. fiber

1. Make marinade by whisking together lime juice, *fish sauce*, and sugar substitute until dissolved. Add jalapeño peppers, and let stand for 20 minutes.

2. Preheat a grill on high, and grill steak for 2 minutes each side.

3. Transfer steak to a cutting board and let rest for 5 minutes. Slice into thin strips; then toss in marinade for 30 minutes.

4. Arrange bean sprouts, basil leaves, mint leaves, and lettuce in a bowl. Pile steak pieces on top, and pour remaining marinade over salad. Toss to coat evenly, and serve in 4 salad bowls.

Nutri Speak

Fish sauce is an extract of scads, herrings, sardines, mackerels, silversides, and slipmouth fish, fermented in the sun. It is similar to Worcestershire sauce, which is made from anchovies. You can use them interchangeably or substitute soy sauce if fish sauce is unavailable in the Asian food section of your market.

Tomato Salad with Cottage Cheese

Makes 4 servings
Prep time: 5 minutes
Cook time: none
Each serving has:
215.7 calories
10.78 g. protein
19.07 g. carbohydrates
12.36 g. total fat
2.22 g. saturated fat
4.76 mg. cholesterol
556.8 mg. sodium
3.9 g. fiber

3 lbs. tomatoes, thickly sliced

8 oz. 2% cottage cheese

2 TB. fresh cilantro, chopped

3 TB. olive oil

1 tsp. sugar substitute, such as Splenda

3 TB. fresh lemon juice

$\frac{1}{2}$ tsp. sea salt

$\frac{1}{2}$ tsp. black pepper, freshly ground

1. Arrange sliced tomatoes on a platter, and spoon cottage cheese over slices. Top with cilantro.

2. Prepare dressing by mixing olive oil, sugar substitute, lemon juice, salt, and pepper together. Pour over salad and serve.

Nutri Notes _____

Heirloom tomatoes have the *real* tomato flavor you get from growing your own in the backyard. Experiment with the many varieties appearing in your supermarket. You'll be amazed at the satisfying flavor they impart to this ordinary "diet" salad.

Warm Scallop and Black Bean Salad

$^1/_2$ lb. scallops

4 oz. canned black beans

1 tsp. garlic, mashed

$2^1/_2$ TB. white wine vinegar

$^1/_4$ cup fresh cilantro, chopped

$^1/_8$ tsp. cayenne

3 TB. olive oil

$^1/_2$ medium red bell pepper, finely diced

2 TB. green onions, sliced on the diagonal

1 tsp. chives, diced

Makes 2 servings
Prep time: 10 minutes
Cook time: 5 minutes
Each serving has:
368.7 calories
24.53 g. protein
20.11 g. carbohydrates
21.51 g. total fat
2.92 g. saturated fat
37.42 mg. cholesterol
185.2 mg. sodium
5.74 g. fiber

1. Rinse scallops and pat dry. Rinse and drain black beans.

2. Dressing: in a bowl, whisk together garlic, vinegar, cilantro, cayenne, and olive oil until well blended or emulsified.

3. Add scallops to dressing, tossing them to coat. In another bowl, toss together beans, bell pepper, and onion.

4. Heat a heavy skillet over moderately low heat. Remove scallops from dressing, reserving it. In the skillet, sauté scallops for 3 to 4 minutes or until they are just cooked through.

5. Remove the skillet from the heat, transferring scallops to a platter. Stir reserved dressing into the skillet to heat. Add simmering dressing to bean mixture, toss bean mixture well, and spoon it around scallops. Top with diced chives and serve.

Tuna Curry Pasta with Cashews

Makes 6 servings
Prep time: 5 minutes
Cook time: 10 minutes
Each serving has:
447.7 calories
24.88 g. protein
36.41 g. carbohydrates
23.11 g. total fat
4.13 g. saturated fat
56.66 mg. cholesterol
490.4 mg. sodium
2.32 g. fiber

1 cup (8 oz.) fresh pasta, not dried

1 cup artichoke hearts in water

³/₄ cup reduced-fat mayonnaise

3 TB. curry powder

1 tsp. vinegar cider

14 oz. tuna, packed in water

3 TB. raisins

1 cup roasted and unsalted cashews

1. Cook fresh pasta according to package directions.

2. Drain artichoke hearts and set aside.

3. For dressing, combine mayonnaise, curry powder, and vinegar, and blend until smooth.

4. Add tuna to pasta, and pour dressing over pasta.

5. Sprinkle raisins and cashews on top and serve at room temperature.

Part 4

Mealtime Stars

This part is a whopper as it covers all the moving sources of protein—fish, poultry, beef, lamb, pork, and game. I've provided you with a variety of cooking techniques, from grilling to poaching, steaming, stove top, or oven cooked. Any way you make them, these recipes will provide you and your family with oodles of healthy nutrition packed with flavor.

I've always enjoyed eating in foreign countries and savoring their unique blend of spices. You'll find recipes from around the world in this part that will open up your senses and fill them with sheer happiness. Promise me you won't make too many yummy sounds at the table! If you're like me, you'll choose some favorites and make them over and over. Once you become more comfortable cooking with total nutrition in mind, you'll easily come up with your own variations. Soon you'll be making your own signature dishes. See how much you've learned?

12

Something's Fishy

In This Chapter

- ◆ Tuna tidbits
- ◆ Be a fatty lover
- ◆ Flash the frozen fish

If you're hooked on fish, you're in good company. Not only is seafood a low-fat replacement for higher-fat foods, but it's also a great source for easily digestible protein and good fats, the kind that can lower your risk of heart disease and strokes. You don't have to get fancy when fixing fish, either, as it lends itself to simple methods of cooking that retain all its healthy benefits.

Unfortunately, the pollution of our environment has resulted in contamination of many species of fish with mercury, a heavy metal that can affect fetuses and young children, causing learning disabilities and neurologic damage. Recent FDA studies show that canned light tuna may contain yellow fin tuna, a species that is heavily contaminated with mercury. However, less than 6 percent of tested light tuna had any noticeable levels of mercury. PCBs and dioxin, chemicals that affect the estrogen receptor, are found in the skin and fat of fish, such as salmon. But simply removing the skin and its fat can eliminate unnecessary exposure. So which fish are safe? No one can guarantee anything, but low-mercury options appear to be shrimp, skinless salmon, Pollock, and catfish. Your best option is to choose a variety of fish and to use canned options no more than once a week.

Fish are an excellent source of omega fatty acids, which can help to reduce your risk of death from a sudden heart attack. They may even help prevent the risk of stroke. However, our bodies can't make omega fatty acids so we are dependent upon food sources for them. Good sources are plant oils, such as canola and olive oil, and fish. If your family members have problems with Type 2 diabetes, omega fatty acids can be important in helping to control inflammation caused by elevated insulin levels. So learn to love the right kinds of fats, and you'll be on your way to cooking with total nutrition in mind.

Frozen fish is extremely convenient as new technology has allowed trawlers to flash freeze the fish minutes after they've hauled it from the sea. When purchasing frozen fish, look to confirm the fish is solidly frozen with no brown spots or discoloration. There should be no fishy odor or evidence of freezer burn, which appears as white, leathery spots. You can store the fish in the freezer for about 2 months. Frozen fish actually cooks up best when still frozen, so adjust any recipe's cooking time and moisture accordingly by a few minutes more, and you'll always have the best total nutrition available for your family.

Broiled Lemon Sole

Makes 4 servings
Prep time: 5 minutes
Cook time: 5 minutes
Each serving has:
209.5 calories
31.1 g. protein
1.78 g. carbohydrate
4.09 g. total fat
1.52 g. saturated fat
78.24 mg. cholesterol
136.6 mg. sodium
0.74 g. fiber

4 TB. plant sterol spread, such as Smart Balance

2 TB. fresh lemon juice

4 slices lemon

4 (6 oz.) Dover sole fillets

2 TB. parsley, coarsely chopped

1 TB. white pepper

1. Heat broiler on high.

2. In a shallow, heatproof baking dish, place sterol spread. Melt under the broiler for 5 seconds; then add lemon juice and slices.

3. Season fillets with parsley and pepper; then place on lemon slices. Broil for 3 minutes or until lightly browned.

 Food for Thought _____

Any thin white fish fillet, such as tilapia, will work well in this recipe, but Dover sole is especially good as it is a very delicate fish and quickly absorbs the flavor of the lemon.

Buttery Steamed Halibut

2 lb. skinless halibut fillets

1 TB. fresh ginger, chopped

1 small serrano pepper, finely diced

1 clove garlic, mashed

1 tsp. fresh lime juice

1 tsp. lime zest

4 TB. plant sterol spread, such as Benecol

Makes 4 servings
Prep time: 10 minutes
Cook time: 7 minutes
Each serving has:
306.1 calories
47.32 g. protein
0.8 g. carbohydrate
7.31 g. total fat
1.78 g. saturated fat
72.57 mg. cholesterol
123.9 mg. sodium
0.15 g. fiber

1. Place fillets onto a plate that will fit inside the steamer.

2. In a small bowl, combine ginger, pepper, garlic, lime juice, and zest. Then sprinkle mixture over fillets. Dot each one with 1 tablespoon of sterol spread.

3. Bring water to a boil in the lower portion of the steamer; then top with the upper portion or basket. Place the plate of fillets inside, cover, and steam for 5 minutes.

4. Using a spatula, transfer fish to serving plates, and pour sauce over top.

Cajun Shrimp

2 TB. plant sterol spread, such as Smart Balance

1/4 cup onion, coarsely diced

1 clove garlic, mashed

1 cup green bell pepper, diced

1/4 cup celery, thinly chopped

1 can (14.5 oz.) tomatoes, crushed

2 shakes Tabasco sauce

1/2 tsp. celery seed

1 tsp. fresh thyme, chopped

1 lb. raw, frozen shrimp (medium-size, 24 count per pound)

Makes 4 servings
Prep time: 10 minutes
Cook time: 30 minutes
Each serving has:
197.9 calories
25.35 g. protein
12.64 g. carbohydrate
3.49 g. total fat
0.97 g. saturated fat
172.4 mg. cholesterol
312.3 mg. sodium
3.18 g. fiber

1. In a 10-inch skillet, melt spread over medium heat. Add onion, garlic, sweet peppers, and celery, and cook until tender, about 5 minutes. Add tomatoes, Tabasco, celery seed, and thyme, and simmer over low heat for about 20 minutes.

2. Add shrimp, and cook until they are pink, about 5 minutes. Serve immediately.

Clams with Whole-Wheat Linguine in Wine Sauce

Makes 4 servings
Prep time: 5 minutes
Cook time: 20 minutes
Each serving has:
539.5 calories
51.96 g. protein
54.76 g. carbohydrate
8.78 g. total fat
2.78 g. saturated fat
115.7 mg. cholesterol
200.4 mg. sodium
0.56 g. fiber

Nutri Speak

To **plate** means to arrange one serving of food on a dish.

¹/₂ lb. whole-wheat linguine

1 TB. olive oil

4 cloves garlic, sliced

¹/₂ cup onion, diced

3 lb. fresh clams

¹/₂ cup dry white wine

2 TB. plant sterol spread, such as Benecol

1 TB. parsley, chopped

1 TB. fresh lemon juice

1. Bring a large pot of water to a boil, and add pasta. Cook until tender. Drain but do not rinse.

2. In a 10-inch skillet, heat olive oil over medium heat. Add garlic and onions, and cook until soft, stirring occasionally, about 5 minutes.

3. Add the wine to the pan and reduce by ¹/₄ volume. Add clams, cover for 2 minutes, then stir clams, looking for them to open. Discard any that do not open after about 5 minutes. Remove clams to a bowl and keep warm.

4. Add sterol spread, parsley, and lemon juice, and return clams to the pan.

5. Divide linguine into 4 portions; *plate*; then top with clams and sauce.

Fish Soft Tacos

$^1/_2$ cup canned tomatoes, crushed

1 small jalapeño pepper, deseeded and diced

$^1/_2$ cup fresh cilantro, chopped

$^1/_2$ cup onion, diced

$^1/_2$ cup avocado, diced

2 TB. fresh lemon juice

1 clove garlic, smashed

Nonstick cooking spray

1 lb. cod, cut into 1-inch pieces

4 La Tortilla Factory low-carb tortillas, 8-inch size

Makes 4 servings
Prep time: 5 minutes
Cook time: 5 minutes
Each serving has:
208.8 calories
26.41 g. protein
16.26 g. carbohydrate
7.89 g. total fat
0.91 g. saturated fat
48.76 mg. cholesterol
250.6 mg. sodium
10.31 g. fiber

1. In a bowl, combine tomatoes, jalapeño, cilantro, onion, avocado, lemon juice, and garlic. Mix together.

2. Spray a medium 10-inch skillet with cooking spray; then heat on medium-high heat. Add cod pieces and stir gently, cooking until they are opaque and flake easily.

3. Take a whole-wheat tortilla, and lay a serving of cod to one side. Top with vegetable mixture, and fold in half.

Variation: Tilapia also works beautifully in this dish.

Grilled Shrimp with Thai Garlic Sauce

2 lb. raw shrimp (medium-size, 24 count per pound)

1 TB. olive oil

1 tsp. red chili paste

2 tsp. fresh lime juice

Makes 6 servings
Prep time: 15 minutes
Cook time: 6 minutes
Each serving has:
180.6 calories
30.72 g. protein
1.53 g. carbohydrate
4.87 g. total fat
0.8 g. saturated fat
229.8 mg. cholesterol
245.5 mg. sodium
0.01 g. fiber

1. In a plastic bag mix olive oil and chili paste to form a paste. Add shrimp and marinate in the bag for one hour or up to six hours in the refrigerator.

2. Heat the grill to moderately high heat, then put shrimp on skewers, threading the skewer through the body near the tail, folding over shrimp and passing the skewer through the body again to the head. Grill or broil, turning once, until shells are bright pink, about 2 to 3 minutes per side. Serve with fresh lime wedges.

It's a Snap Scallop Sauté

Makes 2 servings
Prep time: 5 minutes
Cook time: 4 minutes
Each serving has:
337.4 calories
39.91 g. protein
18.93 g. carbohydrate
4.95 g. total fat
1.77 g. saturated fat
74.84 mg. cholesterol
372.6 mg. sodium
0.85 g. fiber

¹/₄ cup Wondra flour

1 tsp. salt substitute, such as Morton's

1 TB. ground black pepper

Nonstick cooking spray

3 TB. plant sterol spread, such as Smart Balance

1 lb. scallops

4 lemon slices

1. In a small plastic bag, place Wondra flour, and season with salt and pepper.

2. Remove any white hinge pieces from scallops; then drop individually into the plastic bag and shake to coat. Remove to a rack.

3. Heat an 8-inch sauté pan on medium heat. Coat with cooking spray, and add sterol spread to melt. Add scallops, and cook without disturbing them until browned on one side, about 2 minutes. Turn over gently, and brown for another minute. Remove to a plate, and serve with lemon slices.

Mussels with Garlic and Ginger

Makes 4 servings
Prep time: 5 minutes
Cook time: 10 minutes
Each serving has:
152.7 calories
19.85 g. protein
8.59 g. carbohydrate
3.98 g. total fat
0.78 g. saturated fat
42.58 mg. cholesterol
524.6 mg. sodium
0.85 g. fiber

1 cup fish stock

1 cup scallions, sliced

1 TB. fresh ginger, finely chopped

3 cloves garlic, crushed

4 cups mussels

1 tsp. red chili pepper flakes

1. Heat a 10-inch saucepan on high heat, and add fish stock and bring to a boil. Add scallions, ginger, and garlic and mix.

2. Add mussels into the pan. Cover and cook, shaking the pan occasionally, for 5 minutes or until mussels open. Discard any that are still closed. Pour into serving bowls, and top with pepper flakes.

Mussels with Pernod

4 cups mussels

3 TB. plant sterol spread, such as Benecol

$^1/_2$ cup onion, diced

4 cloves garlic, chopped

2 TB. Pernod

1 TB. fresh basil, chopped

2 tsp. fresh lemon juice

2 TB. chives, snipped

Makes 4 servings
Prep time: 5 minutes
Cook time: 8 minutes
Each serving has:
202.6 calories
18.47 g. protein
9.56 g. carbohydrate
5.02 g. total fat
1.43 g. saturated fat
42 mg. cholesterol
431.5 mg. sodium
0.93 g. fiber

1. Clean mussels by soaking in cold water and removing any *beard* from shells.

2. Add 1 tablespoon sterol spread to a 10-inch skillet, add mussels and heat over medium-high heat. Cover and cook, shaking occasionally, for 5 minutes or until the shells open. Discard any shells that have not opened completely.

3. Add onion and garlic; sautéing until soft. Then add Pernod, basil, lemon juice, remaining sterol spread, and chives. Stir to mix and serve.

Nutri Speak

The **beard** is a tuft of strong filaments by which a mussel attaches itself to a surface. To remove it, pull tightly with a small towel holding the mussel.

Poached Red Snapper with Tahitian Sauce

Makes 4 servings
Prep time: 10 minutes
Cook time: 10 minutes
Each serving has:
260 calories
47.21 g. protein
6.86 g. carbohydrate
3.83 g. total fat
0.79 g. saturated fat
83.91 mg. cholesterol
147.4 mg. sodium
1.02 g. fiber

$^1/_2$ cup papaya, diced into $^1/_4$-inch cubes

$^1/_2$ cup mango, diced into $^1/_4$-inch cubes

2 tsp. red onion, finely diced

1 TB. fresh tarragon, finely chopped

1 tsp. shallots, finely diced

2 tsp. fresh ginger, finely chopped

1 clove garlic, smashed

2 lb. skinless red snapper fillets

$^1/_4$ tsp. cayenne

1 tsp. fresh lime juice

1 tsp. macadamia nuts, chopped

1. In a medium bowl, toss together papaya, mango, onion, tarragon, shallots, ginger, and garlic.

2. Fill the bottom portion a two-part steamer with water. Bring to a boil. Line the steamer portion with wax paper; then place the steamer section on top. Season fillets with cayenne, and place each fillet on the wax paper. Cover and steam for about 7 minutes or until fish appears opaque.

3. Add lime juice to fruit mixture. Spoon mixture onto individual serving plates, top with a fish fillet and nuts.

Orange Roughy with Tofu and Black Beans

1 tsp. red chili paste

1 tsp. fresh ginger, finely chopped

¹/₄ tsp. white pepper

1 tsp. sugar substitute, such as Splenda

¹/₄ cup black beans, mashed

1 lb. skinless orange roughy fillets

1 lb. firm tofu, drained and sliced into cubes

¹/₂ cup scallions, sliced

Makes 4 servings
Prep time: 5 minutes
Cook time: 7 minutes
Each serving has:
263 calories
35.82 g. protein
8.8 g. carbohydrate
10.78 g. total fat
1.47 g. saturated fat
22.68 mg. cholesterol
122 mg. sodium
4.03 g. fiber

1. In a bowl, combine chili paste, ginger, pepper, sugar, and beans. Cut fish into strips, and coat with mixture.

2. Bring water to a boil in a steamer. Place the steamer basket into the steamer, and add tofu cubes. Cover and steam for 2 minutes. Place fish strips on top of tofu; cover and steam for 3 more minutes. Serve with sliced scallions.

Salmon and White Beans

2 cups canned cannellini beans

1 cup red onion, thinly sliced

¹/₄ cup celery, diced

2 TB. fresh lemon juice

2 TB. olive oil

Nonstick cooking spray

1 lb. skinless salmon fillets

Makes 4 servings
Prep time: 10 minutes
Cook time: 5 minutes
Each serving has:
358 calories
32.84 g. protein
31.5 g. carbohydrate
11.25 g. total fat
1.72 g. saturated fat
58.97 mg. cholesterol
89.44 mg. sodium
7.35 g. fiber

1. Drain beans and place in a bowl. Combine onion and celery; then drizzle lemon juice and olive oil on top and stir. Divide into 4 portions and plate one quarter of the mixture on each plate.

2. Spray an 8-inch skillet with cooking spray and heat over medium-high heat. Divide salmon into four portions; then quickly sauté on each side until done, about 5 minutes.

3. Place each fillet over bean and onion mixture and serve. Season with pepper or salt as necessary.

Riesling Trout with Fennel

Makes 4 servings

Prep time: 10 minutes

Cook time: 20 minutes

Each serving has:

390.1 calories

48.07 g. protein

4.87 g. carbohydrate

13.35 g. total fat

4.05 g. saturated fat

133.8 mg. cholesterol

92.75 mg. sodium

0.48 g. fiber

2 lb. farm-raised trout

1 tsp. salt substitute, such as Morton's

¼ tsp. ground black pepper

½ cup fennel, thinly sliced

½ cup shallot, finely diced

2 TB. plant sterol spread, such as Smart Balance

¾ cup Riesling or other mild white wine

1. Preheat oven to 425°F.

2. Season trout with salt and pepper. In the center of each trout, place half each of the shallots and fennel slices, and fold back over.

3. Grease an ovenproof baking dish with sterol spread; then lay trout into the pan. Pour wine around fish; cover and place in the oven. Bake for 20 minutes.

4. With a slotted spoon, remove trout to individual serving plates. Peel off skin. Using a spoon, gently push trout meat toward backbone; then gently pull bones from trout by lifting them toward you. Discard bones. Remove fennel pieces from the pan, and serve with fish. Discard cooking liquid.

Salmon and Artichokes in a Paper Heart

Parchment paper

$^1/_2$ **cup artichoke hearts, canned or frozen, defrosted**

1 lb. skinless salmon fillets

$^1/_4$ **cup red bell pepper, finely diced**

1 tsp. onion, finely diced

$^1/_4$ **tsp. fresh tarragon finely chopped**

1 clove garlic, smashed

2 slices lemon

Makes 2 servings
Prep time: 15 minutes
Cook time: 10 minutes
Each serving has:
290.1 calories
46.61 g. protein
5.17 g. carbohydrate
7.89 g. total fat
1.28 g. saturated fat
117.9 mg. cholesterol
363.3 mg. sodium
2.53 g. fiber

1. Cut parchment paper into 2 sheets about 10 inches long.

2. In the center of each piece of paper, place one half of the artichoke hearts, and lay salmon on top. Cover with one half of the red bell pepper, onion, tarragon, and garlic. Lay lemon slices on top.

3. Fold the paper in half over fillet. Begin at the bottom and roll the edges close around fillet, forming a heart shape. Turn all the edges up and inward as you fold. The French call this cooking *en papillote*.

4. Place packets on a rack in the microwave or in a microwaveable dish, and heat on power 7 or medium power for 10 minutes.

5. Place the packets on serving dishes and take scissors to cut open the paper heart. Be careful to avoid any steam. Serve and eat from the paper packet with all juices.

Salmon Crab Cakes

Makes 4 servings
Prep time: 5 minutes
Cook time: 4 minutes
Each serving has:
277.4 calories
22.43 g. protein
37.04 g. carbohydrate
5.04 g. total fat
0.93 g. saturated fat
38.87 mg. cholesterol
519.9 mg. sodium
5.52 g. fiber

3 oz. canned or fresh crab

6 oz. canned salmon

2 cups canned cannellini beans

$^1/_2$ cup red onion, chopped

3 cloves garlic, mashed

2 tsp. curry powder

1 medium red bell pepper, coarsely chopped

$^1/_4$ cup fresh mint leaves

1 tsp. cumin seeds

2 tsp. Tabasco

Nonstick cooking spray

1 cup nonfat yogurt

2 TB. fresh cilantro, chopped

1. In a blender or food processor, combine crab, salmon, beans, onion, garlic, curry, pepper, mint, cumin, and Tabasco. Pulse for just a few seconds to mix, but do not purée.

2. Form into 8 patties.

3. Spray a medium 10-inch skillet with cooking spray and heat over medium-high heat. Gently press patties into the hot pan and cook for 2 minutes on each side or until golden brown.

4. In a separate bowl, combine yogurt and cilantro. Serve with fish cakes.

Scallops *Seviche*

18 large scallops

¹/₂ cup fresh lime juice

¹/₂ cup orange juice

2 TB. Triple Sec

1 clove garlic, crushed

6 leaves romaine lettuce

2 tsp. chives, chopped

Makes 6 servings
Prep time: 5 minutes
Cook time: none
Each serving has:
97.32 calories
13.1 g. protein
6.86 g. carbohydrate
0.66 g. total fat
0.07 g. saturated fat
24.95 mg. cholesterol
123 mg. sodium
0.29 g. fiber

1. Remove any white hinge pieces from scallops, and slice thick scallops in half.

2. In a plastic bag, combine lime and orange juices, Triple Sec, and garlic with scallops, and refrigerate overnight.

3. Place lettuce leaves on a plate, and top with a mound of scallops. Dust with chives and serve.

Nutri Speak

Seviche, also known as Ceviche, is a fish dish marinated in citrus juice. The acids "cook" the fish to a delicate tenderness, turning the fish opaque. Pompano, snapper, and sole are the fish most often selected for this style of cooking.

Scallops with Peppered Bacon and Shallots

Makes 2 servings
Prep time: 5 minutes
Cook time: 5 minutes
Each serving has:
140 calories
23.64 g. protein
6.19 g. carbohydrate
1.43 g. total fat
0.1 g. saturated fat
49.6 mg. cholesterol
375.6 mg. sodium
0 g. fiber

Nonstick cooking spray

4 slices Turkey Peppered Bacon, such as Wellshire, coarsely chopped

¼ cup shallots, diced

8 large scallops

1. Spray an 8-inch sauté pan with cooking spray and heat over medium heat. Add turkey bacon and cook until crisp. Halfway through the cooking, add shallots and cook until soft.

2. Remove any white hinge pieces from scallops; then cut into quarter pieces. Gently add them to bacon and shallot mixture, stirring to cook until they are opaque. Serve immediately.

Sea Bass with Capers

Makes 2 servings
Prep time: 5 minutes
Cook time: 15 minutes
Each serving has:
233.9 calories
34.28 g. protein
15.67 g. carbohydrate
3.89 g. total fat
0.94 g. saturated fat
69.74 mg. cholesterol
359.2 mg. sodium
3.78 g. fiber

Nonstick cooking spray

12 oz. skinless sea bass

1 cup onion, medium diced

2 tsp. capers

1 cup canned tomatoes, crushed

1. Preheat oven to 425°F.

2. Mix together onions, *capers*, and tomatoes.

3. Spray an ovenproof pan with cooking spray and heat on high heat. Place fillets skin side down, and cook for 1 minute. Turn over with a spatula. Remove from the heat, and spoon onion, caper, and tomato mixture over fish. Place the pan into the oven, and cook for 10 minutes.

Sea Bass with Olives and Capers Italiano Style

¹/₂ cup whole Mediterranean Kalmata olives, pitted

¹/₂ cup canned tomatoes, crushed

¹/₄ cup red onion, finely diced

¹/₄ cup fresh basil, chopped

3 TB. capers

2 TB. fresh parsley, chopped

2 TB. balsamic vinegar

1 tsp. garlic, minced

Nonstick cooking spray

2 lb. skinless sea bass

Makes 4 servings
Prep time: 10 minutes
Cook time: 5 minutes
Each serving has:
263.7 calories
43.2 g. protein
6.85 g. carbohydrate
6.67 g. total fat
1.43 g. saturated fat
92.99 mg. cholesterol
498.5 mg. sodium
3.16 g. fiber

1. Heat a double-sided countertop grill on high.

2. Combine olives, tomatoes, onion, basil, capers, parsley, vinegar, and garlic in a bowl. This mixture will make a salsa for fish.

3. Spray each fillet with cooking spray; then grill until firm to the touch, about 5 minutes. Serve with salsa.

Variation: This recipe will work with any moderately firm fish. Consider sablefish, cod, snapper, or striped bass in either fillet or steak cuts.

Seafood Kabobs

1 lb. raw, peeled shrimp (medium-size, 24 count per pound)

¹/₂ lb. scallops

1 large red bell pepper, cut into chunks

1 medium onion, cut into 8 pieces

1 cup canned pineapple chunks, drained

8 wood skewers, soaked in water

Makes 4 servings
Prep time: 10 minutes
Cook time: 8 minutes
Each serving has:
211.3 calories
33.49 g. protein
12.48 g. carbohydrate
2.57 g. total fat
0.44 g. saturated fat
191.1 mg. cholesterol
261.4 mg. sodium
1.81 g. fiber

1. Heat an outdoor grill on high heat.

2. Thread shrimp, scallops, bell pepper, onion, and pineapple onto each skewer alternating as desired.

3. Grill for 4 minutes per side or until shrimp is pink and scallops are firm.

Sesame Ginger Grouper with Bok Choy

Makes 4 servings
Prep time: 10 minutes
Cook time: 5 minutes
Each serving has:
255.4 calories
48.92 g. protein
6.07 g. carbohydrate
3.58 g. total fat
0.71 g. saturated fat
83.91 mg. cholesterol
280.2 mg. sodium
2.72 g. fiber

2 lb. bok choy

1 TB. fresh ginger, finely chopped

2 TB. scallions, sliced

2 TB. sherry vinegar

1 tsp. fresh lime juice

$\frac{1}{4}$ tsp. toasted sesame oil

2 lb. skinless grouper

1 TB. sesame seeds

1. Fill a large stockpot with water and bring to a boil. Blanch bok choy by plunging it into the boiling water for 2 minutes; then drain and immediately place in an ice water bath for 2 minutes. Remove with a slotted spoon to drain. Chop coarsely.

2. In a separate bowl, combine ginger, scallions, vinegar, and lime juice. Mix.

3. Heat a wok or medium 10-inch skillet over medium-high heat and add sesame oil. Immediately place fillets in the pan and cook until toasted on one side, about 3 minutes. Turn over and add bok choy. Stir to toss, which will break up fish.

4. Divide into portions, top with ginger, scallion, and vinegar sauce and serve. Top with sesame seeds.

 Food for Thought _____

Use toasted sesame oil sparingly as it packs a real punch in flavor. Store it away from light in a cool place.

Shrimp in Cilantro Curry Sauce

1 TB. olive oil

6 cloves garlic, whole

¹/₂ cup scallions

1 cup fresh cilantro

1 TB. curry powder

2 lb. raw, peeled shrimp (medium-size, 24 count per pound)

1 tsp. hot pepper flakes

¹/₃ cup fish stock

¹/₄ cup pistachios, chopped

Makes 4 servings
Prep time: 10 minutes
Cook time: 10 minutes
Each serving has:
337.6 calories
49.14 g. protein
8.47 g. carbohydrate
11.31 g. total fat
1.72 g. saturated fat
344.9 mg. cholesterol
376 mg. sodium
2.19 g. fiber

1. Preheat the oven to 500°F.

2. In a blender or food processor, combine olive oil, garlic, scallions, cilantro, and curry powder. Pulse until mixture is well minced or blended. Add pepper flakes to the mixture and pour over shrimp.

3. Place shrimp in an ovenproof roasting pan with all cilantro mixture. Add fish stock, and roast until bubbly, about 10 minutes. Serve immediately, topped with pistachios.

Variation: If you don't have fish stock, simply substitute any vegetable broth or even chicken broth. The flavor will not be significantly different in this recipe.

Shrimp Stir Fry

Makes 4 servings
Prep time: 5 minutes
Cook time: 5 minutes
Each serving has:
242.3 calories
32.58 g. protein
14.38 g. carbohydrate
6.15 g. total fat
1.41 g. saturated fat
190.4 mg. cholesterol
284.6 mg. sodium
2.96 g. fiber

1 cup frozen peas

Nonstick cooking spray

1 tsp. fresh ginger, chopped

1/2 cup scallions, sliced

1/4 lb. prosciutto, coarsely chopped

1 cup water chestnuts, coarsely chopped

1 lb. raw, peeled shrimp (medium-size, 24 count per pound)

1. Cook peas in boiling water for 2 minutes. Drain.

2. Spray a wok or skillet with high-temperature cooking spray, and heat on high. Add ginger and scallions and stir to cook, about 15 seconds. Add prosciutto and water chestnuts and brown slightly.

3. Add shrimp and continue stirring until cooked, about 5 minutes. Serve immediately.

Simple Grilled Halibut Steaks

Makes 4 servings
Prep time: 5 minutes
Cook time: 4 minutes
Each serving has:
254.5 calories
47.45 g. protein
1.12 g. carbohydrate
5.3 g. total fat
0.76 g. saturated fat
72.57 mg. cholesterol
126.2 mg. sodium
0.42 g. fiber

Nonstick cooking spray, high temperature

2 lb. skinless halibut steaks

1 tsp. paprika

4 TB. fresh lemon juice

1 tsp. salt substitute, such as Morton's

1/4 tsp. ground black pepper

1. Heat a grill on medium-high heat.

2. Spray each halibut steak with high-temperature cooking spray, and season with paprika.

3. Grill for 2 minutes on each side or until fish is opaque.

4. Season with lemon juice, salt, and pepper and serve.

Sole O'Mio Lettuce Wraps

8 romaine lettuce leaves

4 TB. tarragon, chopped

4 TB. fat-free mayonnaise, such as Kraft's

1 TB. French mustard

¹/₄ cup dry-roasted peanuts, chopped

¹/₂ lb. cooked, peeled shrimp, coarsely chopped (medium-size, 24 count per pound)

2 lb. Dover sole fillets

1 TB. fresh lemon juice

¹/₄ cup water

Makes 4 servings
Prep time: 10 minutes
Cook time: 12 minutes
Each serving has:
313.4 calories
56.17 g. protein
9.19 g. carbohydrate
9.13 g. total fat
1.04 g. saturated fat
195 mg. cholesterol
464.8 mg. sodium
1.2 g. fiber

1. Bring a pot of water to a boil, and drop lettuce leaves in to simmer for 2 minutes. Remove and drain.

2. Mix together tarragon, mayonnaise, mustard, and peanuts, and add shrimp. Mix to combine.

3. Lay 2 lettuce leaves overlapping, and place fillet on top. Fill with some chopped shrimp mixture; then fold fish to enclose shrimp. Roll lettuce leaves in from sides into a package. Place seam down on a plate. You may secure the closure with a toothpick if desired.

4. Place lettuce packages into a small 8-inch sauté pan. Sprinkle with lemon juice; add water, cover and bring to a simmer to heat. Turn off the heat, and allow packages to gently steam for 10 minutes. Serve immediately.

Variation: You can use savoy cabbage leaves instead of romaine lettuce or even bib lettuce in this recipe. The water necessary to steam the fish is trapped in the leaves making it a snap to cook.

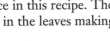

Thai Steamed Garlic Mussels

Makes 4 servings
Prep time: 5 minutes
Cook time: 10 minutes
Each serving has:
145.6 calories
19.51 g. protein
7.25 g. carbohydrate
3.93 g. total fat
0.76 g. saturated fat
42.58 mg. cholesterol
618.2 mg. sodium
0.93 g. fiber

1 cup fish stock

1 TB. red chili paste

4 cups mussels

1 TB. fresh lime juice

2 TB. fresh basil, chopped

1. Heat a 10-inch saucepan on high heat, and add the fish stock. Add chili paste, mix, and put mussels into the pan. Cover and cook, shaking the pan occasionally, for 5 minutes or until mussels open. Discard any that are still closed.

2. Squeeze lime juice over mussels; turn out into serving bowls and top with basil.

Food for Thought

To test if mussels are alive, place them in the freezer for 5 minutes. Discard any shells that don't close.

Tilapia with Zucchini, Fennel, and Onion

³/₄ lb. penne whole-wheat pasta

Nonstick cooking spray

1 cup fennel, thinly sliced

1 cup onion, finely diced

1 cup zucchini, finely diced

1 TB. Paul Prudhomme salmon seasoning

2 cloves garlic, diced

1 lb. tilapia fillets

1 TB. fresh lemon juice

1 TB. fresh basil, coarsely chopped

Makes 4 servings
Prep time: 8 minutes
Cook time: 8 minutes
Each serving has:
245.6 calories
29.63 g. protein
29.71 g. carbohydrate
0.81 g. total fat
0.02 g. saturated fat
56 mg. cholesterol
76.76 mg. sodium
4.72 g. fiber

1. Bring a large pot of water to a boil, and add the pasta. Cook until tender. Drain but do not rinse.

2. While pasta is cooking, spray a 10-inch sauté pan with cooking spray and heat on medium-high heat. Add fennel and onions and cook until softened, about 4 minutes. Add zucchini, seasoning, and garlic and continue to cook until softened. Mix thoroughly; then top with fillets; cover and turn off the heat. Tilapia will cook in about 4 minutes. Serve with basil and squeeze of fresh lemon juice.

Tilapia with Brussels Sprouts and Shredded Carrots

Makes 4 servings
Prep time: 10 minutes
Cook time: 10 minutes
Each serving has:
346.1 calories
53.79 g. protein
11.62 g. carbohydrate
5.77 g. total fat
0.57 g. saturated fat
124.8 mg. cholesterol
411.4 mg. sodium
2.7 g. fiber

¹/₄ cup nonfat yogurt

¹/₄ tsp. lemon zest

1 tsp. lemon juice

2 TB. chives, diced

2 oz. pancetta, coarsely chopped

¹/₂ lb. Brussels sprouts, shredded

¹/₂ cup carrots, shredded

¹/₂ cup shallots, finely diced

2 TB. plant sterol spread, such as Benecol

1 clove garlic, smashed

2 lb. tilapia fillets

1. In a small bowl, whisk together yogurt, lemon zest, juice, and chives.

2. Brown pancetta in a medium 10-inch skillet over medium-high heat until crisp, about 4 minutes. Add Brussels sprouts, carrots, garlic, and shallots, and cook, stirring, until vegetables are soft, about 2 minutes. Turn off the heat and add sterol spread. Stir to mix.

3. Place fillets on top of vegetable mixture, cover, and wait 4 minutes. Serve with yogurt chive sauce.

Food for Thought

I never liked Brussels sprouts, but when shredded, they take on a nutty flavor that is terrific. Be sure to remove the stem and then cut a deep X in the base all the way through to the middle so the tougher center will cook evenly when shredded.

Fowl Play

In This Chapter

- Squawk the talk
- Wipe it clean
- Freezer tips

If you're looking for one of the most versatile, flavorful, and nutritious sources of protein, grab some poultry by the leg. Chicken, especially the lean breast meat, can provide 67.6 percent of your daily protein needs in just 4 ounces. Our fine feathered friends are also a very good source of niacin and selenium, which are amino acids that can help protect against damage to our delicate DNA. Chicken is also a good source of B6, a vitamin that helps with carbohydrate metabolism. No wonder these birds strut so proudly! They can really squawk the talk for total nutrition cooking.

Unfortunately, changes in the feeding and treatment of chickens has resulted in the development of antibiotic-resistant campylobacter infections, which can cause stomach ulcers and heart disease. Because of these issues, it's critical that you follow some important safety guidelines when dealing with raw chicken.

- If you marinate chicken, keep it in the refrigerator. Any room temperature setting can be a breeding ground for bacteria.

♦ Always wipe your counter or cutting area clean with an antibacterial soap, especially if you use plastic cutting boards, as again, any blood from the raw poultry will serve as an invitation for infection.

♦ If you defrost any poultry, do so in the refrigerator and not at room temperature.

♦ When buying chicken, place the package within another plastic bag to prevent any cross contamination with your other foods should the wrapping leak. As soon as you get home, place the chicken in the refrigerator.

Freezing poultry is easy. Simply remove the pieces, if fresh, from the container, and package them in a zip lock freezer bag in portions as needed. You can also over-wrap the store package with airtight heavy duty foil or place the package within another plastic freezer bag. Date it and store it. If frozen continuously, poultry can be safe indefinitely as long as you prevent freezer burn, that grayish brown leathery look that happens when cold air meets food. So start having fun with these recipes, and see how easy it is to give your family a total nutrition cooking feast any night of the week.

Cashew Chicken Tikka

Makes 4 servings
Prep time: 5 minutes
Cook time: 10 minutes
Each serving has:
333.4 calories
54.5 g. protein
4.53 g. carbohydrate
7.82 g. total fat
2.05 g. saturated fat
131.9 mg. cholesterol
161.3 mg. sodium
0.81 g. fiber

2 lb. boneless and skinless chicken breasts

$1/4$ cup nonfat yogurt

$1/4$ cup roasted cashews, unsalted and finely chopped

$1/8$ tsp. ground mace

1 tsp. ground cinnamon

1 tsp. ground coriander

1 tsp. ground ginger

1 tsp. mashed garlic

16 wood skewers, soaked in water

2 TB. plant sterol spread, such as Benecol

$1/2$ tsp. ground fennel

$1/2$ cup fresh cilantro, chopped

1. Cut chicken breasts into 1-inch chunks.

2. In a bowl or plastic bag, combine yogurt, cashews, mace, cinnamon, coriander, ginger, and garlic with chicken. Marinate chicken overnight.

3. Heat a grill on medium-high heat. Thread chicken onto wooden skewers. Toss any remaining marinade. Grill, basting with melted sterol spread until cooked through, about 10 minutes, turning often. Sprinkle fennel and cilantro on top and serve.

Bombay Chicken

1 cup onion, sliced

1 lb. boneless and skinless chicken breasts

1¹/₂ cups canned tomatoes, crushed

1 tsp. ground coriander

1¹/₂ tsp. paprika

1 tsp. ground ginger

³/₄ tsp. salt substitute, such as Morton's

¹/₂ tsp. cayenne

¹/₂ tsp. turmeric

¹/₂ tsp. ground cinnamon

¹/₈ tsp. ground cloves

¹/₂ cup low-salt chicken broth

¹/₃ cup barley

¹/₂ cup water

1 medium green bell pepper, thinly sliced

Makes 6 servings
Prep time: 15 minutes
Cook time: 7 hours
Each serving has:
164.3 calories
21.22 g. protein
16.47 g. carbohydrate
1.78 g. total fat
0.43 g. saturated fat
44.04 mg. cholesterol
140.5 mg. sodium
4.09 g. fiber

1. In a 5¹/₂- to 6-quart slow cooker, add onions and chicken breasts.

2. In a bowl, combine tomatoes, coriander, paprika, ginger, salt, cayenne, turmeric, cinnamon, cloves, broth, barley, and water, and pour over chicken. Cover and cook on low setting for 7 to 8 hours.

3. Add green bell pepper 15 minutes before serving. Cover and let stand. Serve chicken on a platter, spooning sauce over top.

Food for Thought

Look for organic canned tomatoes with sea salt or no salt whenever possible. Brands such as Muir Glenn and Del Monte have tomatoes in a variety of styles, such as crushed, diced, or spiced. Keep several cans in your pantry, and you'll never be at a loss for making a sauce for any dish.

Chicken Mole

Makes 6 servings
Prep time: 10 minutes
Cook time: 7 hours
Each serving has:
161.5 calories
13.34 g. protein
13.03 g. carbohydrate
6.93 g. total fat
1.42 g. saturated fat
28.46 mg. cholesterol
137.3 mg. sodium
3.05 g. fiber

1 can (14.5 oz.) tomatoes, crushed

$^{1}/_{2}$ cup onion, roughly chopped

$^{1}/_{4}$ cup dry-roasted peanuts

3 cloves garlic

1 jalapeño pepper

2 TB. cocoa powder

2 TB. raisins

1 stick cinnamon

$^{1}/_{8}$ tsp. nutmeg

1 TB. sesame seeds

$^{1}/_{8}$ tsp. ground coriander

2 lb. boneless and skinless chicken breasts

1 TB. tapioca

1. Into a blender, place tomatoes, onion, peanuts, garlic, jalapeño, cocoa, raisins, cinnamon, nutmeg, sesame seeds, and coriander, and process until a coarse purée is achieved.

2. Into a 5$^{1}/_{2}$- to 6-quart slow cooker, add chicken and tapioca and cover with sauce mixture. Cook on low heat for 7 to 8 hours.

3. To serve, remove chicken and arrange on a platter. Stir sauce to combine; then pour over chicken and serve.

Food for Thought _____

Tapioca makes a great thickener for any sauce cooked in a slow cooker. You won't get a raw flour flavor from it, and the resistant starch component helps to slow down any blood sugar rise from high glycemic carbs. It can even help to lower cholesterol and triglyceride levels.

Chicken with Apple Cider Vinegar

Nonstick cooking spray, olive oil flavor

1 tsp. fresh rosemary, finely chopped

2 lb. boneless, skinless chicken breasts

Salt substitute, such as Morton's

Freshly ground black pepper

$^1/_2$ cup apple cider vinegar

$^1/_4$ cup water

Makes 4 servings
Prep time: 5 minutes
Cook time: 15 minutes
Each serving has:
336.1 calories
53.65 g. protein
1.81 g. carbohydrate
11.33 g. total fat
3.9 g. saturated fat
141.5 mg. cholesterol
255.7 mg. sodium
0.02 g. fiber

1. Spray a medium skillet with olive oil cooking spray and heat on medium-high heat. Brown chicken breasts on both sides. Season with salt and pepper as desired.

2. Add cider vinegar and $^1/_4$ cup water. Turn the heat down to low and cover. Cook until tender, about 10 minutes.

Chicken with Apples and Hearts of Palm

1 TB. plant sterol spread, such as Smart Balance

1 lb. boneless and skinless chicken breasts

1 cup hearts of palm

2 cups apple with skin, sliced

$^1/_2$ cup reduced-calorie mayonnaise, fat-free

Makes 4 servings
Prep time: 5 minutes
Cook time: 12 minutes
Each serving has:
207.5 calories
27.29 g. protein
15.19 g. carbohydrate
3.24 g. total fat
0.88 g. saturated fat
68.97 mg. cholesterol
469.5 mg. sodium
3.2 g. fiber

1. In a medium saucepan, melt sterol spread over medium-high heat, then sauté chicken breasts until golden and cooked, about 8 minutes per side. Remove chicken from the pan and keep warm.

2. Reduce the heat to medium, add hearts of palm, reserving liquid, and apple slices, and stir to cook until apples are soft. Pour in liquid from hearts of palm, and whisk in mayonnaise to make a sauce. Return chicken breasts to the pan to heat, tossing in sauce.

Food for Thought

Hearts of palm are a great source of fiber and potassium while being low in carbohydrates. Unfortunately, canned versions are high in sodium, so if you need to restrict your salt intake, rinse the hearts thoroughly before using and discard the liquid.

Chicken with Apricots and Prunes

Makes 4 servings
Prep time: 10 minutes
Cook time: 45 minutes
Each serving has:
355.2 calories
53.99 g. protein
27.19 g. carbohydrate
3.07 g. total fat
0.77 g. saturated fat
131.5 mg. cholesterol
151.6 mg. sodium
3.85 g. fiber

2 cups water

$^1/_2$ cup dried apricots, chopped into $^1/_2$-inch cubes

$^1/_2$ cup prunes, chopped into $^1/_2$-inch cubes

Nonstick cooking spray

2 lb. boneless and skinless chicken breasts

1 cup onion, finely chopped

2 tsp. sugar substitute, such as Splenda

$^1/_2$ tsp. ground cinnamon

2 tsp. balsamic vinegar

1. Bring water to a boil in a small saucepan, and add apricots and prunes. Reduce the heat to low and simmer for 20 minutes. Remove fruit with a slotted spoon, and reserve liquid.

2. Spray a cold 10-inch skillet with cooking spray, and heat over medium-high heat. When hot, add chicken breasts and brown, turning as needed, about 12 minutes. Remove chicken to a plate and keep warm.

3. Remove the pan from the heat and spray with more cooking spray. Reduce the heat to low and add onion. Cook until soft and translucent, about 5 minutes. Stir in stewed fruit, sugar, cinnamon, reserved fruit liquid, and vinegar. Turn the heat up to high and cook until reduced 50 percent.

4. Return chicken to the pan, turn to coat, and reheat on medium heat for about 5 minutes.

Chicken with Garden Vegetables Stew

8 oz. mushrooms, thickly
sliced

$^1/_2$ cup carrots, thickly sliced

$^1/_2$ cup onion, finely sliced

$^1/_4$ cup low-salt chicken broth

$^1/_2$ cup water

2 cloves garlic, smashed

4 oz. canned tomatoes,
crushed

$^1/_4$ cup barley

$^1/_2$ tsp. fresh rosemary finely
chopped

$^1/_2$ tsp. fresh thyme

$^1/_4$ tsp. black pepper

1 bay leaf

2 lb. boneless and skinless
chicken legs

Makes 4 servings
Prep time: 15 minutes
Cook time: 8 hours
Each serving has:
178.3 calories
17.45 g. protein
21.82 g. carbohydrate
2.9 g. total fat
0.71 g. saturated fat
47.89 mg. cholesterol
141.3 mg. sodium
4.41 g. fiber

1. Into a $5^1/_2$- to 6-quart slow cooker, place mushrooms, carrots, and onions. Then add broth, water, garlic, tomatoes, barley, rosemary, thyme, pepper, bay leaf, and chicken legs. Cover and cook for 7 to 8 hours on low heat.

2. To serve, transfer chicken and vegetables into bowls. Skim any visible fat from sauce, pour over chicken, and serve.

Chicken with Peppers and Artichokes

Makes 6 servings
Prep time: 10 minutes
Cook time: 7 hours
Each serving has:
199.4 calories
29.16 g. protein
11.04 g. carbohydrate
4.22 g. total fat
0.81 g. saturated fat
65.96 mg. cholesterol
104.6 mg. sodium
2.93 g. fiber

1 TB. olive oil

6 cloves garlic, chopped

1 medium onion, coarsely chopped

8 oz. artichoke hearts

¹/₂ cup reduced-sodium chicken broth

1 TB. tapioca

2 tsp. fresh rosemary

1 tsp. lemon zest

¹/₂ tsp. black pepper

1¹/₂ lb. boneless and skinless chicken breasts

1 medium yellow bell pepper, sliced

1 medium red bell pepper, sliced

1. Heat a small skillet over medium heat, and add olive oil. Sauté garlic and onions until tender and translucent, about 5 minutes.

2. In a 3¹/₂- to 4-quart slow cooker, add artichoke hearts, broth, tapioca, rosemary, lemon zest, pepper, and chicken. Spoon garlic and onion mixture over top. Cover and cook on low heat setting for 6 to 7 hours. Add sweet peppers during the last 15 minutes before serving so they remain somewhat crisp.

Smoke Signals _____

According to the Environmental Working Group's 2003 report "Shopper's Guide to Pesticides in Produce," bell peppers are among the 12 foods on which pesticide residues have been most frequently found. Try to find organic ones whenever possible.

Chicken with Sage and Honey

2 lb. boneless and skinless chicken breasts

Nonstick cooking spray

2 cloves garlic, chopped

10 fresh sage leaves

4 TB. honey

¹/₄ cup fresh lemon juice

¹/₂ cup low-salt chicken broth

Makes 4 servings
Prep time: 5 minutes
Cook time: 15 minutes
Each serving has:
329.1 calories
53.89 g. protein
19.49 g. carbohydrate
3.13 g. total fat
0.84 g. saturated fat
131.8 mg. cholesterol
161.6 mg. sodium
0.13 g. fiber

1. Spray a cold 10-inch skillet with cooking spray and heat over medium-high heat. Brown chicken quickly on both sides; then add garlic and sage on top of the chicken. Reduce heat to low, cover and turn breasts as needed for 10 minutes. Transfer chicken to a plate and keep warm.

2. Add honey, lemon juice, and broth to the pan, and scrape up any bits. Return chicken to the pan, turn to coat, and serve.

Nutri Notes _____

Honey is a natural antibacterial which draws water from a wound, preventing infection. It is rich in antioxidants, in particular pinocembrin, which has antibacterial action against *Staphylococcus aureus*, a common bacteria that can cause infections, especially in open wounds. Darker honeys, specifically honey from buckwheat flowers, sage, and tupelo, contain a greater amount of antioxidants than other honeys. However, processing destroys these properties, so look for raw honey whenever possible.

Chickpea Chicken

Makes 4 servings

Prep time: 10 minutes

Cook time: 30 minutes

Each serving has:

403.1 calories

54.28 g. protein

22.9 g. carbohydrate

10.62 g. total fat

2.53 g. saturated fat

181.7 mg. cholesterol

471.5 mg. sodium

5.37 g. fiber

1 tsp. ground cumin

$1/8$ tsp. ground cardamom

$1/2$ tsp. ground cinnamon

$1/4$ tsp. cayenne

2 lb. boneless and skinless chicken thighs

Nonstick cooking spray

1 lb. zucchini, finely diced

1 cup chickpeas

1 cup canned tomatoes, crushed

$1/2$ cup low-salt chicken broth

1 TB. fresh lemon juice

1 TB. fresh cilantro, chopped

1. In a small bowl, combine cumin, cardamom, cinnamon, and cayenne to blend. Rub all over chicken thighs.

2. Spray a medium-cold skillet with cooking spray, and heat over medium-high heat. Once the pan is hot, add chicken and brown, turning pieces once for about 10 minutes. Remove to a plate and keep warm.

3. Add zucchini, and toss frequently until slightly soft. Add chickpeas and tomatoes, reduce the heat, and cook for about 5 more minutes.

4. Add broth, and bring mixture to a boil over high heat. Reduce the heat, return chicken to the pan, and cover and simmer for 10 minutes. Squeeze lemon juice over mixture, stir, and serve with cilantro.

General Lee Chicken with Orange Sauce

1 lb. boneless and skinless chicken breasts

2 TB. tapioca

³/₄ cup low-salt chicken broth

3 TB. fresh orange juice

2 TB. reduced-sodium teriyaki sauce

1 tsp. dry mustard

1 cup fresh pineapple or canned, drained

1 lb. broccoli, chopped into florets

Makes 4 servings
Prep time: 10 minutes
Cook time: 7 hours
Each serving has:
221.2 calories
32.51 g. protein
17.78 g. carbohydrate
2.71 g. total fat
0.6 g. saturated fat
66.21 mg. cholesterol
255.2 mg. sodium
4.52 g. fiber

1. Place chicken breasts on the bottom of a 5¹/₂- to 6-quart slow cooker.

2. In a bowl, combine tapioca, broth, orange juice, teriyaki sauce, mustard, and pineapple, and stir to blend. Pour over chicken and cover. Cook on low heat for 7 to 8 hours. Place broccoli in sauce 20 minutes before serving so it remains crisp. Cover and let stand.

Grilled Citrus Chicken

Makes 4 servings
Prep time: 15 minutes
Cook time: 15 minutes
Each serving has:
219.7 calories
33.64 g. protein
4.47 g. carbohydrate
6.72 g. total fat
1.71 g. saturated fat
141.2 mg. cholesterol
146.8 mg. sodium
0.12 g. fiber

1½ lb. boneless and skinless chicken thighs

Nonstick cooking spray

½ cup tangerine juice

2 TB. fresh lemon juice

2 TB. fresh lime juice

4 drops Flavors2go guava

4 drops Flavors2go honey

1 tsp. salt substitute, such as Morton's

1 tsp. ground black pepper

1. Spray a cold grill with high-heat cooking spray and then heat on high. Grill chicken thighs until cooked, about 10 minutes per side, then let sit, covered, for 5 minutes.

2. In a bowl, combine tangerine, lemon, and lime juices, guava, and honey. Season to taste with salt and pepper, and serve as a dipping sauce.

Food for Thought ___

I use natural fruit flavorings to enhance the aroma and taste of a dish without the added calories and sugars that come along with fruit juices. Flavors2Go products can be used in heated dishes and are alcohol free. Like liquid Splenda, a drop goes a long way.

Lucky Red Chicken

2 TB. canola oil

2 cups onion, finely diced

2 tsp. garlic, finely chopped

1 tsp. ground ginger

3 jalapeño peppers, deseeded and finely chopped

¼ adobo chili pepper, finely chopped

1 tsp. hot pepper flakes (optional)

1 tsp. ground cinnamon

1 tsp. ground cardamom

⅛ tsp. ground cloves

2 cups canned tomatoes, crushed

4 lb. skinless chicken pieces

2 tsp. salt substitute, such as Morton's

Makes 6 servings
Prep time: 15 minutes
Cook time: 45 minutes
Each serving has:
427.9 calories
63.62 g. protein
11.79 g. carbohydrate
13.15 g. total fat
2.42 g. saturated fat
196.6 mg. cholesterol
333.2 mg. sodium
3.02 g. fiber

1. Heat oil in a 12-inch skillet on medium heat. Add onions, stirring occasionally, until soft, about 10 minutes. Add garlic, ginger, and chilies, and cook stirring gently for about 1 minute. Add pepper flakes, cinnamon, cardamom, and cloves, stir to mix, and then add tomatoes. Cook until mixture breaks down, about 10 minutes.

2. Add chicken pieces, and lower the heat so sauce merely simmers. Cook uncovered for about 30 minutes or until chicken is tender, turning once in the pan. Season with salt to taste.

Food for Thought _____

Adobo chilis in a can are potent, so you can use just some of the sauce if this dish is too spicy for your taste. Always taste a jalapeño, as their degree of hotness varies throughout the year. If jalapeños are too spicy, remove the seeds and veins before chopping.

Moroccan Chicken with Lemon and Carrots

Makes 6 servings
Prep time: 10 minutes
Cook time: 30 minutes
Each serving has:
152.8 calories
18.42 g. protein
12.93 g. carbohydrate
3.66 g. total fat
0.92 g. saturated fat
60.87 mg. cholesterol
110.4 mg. sodium
3.84 g. fiber

2 TB. canola oil

1 lb. skinless chicken thighs

1 cup onion, finely chopped

1 lb. carrots cut on the diagonal

2 tsp. paprika

1 tsp. ground ginger

$^1/_4$ tsp. turmeric

$^1/_8$ tsp. ground cinnamon

1 cup low-salt chicken broth

1 medium lemon, cut into 8 wedges (or one preserved Meyers lemon)

1. Heat oil in heavy skillet over medium-high heat. Season chicken with salt and pepper. Brown on both sides. Transfer to plate and set aside.

2. Add onion to skillet, reduce heat to medium low, and cook until tender, about 8 minutes. Add carrots, and stir 2 minutes to prevent burning. Add paprika, ginger, turmeric, and cinnamon, and stir 1 minute to blend. Return chicken to the skillet, and add broth and lemon. Bring to a boil, cover, and reduce heat. Simmer for 30 minutes. Recipe can be prepared to this point and put into fridge. Reheat on medium heat for 10 minutes to serve.

Food for Thought

Meyers lemons are grown in Morocco and have a soft outer skin. They are very fragrant and have a wonderful true lemon flavor. These are winter lemons which you can preserve in salt for use year-round. Cut the lemons into quarters, but leave the stem portion intact. Pack the cuts with kosher salt. In a clean canning jar, add some salt to the bottom, then pack jar full of lemons, pouring any remaining lemon juice into the jar, and seal. The lemons should be submerged in juice after a few days. If not, add some lemon juice to cover.

Simply The Best Roast Chicken

3¹/₂-lb. roaster chicken

1 TB. peanut oil

2 tsp. fresh tarragon

2 cloves garlic, diced

Makes 6 servings
Prep time: 10 minutes
Cook time: 30 minutes
Each serving has:
316.9 calories
53.95 g. protein
0.43 g. carbohydrate
9.52 g. total fat
2.18 g. saturated fat
172 mg. cholesterol
198.9 mg. sodium
0.05 g. fiber

1. Preheat the oven to 500°F.

2. Clean and rinse chicken, removing bag of giblets, neck, and any excess fat from cavity or up front under skin flap.

3. In a small bowl, combine peanut oil, tarragon, and garlic.

4. Using your hands, lift skin from front of chicken and gently separate it from breast meat using a gentle sweeping motion side to side. Dip your hand into tarragon garlic mixture, and spread it over breast meat on both sides. Coat any remaining mixture liberally over outside of chicken skin.

5. Place chicken breast-up in a roasting pan, and place feet first into the oven on a rack in the middle of the oven. Roast for 30 minutes or until an instant-read thermometer reads 155°F when inserted into thigh. Remove from the oven and let chicken rest in a warm place, loosely covered with foil, for 15 minutes. Cut into serving pieces.

Variation: Omit tarragon, and use oregano, thyme, or marjoram for an Italian version. Or omit tarragon, and use 1 tsp. hot paprika for a Hungarian version.

Variation: This technique works equally well for turkey. For a 14-pound bird, it takes 2 hours to sear roast a bird to perfection with no basting. This is one technique where a continuous instant-read digital thermometer prevents overcooking.

Star Anise Chicken

Makes 6 servings
Prep time: 5 minutes
Cook time: 45 minutes
Each serving has:
257.2 calories
46.4 g. protein
1.03 g. carbohydrate
6.26 g. total fat
1.53 g. saturated fat
147.4 mg. cholesterol
190.5 mg. sodium
0.33 g. fiber

2 quarts water

1 tsp. ground ginger

$^1/_2$ cup green onions, chopped, about 6

2 tsp. crushed star anise

2 TB. salt substitute, such as Morton's

2 TB. sugar substitute, such as Splenda

3-lb. roaster chicken

1. Place water, ginger, onions, anise, salt, and sugar into a large pot. Bring to a boil over high heat.

2. Remove packet of giblets from chicken. Also remove any visible fat from body cavity. Discard the fat and giblets. Gently place chicken breast side up into broth. Cover, reduce the heat to low, and simmer for 20 minutes. Turn off the heat, and let chicken sit for another 20 minutes.

3. Using two forks, lift chicken from the pot and set on a plate to cool. Once cool, remove all skin and cut chicken into serving pieces that can easily be dipped in sauce, such as the Wasabi Ginger Sauce (see Chapter 17).

Steaming Lemon Chicken

2 lb. boneless and skinless chicken breasts

3 TB. reduced-sodium soy sauce

1 TB. oyster sauce

1/4 tsp. ground black pepper

1/2 cup fresh lemon juice

1/4 cup low-salt chicken broth

2 tsp. sugar substitute, such as Splenda

1 tsp. salt substitute, such as Morton's

Makes 4 servings
Prep time: 2 hours
Cook time: 30 minutes
Each serving has:
270 calories
53.92 g. protein
3.69 g. carbohydrate
2.97 g. total fat
0.8 g. saturated fat
131.7 mg. cholesterol
615.1 mg. sodium
0.16 g. fiber

1. Cut chicken breasts into chunks.

2. In a bowl, combine soy sauce, oyster sauce, pepper, lemon juice, chicken broth, sugar, and salt. Add chicken to mixture, and marinate, covered, for up to 2 hours.

3. Choose a pan with a steamer insert. Fill the saucepan with water, then place the steamer on top. Put chicken on a heat-proof plate, place into the steamer, and pour marinade over top. Cover.

4. Bring water to a boil over high heat, and steam chicken for 20 minutes.

Food for Thought _____

Oyster sauce has a very high sodium content and can be omitted if you must restrict your salt intake. Look for brands that do not contain MSG, such as Amoy or Lee Kum Kee.

Tangerine Chicken with Almonds and Raisins

Makes 4 servings
Prep time: 5 minutes
Cook time: 15 minutes
Each serving has:
370.2 calories
55.71 g. protein
15.55 g. carbohydrate
9.01 g. total fat
1.24 g. saturated fat
131.5 mg. cholesterol
155 mg. sodium
2.06 g. fiber

Nonstick cooking spray

2 lb. boneless and skinless chicken breasts

1 tsp. salt substitute, such as Morton's

1 cup mandarin oranges

4 drops Flavors2go tangerine

$^1/_3$ cup slivered almonds

$^1/_4$ cup raisins

1 TB. tangerine zest

1. Spray an 8- to 10-inch skillet with cooking spray. Season chicken breasts with salt and sauté for 5 minutes over medium-high heat. Turn once, and cook for another 4 minutes or until meat lightly springs back to the touch. Remove chicken and keep warm.

2. Keep the pan over medium-high heat, add mandarin oranges with juice, and scrape up any bits of chicken from the pan. Add 3 drops of tangerine flavor, almonds, raisins, and *tangerine* zest. Bring to a medium simmer, and return chicken to the pan, coating with sauce.

Nutri Speak

Tangerine is a widely cultivated member of the mandarin orange family, having deep orange fruit that is easily separated into segments. It originated in Tangier, Morocco. Today, mandarin oranges and tangerines are different varieties, though they are used interchangeably in cooking.

Thai Spicy Sweet Chicken on a Stick

1 tsp. red chili paste

1 tsp. ground ginger

1 TB. sugar substitute, such as Splenda

½ cup water

1 tsp. salt substitute, such as Morton's

1½ lb. boneless and skinless chicken breasts

16 wooden skewers, soaked in water

Makes 4 servings
Prep time: 5 minutes
Cook time: 10 minutes
Each serving has:
187.5 calories
39.28 g. protein
0.08 g. carbohydrate
2.11 g. total fat
0.56 g. saturated fat
98.66 mg. cholesterol
146.3 mg. sodium
0.01 g. fiber

1. In a small saucepan, combine chili paste, ginger, sugar, water, and salt, and bring to a careful boil. Reduce heat and simmer for 5 minutes, then cool. This makes chili sauce.

2. Cut chicken breasts into 4 slices each, then cut each in half to make 16 slices total. Thread one skewer through each piece.

3. Heat the grill on high heat. Place the skewers on the grill and cook until done, turning once.

4. Serve with chili sauce for dipping.

Variation: Add a tablespoon of peanut butter to the mixture along with some hot German-style mustard for a thicker dipping sauce, similar to an Indonesian version.

Duck with Fennel

Makes 2 servings
Prep time: 10 minutes
Cook time: 12 minutes
Each serving has:
403.1 calories
47.85 g. protein
16.68 g. carbohydrate
12.18 g. total fat
4.04 g. saturated fat
174.6 mg. cholesterol
284.4 mg. sodium
7.05 g. fiber

1 lb. duck breasts

1 tsp. ground coriander

1 tsp. ground ginger

1 lb. fennel, thinly sliced

2 TB. plant sterol spread, such as Benecol

1. Season duck breast with coriander and ginger. Discard fennel stalks but chop fronds.

2. In a medium sauté pan, melt sterol spread on medium-high heat. Place duck breast skin side down into the pan, and sear for 4 minutes. Remove from the pan to a warm plate, loosely covered. Reduce the heat to medium, and add fennel slices and fronds. Turn fennel as it cooks until soft but not wilted. Return the duck breasts to the pan and cook for 1 to 2 more minutes. Remove duck to a serving plate, let rest for 5 minutes loosely covered with foil. Divide fennel mixture between the plates, place a duck breast on top of each plate, and serve.

Food for Thought

Duck fat contains 52 percent monounsaturated fatty acids, the good kind. And it is low in sodium. Cook duck breast meat until just pink, but to retain its texture do not overcook.

Duck with Mushrooms and Beans

2 lb. skinless duck breasts

1 lb. mushrooms, thickly sliced

1 TB. tapioca

2 cup water

1 tsp. salt substitute, such as Morton's

1 tsp. ground black pepper

1 bay leaf

$1/2$ tsp. fresh thyme

1 cup onion, coarsely diced

3 cloves garlic, whole

$1/2$ cup red wine vinegar

$1/4$ cup cooked navy beans

Makes 4 servings
Prep time: 10 minutes
Cook time: 7 hours
Each serving has:
353.2 calories
49.84 g. protein
15.41 g. carbohydrate
10.17 g. total fat
3.08 g. saturated fat
174.6 mg. cholesterol
141.6 mg. sodium
3.04 g. fiber

1. Into a 5- to 6-quart slow cooker, put duck breasts. Then add mushrooms, tapioca, water, salt, pepper, bay leaf, thyme, onion, garlic, and vinegar. Cover and cook on low heat setting for 7 hours.

2. Add navy beans 5 minutes before serving, mixing into broth.

Nutri Notes _____

Tapioca derives from the cassava or maniac plant. It is a root starch widely used in South America, Southeast Asia, and Africa as a thickener for bread flour and even a laundry detergent.

Turkey and Shrimp Jambalaya

Makes 8 servings
Prep time: 10 minutes
Cook time: 7 hours
Each serving has:
232.1 calories
33.51 g. protein
13.29 g. carbohydrate
4.99 g. total fat
0.2 g. saturated fat
115.2 mg. cholesterol
304.7 mg. sodium
3.74 g. fiber

1 cup celery, coarsely chopped

1 large onion, coarsely chopped

1 can (14.5 oz.) tomatoes, crushed

1 cup red beans

1 cup water

$\frac{1}{2}$ cup low-salt chicken broth

1 TB. Worcestershire sauce

$1\frac{1}{2}$ tsp. Paul Prudhomme Poultry seasoning

2 lb. skinless turkey thighs

1 cup green bell pepper, coarsely sliced

8 oz. cooked, peeled shrimp (medium-size, 24 count per pound)

1. In a $5\frac{1}{2}$- to 6-quart slow cooker, combine celery, onion, tomatoes, beans, water, broth, Worcestershire sauce, and poultry seasoning. Lay turkey thighs on top. Cover and cook on low heat for 7 to 8 hours.

2. 15 minutes before serving, add green bell pepper and shrimp. Cover and let stand.

Turkey Chipotle Grill

Makes 4 servings
Prep time: 15 minutes
Cook time: 12 minutes
Each serving has:
269 calories
56.41 g. protein
3.73 g. carbohydrate
2.02 g. total fat
0.62 g. saturated fat
140.7 mg. cholesterol
115.5 mg. sodium
1.36 g. fiber

2 lb. boneless and skinless turkey breast

Nonstick cooking spray, high temperature

$\frac{1}{2}$ adobo chili pepper

2 cloves garlic, whole

1. Remove skin from turkey breast.

2. Heat a grill on moderately high heat. Spray turkey breast with a cooking spray for high heat, and grill on both sides for about 10-12 minutes per side.

3. In a blender, combine chili and garlic. Dilute with a small amount of water as needed. Brush turkey with chipotle sauce, and grill for 2 more minutes. Cut into chunks and serve.

Turkey Cutlets

1¹/₂ lb. turkey breast tenderloin slices

1 tsp. salt substitute, such as
Morton's

1 tsp. ground black pepper

1 cup water

¹/₂ cup egg substitute

2 cup panko flakes

3 TB. plant sterol spread,
such as Smart Balance

1 TB. Dijon mustard

1 TB. soy sauce, reduced-
sodium

1 tsp. sugar substitute, such
as Splenda

2 tsp. rice wine vinegar

Makes 4 servings
Prep time: 10 minutes
Cook time: 6 minutes
Each serving has:
380.3 calories
48.97 g. protein
23.52 g. carbohydrate
4.68 g. total fat
1.43 g. saturated fat
105.9 mg. cholesterol
401.3 mg. sodium
0.14 g. fiber

1. Place turkey breast slices between 2 pieces of plastic wrap. Using a bottle or rolling pin, pound cutlets into a flat thin shape, being careful not to tear the plastic wrap. Remove each cutlet from the wrap and season with salt and pepper.

2. Place egg substitute into a bowl, and into another bowl, *panko flakes*. Dip each turkey cutlet into egg mixture, then panko flakes, and set on a plate.

3. Melt sterol spread in a 10-inch skillet on medium-high heat, and add cutlets. Cook for 3 minutes on each side or until lightly golden brown.

4. In a bowl, combine mustard, soy sauce, sugar, and vinegar. Drizzle over cutlets and serve.

Nutri Speak

Panko flakes are Japanese bread crumbs, which make a light, crispy coating when cooked in butter or oil. You can find them in the Asian section of your supermarket.

Turkey in Paprikash Sauce

Makes 6 servings
Prep time: 10 minutes
Cook time: 7 hours 15 minutes
Each serving has:
277.9 calories
43.45 g. protein
18.86 g. carbohydrate
2.7 g. total fat
0.97 g. saturated fat
96.62 mg. cholesterol
124.5 mg. sodium
3.64 g. fiber

1 cup onion, coarsely sliced

$^1/_3$ cup barley

1 TB. tapioca

2 lb. boneless and skinless turkey breast

1 cup low-salt chicken broth

2 TB. paprika

$^1/_2$ tsp. salt substitute, such as Morton's

2 cup green bell pepper, coarsely sliced

1 cup nonfat plain yogurt

1. Into a $5^1/_2$- to 6-quart slow cooker, place onion, barley, tapioca, and turkey.

2. In a small bowl, combine broth, paprika, and salt. Pour over turkey. Cover and cook on low heat for 7 to 8 hours.

3. Remove turkey from the cooker and keep warm. Add green bell pepper and cover for 15 minutes. Stir in yogurt, pour mixture over turkey pieces, and serve.

Variation: You can use a variety of sweet peppers for this dish. Yellow, green, or red ones have different flavors that blend nicely in this dish. Or use all three for a great color effect.

Turkey with Mint and Honey

Makes 4 servings
Prep time: 10 minutes
Cook time: 15 minutes
Each serving has:
329.1 calories
53.89 g. protein
19.49 g. carbohydrate
3.13 g. total fat
0.84 g. saturated fat
131.8 mg. cholesterol
161.6 mg. sodium
0.13 g. fiber

Nonstick cooking spray

2 cloves garlic, coarsely chopped

5 fresh mint leaves

2 lb. boneless and skinless turkey breasts

4 TB. honey

$^1/_4$ cup fresh lemon juice

$^1/_2$ cup low-salt chicken broth

1. Spray a cold 10-inch skillet with cooking spray; then heat over medium-high heat. Cut turkey breasts into 4 portions. Brown turkey quickly on both sides; then add garlic and mint on top of the turkey. Reduce heat to medium, and turn breasts as needed for 10 minutes. Transfer turkey to a plate and keep warm.

2. Add honey, lemon juice, and broth to the pan and scrape up any bits. Return turkey to the pan, turn to coat, and serve.

Turkey Nuggets with Peanut Sauce

1 lb. boneless and skinless turkey breast

3 TB. fresh cilantro, chopped

1/2 tsp. salt substitute, such as Morton's

1 tsp. ground black pepper

6 cloves garlic, 2 whole and 4 finely diced

1/2 cup canned tomatoes, crushed

1 TB. cider vinegar

1 TB. sugar substitute, such as Splenda Brown Sugar Blend

1/2 cup raisins

1/4 cup peanut butter

Makes 4 servings
Prep time: 5 minutes
Cook time: 10 minutes
Each serving has:
293.8 calories
33.25 g. protein
22.13 g. carbohydrate
9.14 g. total fat
1.88 g. saturated fat
70.36 mg. cholesterol
103.9 mg. sodium
2.65 g. fiber

1. Heat oven to 500°F. Cut turkey breast into 8 equal-size pieces. Coat with cilantro and 4 finely diced cloves of garlic, and season with salt and pepper. Place into an ovenproof pan and roast for 10 minutes.

2. In a blender or food processor, combine remaining 2 whole cloves of garlic, tomatoes, vinegar, sugar, raisins, and peanut butter. Thin with water as needed to make dipping sauce. Serve alongside turkey nuggets.

Food for Thought _____

Nut butters are an excellent source of fatty acids that can help prevent heart disease, diabetes, and stroke. Just 1 to 2 ounces of walnuts, cashews, pistachios, or peanuts daily can help you reap this benefit. Some nut butters need to be refrigerated as they contain no stabilizing agents. Merely mix the oil that floats on top back into the mixture before serving.

Turkey Wraps

Makes 4 servings
Prep time: 5 minutes
Cook time: 8 minutes
Each serving has:
195 calories
21.67 g. protein
19.16 g. carbohydrate
7.54 g. total fat
1.59 g. saturated fat
47.06 mg. cholesterol
511.5 mg. sodium
10.71 g. fiber

$^1/_2$ lb. ground turkey

8 oz. fresh spinach leaves

1 cup canned tomatoes, crushed

1 tsp. ground cumin

4 oz. fat-free cream cheese

4 La Tortilla Factory low-carb tortillas, 8-inch size

1. Heat a small 8-inch skillet on high heat; then add ground turkey. Let sit undisturbed for 2 minutes to brown; then stir to cook, about 5 minutes. Add spinach leaves, tomatoes, and cumin, and cook until spinach is wilted. Remove from heat, and stir in cream cheese until melted.

2. Divide mixture into 4 portions. Place mixture to one side of a tortilla. Wrap according to the directions in Southwest Chicken Salad Tortilla (see Chapter 9).

Smoke Signals

According to the Environmental Working Group's 2003 report "Shopper's Guide to Pesticides in Produce," spinach is among the 12 foods on which pesticide residues have been most frequently found. Look for organic produce in this category, or only purchase leaves in sealed bags.

14

The Butcher Shop

In This Chapter

- ◆ Lean and Not so Mean Choices
- ◆ Keep it clean
- ◆ Focus on the Game

From the days of the ancient caveman, humans have been carnivores, or meat eaters. We've burned meat over a fire, eaten it raw, and salted it away for future enjoyment. Entire industries have developed strictly to serve our need to consume an amino-acid-rich source of protein which helps to build strong bones, good teeth, and a better blood profile. But over time our source of meat has drastically changed, shifting from game, rich in omega-3 fatty acids, to the happy cow stuffed with antibiotics and increasing amounts of saturated fat. So to eat healthy, we need to learn how to choose our meat wisely.

Looking for lean, mean sources of animal protein shouldn't make you cranky when you cook with total nutrition in mind. You only need to understand which cuts provide the maximum nutrition with the least saturated fat. When it comes to beef, look for eye of round, top round, round tip, top sirloin, bottom round, top loin, and tenderloin selections. Trimming excess fat can reduce the amount of saturated fat by 50 percent, so keep your knife sharpened when preparing meat for the healthiest choice.

Beef, like other animal protein sources, can easily be contaminated by careless handling. So remember these basic food safety tips:

◆ Never defrost meat on a counter. The bloody liquid can become a breeding ground for bacteria such as E. coli and a serious case of food poisoning.

◆ Keep raw meat from coming in contact with other foods during preparation. This means don't chop vegetables on the same board as you just prepared your meat without washing all utensils first.

◆ Keep meat cold. Store it in the coldest part of your refrigerator in a plastic bag or on a plate to prevent contamination. I place my meats next to the wall of the freezer portion of my refrigerator, but if you have a meat compartment, store it there.

◆ Cook meat properly. The surface of meat can be contaminated with bacteria, but cooking meat to a temperature of 145°F will eliminate any concern. If using a marinade, bring it to a boil for one minute before brushing on any cooked meat.

Choosing a variety of meats will not only help your family develop a healthier palate, but it can also reduce the need for supplements because vitamins and minerals are better absorbed when in whole foods. Game meats, such as buffalo, venison, goat, and rabbit, can provide your family with healthy fats and protein while avoiding the dangers of antibiotics, pesticides, and hormones used in today's meat industry. So be adventuresome, give my recipes a try, and discover how cooking with total nutrition in mind can reap tons of benefits for you and your family.

Asparagus Beef with Noodles

1 lb. top round steak

Nonstick cooking spray

1 cup onion, finely chopped

2 cloves garlic, minced

1 lb. asparagus, cut into
2-inch pieces

¹/₄ cup reduced-sodium fat-free beef broth

³/₄ lb. Dreamfields penne pasta

Makes 4 servings
Prep time: 15 minutes
Cook time: 15 minutes
Each serving has:
473.7 calories
38.06 g. protein
72.95 g. carbohydrate
19.68 g. total fat
3.06 g. saturated fat
69.17 mg. cholesterol
98.18 mg. sodium
9.21 g. fiber

1. Freeze steak for 30 minutes; then slice into thin strips.

2. Spray a wok or 10-inch skillet with cooking spray, and heat on high heat. Sear meat strips on both sides until cooked, about 3 minutes. Transfer to a plate and keep warm.

3. Remove the pan from the heat and spray with cooking spray. Return to the heat and add onion and garlic to the pan and stir for 1 minute. Add asparagus and toss for 30 seconds; then add broth and beef, cover, and turn off the heat.

4. Bring water to boil in a 2-quart saucepan, and cook the pasta until done, about 7 minutes. Drain but do not rinse. Divide into serving portions, top with beef asparagus mixture, including any residual broth, and serve.

Food for Thought _____

Lightly freezing meat will make slicing into thin strips a snap. Be sure to sharpen your knife before slicing so you make clean, straight cuts.

Beef Broccoli and Snow Peas Stir Fry

Makes 8 servings

Prep time: 10 minutes

Cook time: 10 minutes

Each serving has:

255.4 calories

38.15 g. protein

17.55 g. carbohydrate

6.2 g. total fat

2.04 g. saturated fat

31.35 mg. cholesterol

131.9 mg. sodium

7.29 g. fiber

Nutri Speak

Flank steak is a triangular-shaped muscle from the underside or flank of beef. It should be cut across the grain, or horizontally, as thin as possible to remain tender.

$^3/_4$ lb. spaghetti

1 tsp. toasted sesame oil

1 lb. flank steak

Nonstick cooking spray

1 TB. fresh ginger, minced

3 cloves garlic, sliced

1 cup onion, coarsely chopped

2 cups broccoli, cut into small florets

$^1/_2$ cup snow pea pods

2 TB. sugar substitute, such as Splenda Brown Sugar Blend

1 TB. red chili paste

1 TB. oyster sauce

1. Bring water to a boil in a 2-quart saucepan, and cook pasta until just done, about 5 minutes. Drain but do not rinse. Sprinkle sesame oil over pasta in a bowl and toss.

2. Cut *flank steak* into thin strips against the grain.

3. Spray a medium wok or large sauté pan with cooking spray, and heat on medium-high heat. Add ginger and garlic and toss for 30 seconds; then add onion, broccoli, and pea pods and toss for 3 minutes. Remove from the pan. Add meat strips and sauté for a few minutes or until meat has just turned lightly brown. Add pasta, vegetable mixture, and brown sugar, chili paste, and oyster sauce back into the pan and toss until heated through, about 1 minute. Serve immediately.

Beef Fajitas with Salsa

1 lb. top round steak

$^1/_4$ cup fresh lime juice

$^1/_4$ cup shallots, diced

2 cloves garlic, sliced

$^1/_4$ cup fresh cilantro, chopped

1 jalapeño pepper, diced

Nonstick cooking spray

1 cup red bell pepper, sliced

1 cup poblano peppers, sliced

$^1/_4$ tsp. cayenne

$^1/_4$ tsp. ground cumin

$^1/_2$ cup tomato, diced

$^1/_4$ cup onion, diced

1 jalapeño pepper, finely chopped

$^1/_4$ cup fresh cilantro, chopped

8 La Tortilla Factory low-carb tortillas, 8-inch size

$^1/_4$ cup cheddar cheese, shredded

Makes 4 servings
Prep time: 10 minutes
Cook time: 15 minutes
Each serving has:
207.7 calories
16.03 g. protein
33.32 g. carbohydrate
9.25 g. total fat
3.17 g. saturated fat
15.51 mg. cholesterol
511.7 mg. sodium
20.09 g. fiber

1. Freeze steak for 30 minutes, and slice into thin strips. In a plastic bag, combine meat, lime juice, shallots, garlic, cilantro, and jalapeño pepper. Marinate in the refrigerator for 15 minutes.

2. Spray an 10-inch sauté pan with cooking spray; then heat on moderately high heat. Add beef slices, and sauté until cooked, about 4 minutes. Add marinade to the pan and toss to coat. Add red and poblano peppers, cayenne, and cumin, and toss to coat. Cover, turn off the heat, and allow to steam for 5 minutes.

3. In a small bowl, combine tomato, onion, cilantro, and jalapeño pepper to make a salsa. Divide meat mixture between tortillas, and top with salsa. Top with a small amount of shredded cheddar cheese.

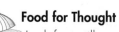

Food for Thought

Look for tortillas made with whole-wheat flour for the best nutritional value. Various brands also have low-fat or low-carb versions.

Beef Stir Fry with Mixed Vegetables

Makes 4 servings
Prep time: 15 minutes
Cook time: 15 minutes
Each serving has:
192.5 calories
28.12 g. protein
9.94 g. carbohydrate
4.68 g. total fat
1.57 g. saturated fat
69.32 mg. cholesterol
126.4 mg. sodium
3.09 g. fiber

Food for Thought

Heat a wok without any added oil for the best results. You can tell if the pan is hot enough by holding your hand over the pan. If you have to remove it by the count of 5 or less, it's *hot!* Now you're ready for searing any protein with minimal oil.

1 lb. top round steak

Nonstick cooking spray

½ cup onion, diced

1 clove garlic, sliced

1 TB. fresh ginger, diced

1 cup broccoli, cut into florets

1 cup cauliflower, cut into florets

1 cup bok choy, coarsely chopped

1 cup mushrooms, sliced

¼ cup low-salt chicken broth

½ cup red bell pepper, sliced

1 small jalapeño pepper, diced

1 TB. oyster sauce

1 tsp. cornstarch

1. Cut round steak into strips.

2. Spray a 10-inch skillet or wok with cooking spray; then heat on high. Add steak strips, cooking in batches as needed until just turning brown on edges. Pieces should still have some pink visible and not be cooked through. Remove meat to a plate and keep warm, covered loosely with foil.

3. Remove the pan from the heat and spray with cooking spray. Return to the heat and add onion, garlic, and ginger to the sauté pan, and stir frequently to cook until onions are translucent, about 2 minutes. Add broccoli, cauliflower, and bok choy, and toss to cook. Add mushrooms, broth, and peppers and cover. Lower heat and steam for 3 minutes.

4. In a small bowl, combine oyster sauce and cornstarch. Add a few spoonfuls of hot chicken broth to mixture; then add to the sauté pan, tossing to coat thoroughly. Add meat back to mixture, toss to heat, and then serve.

Beef Tostada

1/2 lb. top round steak

1/2 tsp. ground cumin

1/2 tsp. chili powder

1 clove garlic, minced

Nonstick cooking spray

4 La Tortilla Factory low-carb tortillas, 8-inch size

2 cups lettuce, romaine, shredded

1/2 cup onion, finely diced

1 cup canned black beans, drained

1 cup tomatoes, coarsely diced

1 jalapeño pepper, deseeded and finely diced

1/2 cup nonfat sour cream

1/2 cup feta cheese, crumbled

Makes 4 servings
Prep time: 10 minutes
Cook time: 5 minutes
Each serving has:
298.5 calories
27.09 g. protein
31.27 g. carbohydrate
10.89 g. total fat
5.26 g. saturated fat
64.04 mg. cholesterol
590.7 mg. sodium
13.02 g. fiber

1. Freeze steak for 30 minutes, and slice into thin strips. In a plastic bag, combine cumin, chili powder, and garlic, and add meat to coat thoroughly.

2. Spray an 8-inch sauté pan with cooking spray; then heat on moderately high heat. Remove steak strips from the bag, and quickly sauté until cooked, about 4 minutes.

3. Toast tortillas in a toaster until crisp.

4. In a bowl, combine onion, beans, tomatoes, and peppers to make salsa.

5. Place toasted tortilla on a plate, and add meat mixture. Top with lettuce and some salsa mixture. Add some sour cream and crumbled feta cheese and serve.

Smoke Signals

If you are pregnant, avoid unpasteurized cheeses such as feta, brie, and goat's milk cheese, which might be contaminated with listeria, a bacteria which causes severe problems with the fetus. Substitute any hard cheese for these cheeses in any recipe.

Beef with Chipotle and Green Chili Sauce

Makes 4 servings
Prep time: 10 minutes
Cook time: 20 minutes
Each serving has:
187.1 calories
26.22 g. protein
10.75 g. carbohydrate
4.54 g. total fat
1.53 g. saturated fat
69.17 mg. cholesterol
118.2 mg. sodium
3.67 g. fiber

1 lb. top round steak

1 tsp. salt substitute, such as Morton's

1 tsp. black pepper

1 tsp. chili powder

1 tsp. ground cumin

1 tsp. ground coriander

Nonstick cooking spray

1 cup onion, diced

5 cloves garlic, minced

1 cup fresh tomatoes, chopped

1/4 cup fresh lime juice

1 1/2 TB. chipotle pepper in adobo sauce

1/2 cup poblano peppers, sliced

1 cup water

1. Freeze steak for 30 minutes, and slice thinly into strips.

2. Combine salt, pepper, chili powder, cumin, and coriander, and toss with steak.

3. Spray a 10-inch skillet with cooking spray, and heat on medium-high heat. Quickly brown meat on both sides, about 4 minutes. Add onion and garlic, and cook for another 2 minutes or until soft. Add tomatoes, lime juice, chipotle pepper, poblano peppers, and water. Bring to a boil, cover and reduce the heat to low, and simmer for 10 minutes.

Beef with Winter Squash and Fennel

1½ lbs. beef bottom round

Nonstick cooking spray

1 cup onion, diced

2 cloves garlic, minced

1 cup mushrooms, sliced

2 cups carrots, chopped

1 can (14.5 oz.) tomatoes, crushed

1 cup water

2 tsp. fresh thyme

½ tsp. black pepper

3 cups butternut squash, peeled and cubed

1 cup fennel, sliced

Makes 8 servings
Prep time: 15 minutes
Cook time: 1 hour
Each serving has:
228.8 calories
26.7 g. protein
16.44 g. carbohydrate
6.62 g. total fat
2.19 g. saturated fat
66.34 mg. cholesterol
142.8 mg. sodium
2.89 g. fiber

1. Cut steak into 1-inch cubes.

2. Spray a Dutch oven with cooking spray, and heat on medium-high heat. Quickly sear the meat on both sides but do not cook through. Remove meat to a plate. Add onion and garlic to the pan and sauté until soft, stirring often to avoid burning, about 4 minutes. Return steak to the pan, and add mushrooms, carrots, tomatoes, water, thyme, pepper, squash, and fennel. Cover, reduce heat to low, and simmer for 1 hour. Test squash for doneness and serve.

Food for Thought _____

If you need to watch your salt intake, use fresh tomatoes rather than canned ones. Once the tomatoes are cooked, you can easily remove the skins from the sauce before serving without having to blanch the tomatoes.

Brisket in Guinness

Makes 6 servings
Prep time: 5 minutes
Cook time: 8 hours
Each serving has:
309.2 calories
34.7 g. protein
15.4 g. carbohydrate
9.78 g. total fat
3.09 g. saturated fat
89.21 mg. cholesterol
114.8 mg. sodium
3.19 g. fiber

2 lbs. beef brisket

1 cup onion, sliced

1 bay leaf

$^1/_2$ cup barley

12 oz. Guinness beer

2 TB. sugar substitute, such as Splenda Brown Sugar

$^1/_2$ tsp. thyme

1 clove garlic, sliced

12 oz. water

1. Trim any visible fat from brisket, cut into pieces, and place into a 5- to 6-quart slow cooker.

2. Add onions, bay leaf, and barley.

3. In a medium bowl, combine beer, brown sugar, thyme, garlic, and water. Pour over brisket, cover, and cook on low heat setting for 8 hours. Serve with beer broth.

Eye of Round Roast with Home Vegetables

Makes 6 servings
Prep time: 15 minutes
Cook time: 4 to 6 hours
Each serving has:
290.5 calories
36.47 g. protein
16.74 g. carbohydrate
8.01 g. total fat
2.62 g. saturated fat
81.65 mg. cholesterol
337.1 mg. sodium
2.96 g. fiber

2 lbs. choice eye of round roast

1 TB. tapioca

1 cup carrots, cut into 1-inch lengths

1 cup onion, sliced

1 bay leaf

1 cup cannellini beans, drained

1 can (14.5 oz.) reduced-sodium, fat-free beef broth

1 cup red bell pepper, sliced

1. Line a 5- to 6-quart slow cooker with a liner. Place tapioca, carrots, onion, bay leaf, and beans into the cooker; then top with roast. Add beef broth, cover, and set for 6 hours if you want shredded meat or 4 hours if you want to be able to cut it into chunks.

2. 15 minutes before serving, raise the temperature to high, add pepper slices, cover, and cook. Serve with sauce.

Grilled Flank Steak

2 tsp. ancho chili powder

2 tsp. paprika

2 tsp. Mexican or Greek oregano

1 tsp. ground cumin

1 tsp. mustard powder

1 clove garlic, minced

1 cup rolled oats

Nonstick cooking spray

1 lb. flank steak

Makes 6 servings
Prep time: 5 minutes
Cook time: 10 minutes
Each serving has:
255 calories
25.7 g. protein
18.54 g. carbohydrate
8.38 g. total fat
2.93 g. saturated fat
41.8 mg. cholesterol
54.14 mg. sodium
3.28 g. fiber

1. In a blender, combine chili powder, paprika, oregano, cumin, mustard, garlic, and oats. Place mixture into a plastic bag, and add steak. Coat thoroughly.

2. Spray a countertop grill with high heat tolerant cooking spray. Heat the grill on high heat. Cook steak on the grill until outside is crisp, about 7 minutes. Slice across the grain and serve.

Food for Thought

Mexican or Greek oregano has a distinctly different aroma and flavor than Italian varieties. You will find this oregano in any Latin foods market or in the grocery store in the Latin foods section.

Grilled Thai Steak

Makes 6 servings
Prep time: 25 minutes
Cook time: 4 minutes
Each serving has:
118.4 calories
17.64 g. protein
5.25 g. carbohydrate
2.99 g. total fat
1.01 g. saturated fat
46.12 mg. cholesterol
298.3 mg. sodium
1.54 g. fiber

1 lb. top round steak
2 TB. fresh lime juice
5 TB. shallots, minced
4 cloves garlic, minced
1/4 cup green onions, finely chopped
1/2 cup fresh cilantro, chopped

1/2 cup fresh mint leaves, chopped
1 jalapeño pepper, diced
3 TB. ground lemongrass
1 TB. fish sauce
1/4 cup red onion, diced
6 cups romaine lettuce, full leaves

1. Heat a countertop grill on high heat. Grill steak until cooked medium rare, about 4 minutes. Remove and slice into strips.

2. In a bowl, combine lime juice, shallots, garlic, scallions, cilantro, mint, jalapeño, lemongrass, fish sauce, and onion. Add steak strips and any juices. Toss to coat, and let marinate for 20 minutes.

3. Place lettuce on serving plates, and top with mixture.

Grilled Steak with Caribbean Sauce

1½ lbs. top round steak

Nonstick cooking spray

1 tsp. chili pepper paste

½ tsp. ground allspice

¼ cup fresh lime juice

½ cup green onions, finely chopped

¼ cup fresh orange juice

¼ cup boiling water

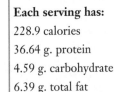

Makes 4 servings
Prep time: 5 minutes
Cook time: 8 minutes
Each serving has:
228.9 calories
36.64 g. protein
4.59 g. carbohydrate
6.39 g. total fat
2.23 g. saturated fat
103.8 mg. cholesterol
134.4 mg. sodium
0.5 g. fiber

1. Heat a countertop grill on high. Spray steak with cooking spray, and then grill until cooked, about 8 minutes.

2. In a bowl, combine chili pepper paste, allspice, lime juice, scallions, orange juice, and water. Serve mixture as sauce for steak.

Food for Thought

Countertop grills allow you to cook both sides of your entrée at the same time. Be sure to heat the grill 10 minutes longer than the ready light says to ensure your grill is hot enough to make nice grill marks on the food.

Liver with Garlic and Onions

2 TB. plant sterol spread, such as Smart Balance

1½ lbs. calf's liver

2 cloves garlic, sliced

1 cup onion, sliced

½ cup white wine

6 fresh leaves sage

2 TB. lemon juice

Makes 4 servings
Prep time: 10 minutes
Cook time: 15 minutes
Each serving has:
305.9 calories
36.65 g. protein
10.42 g. carbohydrate
7.12 g. total fat
0.53 g. saturated fat
564 mg. cholesterol
136 mg. sodium
0.83 g. fiber

1. Heat a 10-inch skillet on medium-high heat, and add sterol spread. Brown liver on both sides for about 4 minutes each; then transfer to a plate to keep warm, loosely covered with foil. Do not overcook liver, as it will continue to cook while resting.

2. Add garlic and onions to the skillet, and cook over medium heat until soft, about 5 minutes. Add wine and sage leaves, and cook until wine has reduced about 50 percent. Add lemon juice. Pour sauce over liver and serve.

Liver with Sage

Makes 4 servings
Prep time: 5 minutes
Cook time: 10 minutes
Each serving has:
323.43 calories
38.26 g. protein
16.74 g. carbohydrate
7.831 g. total fat
0.67 g. saturated fat
564 mg. cholesterol
134.1 mg. sodium
1.98 g. fiber

1½ lbs. calf's liver

¼ cup ground rolled oats

2 TB. plant sterol spread, such as Benecol

1 cup onion, diced

1 tsp. fresh thyme

1 tsp. ground sage

2 cloves garlic, minced

1. Cut liver into strips. Toss into oat flour to coat.

2. Heat a 10-inch skillet on medium-high heat, and melt 1 table-spoon sterol spread. Add onion, thyme, sage, and garlic, and cook until soft, about 5 minutes. Remove to a bowl and keep warm.

3. Melt remaining 1 tablespoon plant sterol spread. Quickly brown liver pieces in the skillet, about 4 minutes. Add onion mixture to the pan, toss to coat, and serve.

Food for Thought _____

You can make oat flour simply by grinding rolled oats in a food processor or blender. Oat flour is an excellent source of fiber and will keep in a sealed jar for 3 weeks, so keep plenty on hand to use in your recipes.

Liver with Thyme and Lemon Pepper

1 lb. calf's liver, sliced into
¹/₄-inch thick slices

1 TB. plant sterol spread,
such as Smart Balance

6 sprigs fresh thyme

1 TB. lemon pepper

Makes 4 servings
Prep time: 5 minutes
Cook time: 5 minutes
Each serving has:
173.3 calories
24 g. protein
4 g. carbohydrate
4.52 g. total fat
0.26 g. saturated fat
376 mg. cholesterol
88.26 mg. sodium
0 g. fiber

1. Heat an 8-inch skillet over medium-high heat, and add sterol
   spread. Quickly sauté liver strips until just pink, about 2 minutes. Add thyme leaves and lemon pepper, and cook for one
   more minute.

Food for Thought

Find lemon pepper in the seasoning section of your grocery
store or make your own. Just combine equal mounts of lemon
zest and whole black peppercorns to a spice grinder. Coarsely
chop; then pour out onto a baking sheet and place in a 200°F
oven overnight. Pulverize in a spice grinder the next day and
keep in a sealed jar. If you desire more lemon, increase the ratio
of lemon zest by 50 percent.

Mexican Steak Olé

Makes 6 servings
Prep time: 10 minutes
Cook time: 8 hours
Each serving has:
247.6 calories
26.97 g. protein
19.07 g. carbohydrate
7.03 g. total fat
2.72 g. saturated fat
41.8 mg. cholesterol
49.24 mg. sodium
6.39 g. fiber

1½ lbs. flank steak

10 oz. tomatoes, chopped

1 small jalapeño pepper, diced

2 cloves garlic, sliced

1 cup onion, sliced

1 TB. Mexican or Greek oregano

1 tsp. chili powder

1 tsp. ground cumin

2 medium poblano peppers, sliced

12 oz. black beans, drained

1. Trim any visible fat from the meat. Cut into 4 pieces, and place in a 5- to 6-quart slow cooker.

2. Add tomatoes, jalapeño, garlic, onion, oregano, chili powder, and cumin. Cover and cook on low heat for 8 hours.

3. Turn the setting to high, and add poblano peppers and beans. Cook for another 15 minutes. Remove meat and shred with forks. Serve with sauce.

Moghul Beef Biryani

Nonstick cooking spray

2 lbs. top round steak, cut into 1-inch cubes

1 cup onion, sliced

2 cloves garlic, sliced

2 TB. fresh ginger, minced

1 cup nonfat yogurt

1 tsp. cumin seeds

3 seeds cardamom

6 cloves garlic, whole

1 stick cinnamon

$^1/_2$ cup chana dal lentils

1 cup water

1 cup peas

$^1/_2$ tsp. saffron threads soaked in $^1/_4$ cup hot water

$^1/_4$ cup fresh cilantro, chopped

Makes 8 servings
Prep time: 10 minutes
Cook time: 6 hours 30 minutes
Each serving has:
215.6 calories
29.75 g. protein
12.97 g. carbohydrate
4.77 g. total fat
1.49 g. saturated fat
69.8 mg. cholesterol
103.7 mg. sodium
2.65 g. fiber

1. Spray a medium skillet with cooking spray, and heat on medium-high heat. Brown steak cubes on all sides, about 10 minutes. Add onions and cook until translucent, about 2 minutes. Add garlic and ginger and cook for 3 minutes, stirring often.

2. In a spice grinder, combine cumin, cardamom, garlic, and cinnamon. Grind to blend. Add to meat mixture, stir to blend, and then add yogurt.

3. Transfer meat mixture to a slow cooker, and add water and chana dal. Cover and cook on low for 6 hours. Turn the heat to high, and add peas and saffron water mixture. Cook for 10 minutes longer. Garnish with cilantro.

Smoke Signals

Lentils, such as chana dal, contain purines that can cause problems for people who suffer from gout or uric acid kidney stones. If you or your family members have this problem, avoid lentils.

Raja's Beef Roast

Makes 6 servings
Prep time: 10 minutes
Cook time: 8 hours
Each serving has:
287.4 calories
30.71 g. protein
18.09 g. carbohydrate
9.89 g. total fat
3.65 g. saturated fat
98.28 mg. cholesterol
163.9 mg. sodium
4.41 g. fiber

2 lbs. boneless chuck roast

1 tsp. ginger powder

1 tsp. curry powder

1 tsp. turmeric

$\frac{1}{2}$ tsp. ground cloves

1 cup onion, sliced

1 lb. carrots, sliced

2 cloves garlic, sliced

1 TB. tapioca

$\frac{1}{2}$ cup reduced-sodium fat-free beef broth

1. Trim fat from meat.

2. In a small bowl, combine ginger, curry powder, turmeric, and cloves, and rub over meat.

3. In a 5- to 6-quart slow cooker, place onion, carrots, garlic, and tapioca; then place meat on top. Add broth, cover, and cook for 8 hours. Serve with juices.

Food for Thought

You need to trim chuck roasts of any visible fat chunks, so don't be afraid to get ruthless with your knife. Saturated beef fat contains hormones, pesticides, and antibiotics, so you want to eliminate as much fat as possible for a healthier meal.

Ropa Viejo

1¹/₂ lbs. flank steak, quartered

¹/₂ cup onion, sliced

2 cloves garlic, sliced

1 cup water

1 cup canned tomatoes, crushed

2 medium jalapeño peppers, diced

1 tsp. ground oregano

1 tsp. ground cumin

1 cup black beans

Makes 8 servings
Prep time: 10 minutes
Cook time: 4 hours 30 minutes
Each serving has:
209.4 calories
26.23 g. protein
8.6 g. carbohydrate
7.4 g. total fat
2.96 g. saturated fat
47.03 mg. cholesterol
89.04 mg. sodium
2.73 g. fiber

1. Into a pressure cooker, place steak, onion, garlic, and water. Cover and bring to a boil over high heat. Slightly reduce the heat, and pressure cook for 20 minutes. Turn off the heat, and allow cooker to cool down on its own. Dish may be made ahead to this point.

2. In a slow cooker, place meat mixture, tomatoes, jalapeños, oregano, and cumin. Cover and cook on low setting for 4 hours. Add beans; heat for 10 minutes and serve.

Saigon Beef BBQ

Makes 4 servings
Prep time: 1 hour
Cook time: 4 minutes
Each serving has:
149.6 calories
24.49 g. protein
1.96 g. carbohydrate
4.24 g. total fat
1.48 g. saturated fat
69.17 mg. cholesterol
122.9 mg. sodium
0.39 g. fiber

1 lb. top round steak

1 TB. sugar substitute, such as Splenda Brown Sugar

2 TB. oyster sauce

1 TB. rice wine vinegar

1 tsp. fresh ginger, minced

3 cloves garlic, minced

Nonstick cooking spray

$\frac{1}{2}$ cup scallions, sliced in half

1. Freeze steak in plastic wrap for 30 minutes. Then slice frozen steak into thin strips.

2. Combine sugar, oyster sauce, vinegar, ginger, and garlic in a plastic bag. Add beef, and marinate in the refrigerator for at least 1 hour or longer.

3. Spray a countertop grill with cooking spray; then heat on high. Grill meat until crisp on edges. Add scallions to the grill to cook for 1 minute. Serve immediately.

Food for Thought _____

It's not necessary to use sugar substitute if you are not sensitive to carbohydrates, as the amount is low. Just measure accurately to avoid dumping too much sugar into the bag.

Spanish Liver

2 lbs. calf's liver

$^1/_2$ cup carrots, sliced

$^1/_2$ cup celery, sliced

1 cup onion, sliced

1 can (14.5 oz.) tomatoes, crushed

1 bay leaf

1 cup cannellini beans

$^3/_4$ lb. Dreamfields penne pasta

Makes 6 servings
Prep time: 10 minutes
Cook time: 8 hours
Each serving has:
495.2 calories
42.73 g. protein
66.51 g. carbohydrate
16.21 g. total fat
1.1 g. saturated fat
501.3 mg. cholesterol
345 mg. sodium
7.88 g. fiber

1. Place liver in the slow cooker; then add carrots, celery, onion, tomatoes, bay leaf, and beans. Cook on low for 6 to 8 hours.

2. Bring a 2 quart saucepan with water to a boil, and cook pasta until just done. Drain but do not rinse. Serve liver mixture over top of pasta.

Food for Thought

You can use whole-wheat or soy pasta if you can't locate a carb-controlled pasta at your grocery store. Look for a high-fiber product to help keep blood sugar levels in line.

Spicy Beef with Basil

Makes 4 servings
Prep time: 10 minutes
Cook time: 5 minutes
Each serving has:
151.2 calories
24.7 g. protein
2.17 g. carbohydrate
4.34 g. total fat
1.49 g. saturated fat
69.17 mg. cholesterol
95.69 mg. sodium
0.92 g. fiber

1 tsp. black peppercorns

2 cloves garlic, whole

1 TB. fresh ginger

2 TB. fresh cilantro

2 tsp. lime zest

2 medium jalapeño peppers

1/2 cup + 1 TB. fresh basil

1 lb. top round steak

1 TB. oyster sauce

1 TB. fresh lime juice

1. In a blender or food processor, combine peppercorns, garlic, ginger, cilantro, lime zest, peppers, and 1/2 cup basil, and grind into paste.

2. Cut steak into strips, and toss into a bowl with paste to coat.

3. Heat a skillet on high heat; then *sear* beef, stirring constantly to cook, about 5 minutes. Add in oyster sauce and lime juice; stir to coat; then serve topped with remaining tablespoon of basil.

Nutri Speak

Sear means to quickly char, burn, or scorch the surface with a hot instrument. It also means to brown meat quickly with very high heat.

St. Petersburg Beef Stroganoff

1 lb. beef sirloin steak

Nonstick cooking spray

2 cups mushrooms, dried

1 cup onion, sliced

2 cloves garlic, sliced

$^1/_2$ cup reduced-sodium fat-free beef broth

$^1/_2$ cup water

$^1/_2$ cup nonfat yogurt

$^1/_4$ cup red burgundy wine

2 tsp. poppy seeds

$^3/_4$ lb. egg noodles

Makes 6 servings
Prep time: 15 minutes
Cook time: 12 minutes
Each serving has:
582.4 calories
33.87 g. protein
104.5 g. carbohydrate
6.73 g. total fat
1.89 g. saturated fat
86.09 mg. cholesterol
115.6 mg. sodium
11.2 g. fiber

1. Partially freeze steak for 30 minutes; then slice into strips.

2. Spray a Dutch oven with cooking spray, and heat on medium-high heat. Add steak, mushrooms, onion, and garlic. Sauté for 7 minutes or until steak is just browned and vegetables are soft. Remove contents from the heat and keep warm on a plate.

3. Add beef broth and water, and bring to a simmer. Add yogurt, wine, and poppy seeds; cover and lower heat to a simmer. Do not allow to boil, or yogurt mixture will curdle. Return meat and vegetable mixture to sauce; cover and turn off the heat.

4. Bring a 2-quart saucepan of water to boil, cook noodles until tender, about 7 minutes, then drain. Serve meat and sauce over noodles.

Food for Thought

Be sure to use a scale to measure the pasta as it is too easy to cook mega portions, which increase the calories and blood sugar response in your body. After you do this several times, you'll be able to eyeball the right portion size for your family.

Steak with Peppercorns

Makes 4 servings
Prep time: 10 minutes
Cook time: 10 minutes
Each serving has:
251.2 calories
36.7 g. protein
3.06 g. carbohydrate
7.54 g. total fat
2.76 g. saturated fat
103.8 mg. cholesterol
141.5 mg. sodium
0.86 g. fiber

2 TB. black peppercorns

1¹/₂ lbs. top round steak

2 TB. plant sterol spread, such as Smart Balance

2 TB. shallots, diced

2 tsp. Dijon mustard

¹/₄ cup water

1. Place peppercorns in a spice grinder, and process until just cracked. Press peppercorns into steaks to form an even coating.

2. Heat a 10-inch skillet on medium-high heat, and melt sterol spread. Add steaks, increase the heat to high, and sear on both sides, about 3 minutes per side. Lower the heat to medium, and cook for another 3 minutes. Remove steaks from the pan and keep warm.

3. Add shallots and cook until soft, about 3 minutes, scraping up any bits in the pan. Add mustard and water, and blend. Pour sauce over steaks and serve.

Food for Thought _____

A coffee grinder makes an excellent spice grinder. To clean it between grinds, just use a piece of dried bread. Grind for one minute and toss. Your grinder will now be clean for either coffee or your latest spice mixture creation.

Swiss Steak American Style

1 cup Wondra Instant Flour

1 tsp. McCormick Grill Mates Salt Free Steak Seasoning

1 cup onion, halved and sliced

Nonstick cooking spray

1½ lbs. skirt steak

½ lb. carrots, 1-inch lengths

1 cup fresh tomatoes, diced

Makes 4 servings
Prep time: 10 minutes
Cook time: 6 hours
Each serving has:
437.6 calories
42.22 g. protein
33.93 g. carbohydrate
14.64 g. total fat
5.55 g. saturated fat
83.38 mg. cholesterol
132.8 mg. sodium
2.83 g. fiber

1. In a plastic bag, place flour and steak seasoning. Place *skirt steak* in the bag and shake to coat. Remove steak, put onion into bag, and shake to coat.

2. Spray a 10-inch sauté pan with cooking spray, and heat over medium-high heat. Brown steak on both sides. Remove. Brown onion and remove. Transfer steak and onions to a 5- or 6-quart slow cooker.

3. Add carrots and tomatoes, and cook for 6 hours.

Nutri Speak

Skirt steak is a piece of meat cut from the diaphragm of the cow. It freezes well and can be cut horizontally before grilling but should not be overcooked.

Swiss Steak with Mushrooms

Makes 4 servings
Prep time: 10 minutes
Cook time: 45 minutes
Each serving has:
221 calories
27.44 g. protein
12.7 g. carbohydrate
5.63 g. total fat
1.89 g. saturated fat
69.17 mg. cholesterol
107.4 mg. sodium
2.63 g. fiber

1 lb. top round steak

¼ cup ground rolled oats

Nonstick cooking spray

1 TB. plant sterol spread, such as Benecol

½ cup onion, sliced

½ cup fresh tomatoes, diced

¼ cup mushrooms, sliced

½ cup green bell pepper, sliced

1. Ask your butcher to put steak through a tenderizer. Cut into serving-size pieces. Lightly dust with oat flour.

2. Spray a 10-inch skillet with cooking spray, and heat on medium-high heat. Add sterol spread, and brown steak on both sides, about 4 minutes. Add onions, tomatoes, and mushrooms; cover and reduce the heat to simmer. Cook for 30 minutes. Add peppers, and cook for 15 minutes uncovered on simmer. Serve with sauce.

Food for Thought _____

You can tenderize meat with a cross-hatched hammer available in the utensil section of your grocery store. The shape breaks the meat fibers up into small portions. A butcher has a machine that does the same thing without the noise, but it won't keep your arms in shape!

Tangerine Beef Stir Fry

1 lb. top round steak
2 tsp. ground ginger
1 tsp. tangerine rind
¹/₂ cup tangerine juice
2 TB. oyster sauce
2 tsp. cornstarch

Nonstick cooking spray
¹/₂ lb. snow peas
1 cup bean sprouts
¹/₂ cup mushrooms, dried
³/₄ cup celery, sliced

Makes 6 servings
Prep time: 30 minutes
Cook time: 10 minutes
Each serving has:
197.4 calories
20.4 g. protein
24.24 g. carbohydrate
3.21 g. total fat
1.07 g. saturated fat
46.12 mg. cholesterol
99.2 mg. sodium
3.57 g. fiber

1. Freeze steak for 30 minutes; then slice thinly into strips.

2. In a bowl, combine ginger, tangerine rind and juice, and oyster sauce. Marinate steak in mixture for 30 minutes.

3. Drain steak, reserving marinade. Add cornstarch to marinade, mix, and set aside.

4. Spray cooking spray into cold 10-inch sauté pan or wok and heat on high. Add steak, and stir-fry for 5 minutes. Add snow peas, bean sprouts, mushrooms, and celery to the pan, and stir-fry for 3 minutes or until mushrooms are moist. Add marinade, and stir-fry until slightly thickened.

Top Round Roast with Mushroom Dust

Makes 4 servings
Prep time: 10 minutes
Cook time: 1 hour
Each serving has:
468.3 calories
54.44 g. protein
47.31 g. carbohydrate
9.06 g. total fat
3.11 g. saturated fat
138.4 mg. cholesterol
142 mg. sodium
7.53 g. fiber

1 cup dried mushrooms

1 TB. dried parsley

1 TB. garlic powder

1 TB. black peppercorns

2 lbs. top round steak

1. In a spice grinder place mushrooms, parsley, garlic powder, and peppercorns. Grind into fine powder.

2. Cover roast all over with mushroom mixture.

3. Heat an oven to 300°F. Place roast in an ovenproof pan and place in the oven. Cook for 1 hour or until the temperature on an instant thermometer shows 123°F for rare, 130°F for medium. Remove from the oven, and let sit for 5 minutes before carving, loosely covered with foil.

Food for Thought

Dried mushrooms make a great powdered flavoring for beef. I particularly like to use dried porcini mushrooms when making my mushroom dust. Keep the extra ground mushrooms in a sealed jar, and they will be good for a year.

Apricot Honey Mustard Pork Tenderloin

1 lb. pork tenderloin

¹/₄ cup balsamic vinegar

2 TB. honey mustard

¹/₄ cup dried apricots, chopped

1. Preheat the oven to 400°F.

2. Split tenderloin halfway down middle, laying it open.

3. Combine vinegar and honey mustard, and brush tenderloin with mixture. Top with apricots, and place in an ovenproof baking dish. Bake in the oven for 20 minutes or until meat thermometer registers 155°F. Remove from the oven and allow to rest for 5 minutes; then slice and serve.

Food for Thought

Letting meat "rest" after cooking is an important step as it lets the juices come back into the meat, rather than run out onto the plate when cut immediately after cooking.

Makes 4 servings
Prep time: 15 minutes
Cook time: 20 minutes
Each serving has:
181.5 calories
24.51 g. protein
10.31 g. carbohydrate
4.14 g. total fat
1.34 g. saturated fat
73.71 mg. cholesterol
67.32 mg. sodium
1 g. fiber

Gingersnap Pork Tenderloin

Makes 4 servings
Prep time: 15 minutes
Cook time: 20 minutes
Each serving has:
311.2 calories
25.68 g. protein
30.44 g. carbohydrate
9.41 g. total fat
2.86 g. saturated fat
74.84 mg. cholesterol
369.7 mg. sodium
1.91 g. fiber

1 lb. pork tenderloin

$^1/_2$ cup dried apricots, chopped into small pieces

2 TB. Dijon mustard

$^1/_3$ cup sugar substitute, such as Splenda Brown Sugar

$^1/_2$ cup gingersnap cookies, crushed

$^1/_2$ tsp. ground allspice

$^1/_2$ tsp. ground cinnamon

1. Trim pork tenderloin of any visible outer fat.

2. In a bowl, combine apricots, mustard, sugar, cookies, allspice, and cinnamon. Spread mixture over tenderloin to coat.

3. Heat an oven to 425°F. Place tenderloin on a rack in a foil-lined ovenproof baking pan, and roast for 20 minutes or until meat thermometer registers 160°F. Let sit for 5 minutes before carving into thin slices.

Food for Thought

A quick way to crush cookies is to put them into a sealable plastic bag and then pound with a rolling pin or empty bottle until cookies are crushed to a desirable level.

Grilled Pork Chops with Roast Peaches

2 TB. apple cider vinegar

1/4 cup sugar substitute, such as Splenda Brown Sugar

1 tsp. chili powder

1/4 tsp. paprika

1/4 cup rolled oats

1 1/2 lbs. boneless pork chops

4 medium unpeeled peaches

Makes 4 servings
Prep time: 10 minutes
Cook time: 7 minutes
Each serving has:
232.8 calories
24.71 g. protein
18.11 g. carbohydrate
6.94 g. total fat
2.29 g. saturated fat
66.46 mg. cholesterol
54.52 mg. sodium
3.14 g. fiber

1. Combine vinegar, sugar, chili powder, paprika, and oats in a blender. Coat pork chops with mixture.

2. Heat a countertop grill on high. Slice peaches into quarters. Place pork and peaches on the grill, and cook for 7 minutes or until pork is done and peaches are softened with nice grill marks.

Nutri Notes —————

Apple cider vinegar can help keep your blood sugar response in line, much like several oral medications used to treat diabetes. Just one tablespoon with your meal can help keep unwanted belly fat on the run.

Grilled Pork Satay

Makes 6 servings
Prep time: 20 minutes
Cook time: 7 minutes
Each serving has:
153.8 calories
24.35 g. protein
1.29 g. carbohydrate
5.15 g. total fat
1.52 g. saturated fat
73.71 mg. cholesterol
109.1 mg. sodium
0.47 g. fiber

1½ lbs. pork tenderloin

2 TB. oyster sauce

1 TB. shallot, diced

2 TB. sesame seeds

2 TB. lemongrass

1 clove garlic, minced

12 wood skewers, soaked in water

1. Cut pork tenderloin into 1-inch cubes.

2. In a bowl, combine oyster sauce, shallot, sesame seeds, lemon-grass, and garlic, and add tenderloin pieces. Toss to coat, and marinate for 15 minutes. Recipe can be made ahead to this point and left in the refrigerator overnight.

3. Thread pork cubes onto the skewers.

4. Heat a countertop grill on high, and grill pork until cooked, about 7 minutes.

Food for Thought _____

Dice shallots by cutting slices straight across the shallot without cutting all the way through, then cutting slices horizontally before slicing vertically.

Lemon Pork Stir Fry

¾ lb. pork tenderloin

2 TB. lemon juice

1 tsp. honey

1 TB. oyster sauce

1 TB. cornstarch

½ cup water

Nonstick cooking spray

½ cup carrots, sliced

¼ cup green onions, coarsely chopped

1 cup bean sprouts

1 cup bok choy, coarsely chopped

½ cup dried mushrooms

8 drops Flavors2Go honey

Makes 4 servings
Prep time: 10 minutes
Cook time: 5 minutes
Each serving has:
246.7 calories
22.68 g. protein
32.06 g. carbohydrate
5.07 g. total fat
1.69 g. saturated fat
56.13 mg. cholesterol
87.56 mg. sodium
4.6 g. fiber

1. Place tenderloin in the freezer for 30 minutes. Slice into strips.

2. In a small bowl, combine lemon juice, honey, oyster sauce, cornstarch, and water, and mix well.

3. Spray a 10-inch sauté pan or wok with cooking spray, and heat on high. Add pork and stir-fry for 3 minutes. Remove and set aside.

4. Stir-fry carrots, then scallions for 30 seconds. Add bean sprouts, bok choy, mushrooms, and cornstarch mixture. Stir-fry for 1 minute, and add pork. Stir to mix, add honey drops, and serve.

Mocha Cinnamon Pork Tenderloin

Makes 4 servings
Prep time: 35 minutes
Cook time: 10 minutes
Each serving has:
252.2 calories
27.62 g. protein
17.74 g. carbohydrate
8.15 g. total fat
2.47 g. saturated fat
74.84 mg. cholesterol
105 mg. sodium
3.76 g. fiber

1 lb. pork tenderloin

$^1/_3$ cup coffee beans

1 TB. brown mustard

2 TB. sugar substitute, such as Splenda Brown Sugar

2 TB. apple cider vinegar

2 TB. paprika

2 TB. black peppercorns

1 tsp. salt substitute, such as Morton's

$^1/_2$ cup rolled oats

1. Trim pork tenderloin of any visible fat.

2. In a blender, combine coffee beans, mustard, sugar, vinegar, paprika, peppercorns, salt, and oats. Process into a paste. Coat tenderloin with mixture and marinate for 30 minutes.

3. Heat a countertop grill on high; then grill tenderloin for 10 minutes or until a thermometer registers 160°F.

4. Place pork on a platter, and let sit for 5 minutes loosely covered with foil before slicing.

Pepper Pork

Makes 4 servings
Prep time: 5 minutes
Cook time: 4 minutes
Each serving has:
145.2 calories
24.2 g. protein
1.87 g. carbohydrate
4.16 g. total fat
1.4 g. saturated fat
73.71 mg. cholesterol
57.79 mg. sodium
0.67 g. fiber

1 lb. pork tenderloin

2 tsp. paprika

1 tsp. thyme

$^1/_2$ tsp. oregano

$^1/_2$ tsp. fresh rosemary

$^1/_4$ tsp. black peppercorns

$^1/_8$ tsp. cayenne

2 cloves garlic

1 tsp. red chili pepper flakes

1. Cut tenderloin into 1-inch chunks.

2. In a blender or food processor, grind together paprika, thyme, oregano, rosemary, peppercorns, cayenne, garlic, and pepper flakes. Coat meat with pepper mixture.

3. Heat a countertop grill on high heat; grill pork chunks until browned, about 4 minutes.

Pork and Asparagus Stir Fry

1 lb. pork tenderloin

Nonstick cooking spray

1 clove garlic, minced

$^1/_2$ cup green onions, coarsely chopped

2 cup asparagus, sliced into 1-inch pieces

$^1/_2$ cup reduced-sodium fat-free chicken stock

1 TB. oyster sauce

1 tsp. toasted sesame oil

Makes 4 servings
Prep time: 5 minutes
Cook time: 5 minutes
Each serving has:
176.3 calories
26.93 g. protein
4.54 g. carbohydrate
5.48 g. total fat
1.63 g. saturated fat
74 mg. cholesterol
100.4 mg. sodium
1.75 g. fiber

1. Cut pork tenderloin into strips.

2. Spray a wok or 10-inch skillet with cooking spray, and heat on medium-high heat. Quickly stir-fry pork until just browned; then add garlic. Stir for one minute. Add scallions, asparagus, chicken stock, oyster sauce, and sesame oil. Stir for two more minutes and serve.

Smoke Signals

Oyster sauce for vegetarians doesn't contain any oysters, unlike standard oyster sauce. It is made from soybeans, sugar, Chinese mushrooms, and modified cornstarch or MSG. If you are allergic to MSG, try an oyster sauce made by Amoy or Lee Kum Kee.

Pork and Coconut Stir Fry

Makes 6 servings
Prep time: 5 minutes
Cook time: 5 minutes
Each serving has:
168.8 calories
25.22 g. protein
3.91 g. carbohydrate
5.55 g. total fat
2.76 g. saturated fat
73.71 mg. cholesterol
59.22 mg. sodium
0.49 g. fiber

1½ lbs. pork tenderloin

Nonstick cooking spray

2 cloves garlic, minced

1 medium jalapeño pepper, diced

¼ cup rice wine vinegar

1 cup bean sprouts

1 TB. unsweetened coconut

1. Cut pork tenderloin into strips.

2. Spray a wok or 10-inch skillet with cooking spray, and heat on medium-high heat. Add pork strips and quickly stir to sear on all sides. Add garlic and toss for 1 minute. Add jalapeño, vinegar, bean spouts, and coconut, and stir for 2 minutes. Serve immediately.

Food for Thought

Unsweetened coconut is available in health food stores or chains such as Whole Foods or Wild Oats. It's healthier for you than commercially sweetened brands, which are not suitable for this dish.

Pork and Turkey Pot Stickers

¹/₂ lb. pork tenderloin	1 clove garlic, whole
¹/₂ lb. ground turkey	24 small won ton wrappers
1 tsp. dried spearmint	¹/₂ cup water
¹/₄ cup onion, sliced	1 tsp. olive oil

Makes 6 servings
Prep time: 20 minutes
Cook time: 10 minutes
Each serving has:
179.6 calories
16.62 g. protein
15.14 g. carbohydrate
5.13 g. total fat
1.38 g. saturated fat
56.38 mg. cholesterol
126.7 mg. sodium
0.53 g. fiber

1. In a food processor, combine tenderloin, turkey, spearmint, onion, and garlic, and process to a coarse grind.

2. Take a won ton wrapper and lay spoonful of meat mixture in center; then wet edges of wrapper with water and fold over edges, making a triangular piece. Press to seal. Repeat with remaining mixture and wrappers. These wraps can be made ahead to this point and kept covered in the refrigerator.

3. Into an 8-inch skillet, add water and olive oil. Place pot stickers in water bath; cover and bring to a boil. Once it boils, reduce the heat and simmer until all but ¹/₄ of water is absorbed, about 4 minutes. Lower the heat, remove the lid, and continue to cook uncovered until remaining water evaporates and pot stickers begin to brown. Turn them to brown on both sides in the dry pan. Serve with the Wasabi Ginger Sauce found in this book.

Pork Burgundy Stew

Makes 4 servings

Prep time: 5 minutes

Cook time: 6 hours 10 minutes

Each serving has:

357.5 calories

39.97 g. protein

26.2 g. carbohydrate

7.06 g. total fat

2.41 g. saturated fat

110.6 mg. cholesterol

148 mg. sodium

5.86 g. fiber

Nonstick cooking spray

1 TB. plant sterol spread, such as Benecol

1 1/2 lbs. pork tenderloin, cut into cubes

1 cup onion, sliced

1 clove garlic, sliced

1/4 cup pearl onions, about 20

1/2 cup red burgundy wine

2 bay leaves

1/2 tsp. ground cinnamon

3/4 cup canned tomatoes, crushed

1/4 cup red wine vinegar

1/4 cup water

1/2 cup barley

1. Spray a 10-inch skillet with cooking spray; then melt sterol spread in the pan. Quickly sauté pork cubes until browned on all sides. Remove and place in the slow cooker.

2. In the skillet, sauté onion, garlic, and pearl onions until lightly browned. Add to the slow cooker. Place wine, bay leaves, cinnamon, tomatoes, vinegar, water, and barley into the slow cooker, cover, and set on low for 6 hours.

 **Food for Thought** _____

Always use a wine you would drink when adding it to any dish. Cheap, acrid wines will ruin a great dish faster than you can say "corkscrew," so always taste your selection before mixing it into a dish.

Pork Chops with Apples and Ginger

Nonstick cooking spray

1¹/₂ lbs. boneless pork chops

1 TB. sugar substitute, such as Splenda Brown Sugar

1 tsp. star anise, whole, about 2 pieces

1 TB. ground ginger

1 tsp. ground cinnamon

1 cup apples, sliced

2 tsp. apple cider vinegar

¹/₂ cup apple cider

Makes 4 servings
Prep time: 10 minutes
Cook time: 20 minutes
Each serving has:
177.2 calories
22.51 g. protein
7.64 g. carbohydrate
6.31 g. total fat
2.17 g. saturated fat
66.46 mg. cholesterol
54.83 mg. sodium
1.26 g. fiber

1. Spray 10-inch skillet with cooking spray, and heat on medium-high heat. Brown pork chops on both sides, and cook until done, about 8 minutes. Remove chops from the pan to a plate and keep warm, loosely covered with foil.

2. Add brown sugar to the pan along with star anise, ginger, and cinnamon, and stir over medium-high heat until melted. Add apple slices, and cook until caramelized, about 6 minutes. Remove apples from the pan and add to pork. Stir in vinegar and cider, and scrape up any bits left in the pan. Pour sauce over apples and pork and serve.

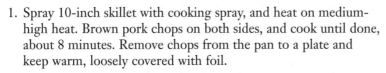

Food for Thought _____

To substitute anise seeds for star anise, increase the quantity by 50 percent. Star anise is the principal ingredient in Chinese Five Spice Powder. It pairs especially well with fruit, such as pears or plums.

Pork Chops with Applesauce

Makes 4 servings
Prep time: 5 minutes
Cook time: 10 minutes
Each serving has:
181.1 calories
22.55 g. protein
8.19 g. carbohydrate
6.21 g. total fat
2.18 g. saturated fat
66.46 mg. cholesterol
56.09 mg. sodium
1.23 g. fiber

Nonstick cooking spray
1½ lbs. boneless pork chops
2 tsp. fresh rosemary, chopped
2 tsp. fresh thyme

1 clove garlic, minced
1 cup applesauce
1 TB. apple cider vinegar
¼ tsp. ground allspice
½ tsp. ground cinnamon

1. Spray a 10-inch skillet with cooking spray, and heat on medium-high heat. Season pork chops with rosemary and thyme.

2. Add pork chops and brown on both sides, about 4 minutes. Reduce the heat to low and add garlic on top of the pork. Cook until tender, turning once, about 5 minutes.

3. In a bowl, combine applesauce, vinegar, allspice, and cinnamon, and pour over pork chops in the pan. Toss to mix, scraping up any bits. Remove pork chops to a serving dish, and cover with applesauce mixture.

Food for Thought

Use an unsweetened applesauce for the best health benefits. If you have time, merely core and peel 3 pounds of apples, place in a saucepan with a cup of water, cover, bring to a boil, and simmer for 30 minutes. You can freeze any leftovers.

Pork Chops with Black Beans and Garlic

Nonstick cooking spray

1¹/₂ lbs. boneless, thin-cut pork chops

4 cloves garlic, minced

¹/₂ cup green onions, coarsely chopped

1 cup black beans, drained

1 TB. fresh ginger, minced

1 TB. sherry

¹/₂ cup water

Makes 4 servings
Prep time: 5 minutes
Cook time: 12 minutes
Each serving has:
216.9 calories
26.34 g. protein
11.57 g. carbohydrate
6.34 g. total fat
2.21 g. saturated fat
66.46 mg. cholesterol
56.44 mg. sodium
3.83 g. fiber

1. Spray a wok or 10-inch skillet with cooking spray, and heat on medium-high heat. Quickly brown pork chops on both sides, about 4 minutes each side. Remove from the pan and keep warm.

2. Add garlic and green onions to the pan, stir for 30 seconds; then add black beans, ginger, sherry, and water. Stir to mix and bring to a boil. Return pork chops to the pan, lower the heat to simmer, cover, and cook for 5 minutes or until pork chops are tender.

Food for Thought _____

If you don't have sherry, you can add white wine, apple cider, or a nice wine vinegar to this dish. It will taste great!

Pork Chops with Cranberry Sauce

Makes 4 servings
Prep time: 5 minutes
Cook time: 12 minutes
Each serving has:
278 calories
22.69 g. protein
34.6 g. carbohydrate
7.15 g. total fat
2.18 g. saturated fat
66.46 mg. cholesterol
58.08 mg. sodium
2.76 g. fiber

1½ lbs. boneless pork chops

1 tsp. ground black pepper

⅓ cup apple cider

1¼ cup dried cranberries

1 TB. fresh thyme

1 TB. sugar substitute, such as Splenda

1 TB. apple cider vinegar

½ cup green onions, finely chopped

1. Season pork chops with black pepper.

2. Heat a skillet on high heat, and brown pork chops on both sides, about 6 minutes. Add pepper, cider, cranberries, thyme, sugar, vinegar, and scallions. Scraping up any brown bits in the pan, cover and lower heat to simmer. Cook for 10 minutes or until cranberries are soft.

Pork Chops with Prunes and Apples

Makes 4 servings
Prep time: 5 minutes
Cook time: 30 minutes
Each serving has:
359.5 calories
23.66 g. protein
36.32 g. carbohydrate
11.17 g. total fat
2.78 g. saturated fat
66.46 mg. cholesterol
170.1 mg. sodium
4.03 g. fiber

2 TB. plant sterol spread, such as Smart Balance

1½ lbs. boneless pork chops

1 tsp. fresh thyme

2 cloves garlic, minced

1 cup white wine

1 cup dried pitted prunes

1 cup apple, peeled and coarsely chopped

3 TB. fat-free mayonnaise, such as Kraft's

1. Heat a 10-inch skillet on medium-high heat, and add sterol spread. Add pork chops and brown on both sides, about 5 minutes. Add thyme and garlic; then lower the heat.

2. Add wine, prunes, and apples, cover, and simmer for 20 minutes.

3. Transfer pork chops to a platter and keep warm. Reduce sauce to about ½ cup over medium heat. Whisk in mayonnaise, mix thoroughly, and then pour fruit and sauce over pork chops and serve.

Pork Curry

2¹/₂ lbs. pork tenderloin

3 TB. paprika

2 tsp. cumin

2 tsp. fennel seeds

2 tsp. cayenne

1 TB. turmeric

1 tsp. cardamom

¹/₃ tsp. cinnamon

¹/₂ tsp. cloves

2 TB. fresh ginger

1 cup reduced-sodium fat-free chicken broth

Nonstick cooking spray

1 cup onion, diced

1 cup canned tomatoes, crushed

¹/₂ cup chickpeas, drained

Makes 8 servings
Prep time: 1 hour
Cook time: 1 hour
Each serving has:
248.3 calories
32.61 g. protein
9.21 g. carbohydrate
8.92 g. total fat
2.87 g. saturated fat
93.84 mg. cholesterol
125.1 mg. sodium
2.54 g. fiber

1. Cut pork tenderloin into 1-inch cubes.

2. In a blender, combine paprika, cumin, fennel seeds, cayenne, turmeric, cardamom, cinnamon, cloves, and ginger, and blend. Empty mixture into a large plastic bag, and add pork cubes. Toss to coat; then marinate in the refrigerator for one hour or overnight.

3. In a pressure cooker, place chicken broth and pork. Close and bring to a boil. Cook for 10 minutes; then turn off the heat and allow the pressure to return to normal. The dish can be prepared to this point and refrigerated.

4. Spray a 10-inch skillet with cooking spray, and heat over medium heat. Add the onions, and cook until translucent, about 5 minutes. Add pork mixture with its liquid, tomatoes, and chickpeas, and cook on low heat uncovered for 20 minutes.

Food for Thought

You can serve this dish over wilted spinach or basmati rice for a final touch. It also reheats well.

Pork Cutlets *Milanese*

Makes 4 servings
Prep time: 10 minutes
Cook time: 5 minutes
Each serving has:
226.7 calories
23.97 g. protein
11.59 g. carbohydrate
7.13 g. total fat
2.4 g. saturated fat
66.46 mg. cholesterol
170.9 mg. sodium
0.02 g. fiber

1½ lbs. boneless pork chops

1 TB. Dijon mustard

1 cup panko flakes

Nonstick cooking spray

1 TB. plant sterol spread, such as Smart Balance

1. Pound pork chops between 2 pieces of plastic wrap until thin. Spread mustard on both sides of pork chops and coat with panko flakes.

2. Spray a 10-inch skillet with cooking spray, heat on medium-high heat, and add sterol spread. Quickly sauté pork chops for 2 minutes per side or until coating is crisp and pork chops are cooked. Serve.

 Nutri Speak _____

Milanese means in the style of Milan. Typically it's a dish dipped in egg, coated with bread crumbs and Parmesan cheese, and then fried in butter.

Pork Medallions with Grilled Fennel, Onions, and White Squash

1 lb. pork tenderloin

1 TB. herbs de Provence

1 lb. fresh fennel

1 lb. onion, quartered

1 lb. white squash, cut into cubes

8 wood skewers, soaked in water

Makes 4 servings
Prep time: 20 minutes
Cook time: 10 minutes
Each serving has:
237 calories
27.86 g. protein
22.99 g. carbohydrate
4.51 g. total fat
1.42 g. saturated fat
73.71 mg. cholesterol
121.3 mg. sodium
7.71 g. fiber

1. Cut pork tenderloin into 12 slices or round medallions. Season with herbs de Provence or your favorite seasoning mix.

2. Split fennel bulbs into 3 sections and soak in cold water for 15 minutes. Drain.

3. Thread pork medallions on skewers, alternating with chunks of onion and squash.

4. Heat a countertop grill on high. Quickly char fennel sections to soften, about 3 minutes. Remove from the grill, and bring grill back to temperature.

5. Place pork skewers on the grill and cook for 5 minutes or until done. Serve with fennel sections.

Food for Thought _____

Soaking fennel in water eliminates the need for any fat when charring this vegetable. The cold water steams the fennel, making it soft and tender when grilled.

Pork Medallions with Mustard and Leeks

Makes 6 servings
Prep time: 10 minutes
Cook time: 15 minutes
Each serving has:
211.7 calories
32.44 g. protein
3.41 g. carbohydrate
5.38 g. total fat
1.81 g. saturated fat
98.28 mg. cholesterol
122.1 mg. sodium
0.51 g. fiber

2 lbs. pork tenderloin

Nonstick cooking spray

1 cup leeks, white and just first one third of green section only, chopped

$^{1}/_{2}$ cup white wine

2 cloves garlic, minced

1 TB. Dijon mustard

2 TB. chives, chopped

1 TB. fresh tarragon, chopped

2 TB. fresh parsley, chopped

1. Slice tenderloin into 12 pieces crosswise, making medallions or small round steaks.

2. Spray a 10-inch skillet with cooking spray, and heat on high heat. Sear medallions on both sides, and cook for 4 minutes. Remove from the pan and keep warm.

3. Add leeks and toss to cook until soft, about 4 minutes. Add wine, garlic, mustard, chives, tarragon, and parsley to the pan. Bring to a boil, reduce to low heat, and simmer until sauce is reduced in half, scraping up any bits from the pan. Return pork to the skillet, and coat with sauce.

Pork *Scallopine* with Pasta

1½ lbs. pork tenderloin

¾ cup Dreamfields linguine pasta

½ cup chives, chopped

2 TB. fresh tarragon, chopped

1 tsp. capers, rinsed and drained

2 TB. plant sterol spread, such as Benecol

½ cup dry vermouth

Makes 4 servings
Prep time: 10 minutes
Cook time: 12 minutes
Each serving has:
421.2 calories
41.83 g. protein
34.57 g. carbohydrate
14.86 g. total fat
3.36 g. saturated fat
110.6 mg. cholesterol
110.7 mg. sodium
3.43 g. fiber

1. Cut pork tenderloins into 8 pieces, place between sheets of plastic wrap, and pound into thin steak.

2. Bring a 2 quart saucepan with water to a boil and add linguine. Cook until done, about 7 minutes. Drain but do not rinse. Add chives, tarragon, and capers, and toss to mix.

3. Heat a 10-inch skillet on medium-high heat and add sterol spread. Quickly brown pork scallops on both sides, about 3 minutes. Remove to a plate to keep warm, loosely covered with foil.

4. Add vermouth to the pan and scrape up any brown bits. Reduce sauce. Divide pasta between serving plates, top with pork scallop, and drizzle vermouth sauce on top.

Nutri Speak _____

Scallopine in Italian means to form a shell or scallop shape. It occurs when meat is pounded very thin into a rounded shape like a sea scallop shell.

Pork Stir Fry with Garlic and Black Beans

Makes 4 servings
Prep time: 5 minutes
Cook time: 5 minutes
Each serving has:
258.6 calories
38.27 g. protein
7.95 g. carbohydrate
6.54 g. total fat
2.31 g. saturated fat
110.6 mg. cholesterol
117.2 mg. sodium
2.75 g. fiber

1 TB. plant sterol spread, such as Smart Balance

2 cloves garlic, minced

2 medium jalapeño peppers, diced

1 1/2 lbs. pork tenderloin, cut into strips

1 cup green onions, finely chopped

1 TB. oyster sauce

1/2 cup black beans, drained

1. Heat a 10-inch skillet on medium-high heat. Add sterol spread, garlic, and chilies and cook for one minute.

2. Add pork strips and stir for one minute. Then add green onions and toss to mix. Add oyster sauce and black beans, stir to combine, and serve.

Food for Thought _____

To make jalapeño peppers less spicy, remove the seeds and the veins attached to them from inside the pepper before using. Be sure to wash your hands before touching your eyes, or you'll be in for a very unpleasant surprise!

Pork Tacos

1 TB. ancho chili powder

1 tsp. garlic powder

2 TB. sugar substitute, such as Splenda Brown Sugar

1 lb. pork tenderloin

8 La Tortilla Factory low-carb tortillas, 8-inch size

2 cup onion, diced

1/2 cup tomatoes, diced

1/4 cup avocado, diced

1/2 cup fresh cilantro, chopped

Makes 4 servings
Prep time: 10 minutes
Cook time: 20 minutes
Each serving has:
319.6 calories
34.98 g. protein
31.92 g. carbohydrate
12.88 g. total fat
2.53 g. saturated fat
74.84 mg. cholesterol
425.2 mg. sodium
18.75 g. fiber

1. Blend chili powder, garlic powder, and sugar substitute together, and rub all over tenderloin.

2. Heat oven to 425°F. Place tenderloin on a foil-lined baking pan, and roast for 20 minutes or until a meat thermometer registers 160°F. Let rest 5 minutes before cutting into thin strips.

3. Take tortilla and place tenderloin in center. Top with diced onions, tomatoes, avocado, and cilantro. Fold in half and serve.

Pumpkin Pork and Noodles

1 lb. pork tenderloin

Nonstick cooking spray

1 cup onion, sliced

1/2 cup celery, sliced

3/4 cup reduced-sodium fat-free chicken broth

1/4 cup champagne vinegar

1 cup tomatoes, diced

1/2 tsp. pumpkin pie spice

1/4 tsp. thyme

6 oz. dried apricots

1 cup pumpkin purée

3/4 lb. Dreamfields linguine pasta

Makes 6 servings
Prep time: 15 minutes
Cook time: 30 minutes
Each serving has:
361.3 calories
25.35 g. protein
56.81 g. carbohydrate
14.85 g. total fat
2.61 g. saturated fat
50.19 mg. cholesterol
64.79 mg. sodium
7.11 g. fiber

1. Freeze pork tenderloin for 30 minutes, and slice into strips.

2. Spray a 10-inch skillet with cooking spray, and heat on medium-high heat. Add onion and sauté until soft, about 2 minutes. Add tenderloin strips and celery, and cook until pork is browned. Add broth, vinegar, tomatoes, pumpkin pie spice, thyme, apricots, and pumpkin purée. Bring to a boil, reduce heat, and simmer for 10 minutes or until almost all liquid is gone. Add water as needed to finish cooking.

3. Bring a 2-quart saucepan with water to a boil, and add pasta. Cook until done, about 7 minutes. Drain but do not rinse.

4. Divide pasta into serving portions, top with pork mixture, and serve.

Food for Thought

You can make your own pumpkin pie spice by combining $^1/_2$ teaspoon ground cinnamon with $^1/_4$ teaspoon ground ginger and $^1/_8$ teaspoon each ground allspice and ground nutmeg.

Roast Pork South American Style

Makes 8 servings
Prep time: 5 minutes
Cook time: 1 hour 15 minutes
Each serving has:
292.5 calories
48.03 g. protein
4.91 g. carbohydrate
7.82 g. total fat
2.69 g. saturated fat
147.4 mg. cholesterol
114.3 mg. sodium
0.44 g. fiber

1 cup onion, diced

$^3/_4$ cup fresh orange juice

$^1/_4$ cup fresh lime juice

2 tsp. red wine vinegar

1 tsp. sugar substitute, such as Splenda

1 tsp. ground sage

4 lbs. pork tenderloin

1. Combine onion, orange juice, lime juice, vinegar, sugar, and sage.

2. Heat the oven to 400°F.

3. Place tenderloins into a deep baking dish, and make slashes through meat with a knife point. Pour half juice and onion mixture over meat; then turn it over and repeat the slashing and finish with mixture. Cover the pot and bake for 10 minutes.

4. Take the pot from the oven, pour out all juices, reserving them for sauce. Uncover and bake for another 10 minutes. Slice and serve with juice mixture.

Simple Grilled Pork Chops

1 tsp. garlic powder

1 tsp. cayenne

1 tsp. dried thyme

Nonstick cooking spray

1¹/₂ lbs. boneless pork chops

Makes 4 servings
Prep time: 5 minutes
Cook time: 5 minutes
Each serving has:
154.5 calories
22.51 g. protein
0.99 g. carbohydrate
6.19 g. total fat
2.17 g. saturated fat
66.46 mg. cholesterol
54.58 mg. sodium
0.32 g. fiber

1. Combine garlic powder, cayenne, and thyme in a spice grinder and mix. Sprinkle on pork chops about 5 minutes before grilling.

2. Spray a countertop grill with cooking spray, and heat on high. Grill chops covered for 5 minutes or until lightly browned. Let sit 4 minutes before serving.

Nutri Notes

Cayenne contains capsaicin, which is a potent anti-inflammatory agent used to treat arthritic symptoms. It can also help to prevent gastric ulcers.

Sweet and Sour Apple Pork Tenderloin

1 tsp. apple jelly

2 tsp. apple cider vinegar

2 TB. sugar substitute, such as Splenda Brown Sugar

1 tsp. cumin

1 tsp. ground black pepper

2 lbs. pork tenderloin

¹/₂ lb. apples, sliced

Makes 4 servings
Prep time: 30 minutes
Cook time: 20 minutes
Each serving has:
313.22 calories
47.8 g. protein
10.69 g. carbohydrate
7.97 g. total fat
2.72 g. saturated fat
147.42 mg. cholesterol
114.24 mg. sodium
2 g. fiber

1. Preheat oven to 400°F.

2. Heat apple jelly with vinegar in the microwave on high for 15 seconds. Stir to mix. Combine sugar, cumin, and pepper in a plastic bag, add pork, and marinate for 30 minutes in the refrigerator. Remove pork from the bag and discard mixture.

3. Place pork in a heat-proof glass baking dish, top with apple slices, sprinkle more brown sugar over apples and bake for 20 minutes or until meat thermometer registers 155°F. Remove from the oven, let sit for 10 minutes, loosely covered with foil, and slice and serve with baked apples.

Smoky Pork Tenderloins in Argentine Spices

Makes 6 servings
Prep time: 15 minutes
Cook time: 5 minutes
Each serving has:
189.5 calories
32.01 g. protein
1.9 g. carbohydrate
5.29 g. total fat
1.83 g. saturated fat
98.28 mg. cholesterol
76.85 mg. sodium
0.79 g. fiber

2 lbs. pork tenderloin

2 TB. smoky paprika powder

4 cloves garlic

2 TB. dried thyme

1 tsp. fresh rosemary

1 tsp. cumin, whole

1 cup fresh cilantro, chopped

1/2 cup canola oil

1. Cut pork into 6 sections. Place each section between plastic wrap and pound into thin steak, about 1/4-inch thick.

2. In a blender or food processor, combine paprika, garlic, thyme, rosemary, cumin, and cilantro, and blend into a paste. In a plastic bag, add vegetable oil, herbal paste, and meat. Massage mixture into meat and let marinate. Make ahead to this point and refrigerate for up to 8 hours.

3. Heat a countertop grill on high heat. Drain meat from marinade and discard marinade. Grill steaks until cooked, about 3 minutes.

Food for Thought

To keep cilantro fresh in the refrigerator, wrap the herb in a damp paper towel and place inside an open plastic bag. When chopping cilantro, toss the chopped pieces several times to separate the heavier stem sections from the lighter leaves for the best taste.

English Leg of Lamb with Mint Sauce

3 lbs. boneless leg of lamb

2 cloves garlic, sliced

10 cloves garlic, whole

1 TB. fresh parsley, chopped

1 TB. fresh thyme

2 cups rolled oats

Water as necessary

1 TB. whole or ground black pepper

1 TB. chives, chopped

¼ cup red wine vinegar

2 cup fresh mint leaves

½ cup apple cider vinegar

1 tsp. sugar substitute, such as Splenda

Makes 8 servings
Prep time: 15 minutes
Cook time: 2 hours 10 minutes
Each serving has:
396.9 calories
42.2 g. protein
30.33 g. carbohydrate
11.48 g. total fat
3.61 g. saturated fat
112.3 mg. cholesterol
113.9 mg. sodium
5.19 g. fiber

1. Preheat oven to 425°F. Remove any visible fat from lamb and cut slits into the meat. Insert garlic slices.

2. In a blender, combine garlic, parsley, thyme, oats, pepper, chives, and wine vinegar. Blend into a paste, adding water as necessary, and spread over lamb. Place lamb on a broiler pan. Bake at 425°F for 10 minutes; then lower the temperature to 325°F and bake for 1 more hour or until a meat thermometer registers 140°F. Remove lamb from the rack, place on a platter, and allow to rest for 15 minutes.

3. In a blender, combine mint leaves, cider vinegar, and sugar to make mint sauce. Serve alongside lamb.

Lamb and Green Beans

Makes 4 servings
Prep time: 15 minutes
Cook time: 8 hours
Each serving has:
301.1 calories
28.82 g. protein
25.58 g. carbohydrate
8.36 g. total fat
3.34 g. saturated fat
80.51 mg. cholesterol
193.2 mg. sodium
7.54 g. fiber

1 lb. boneless lamb shoulder, cut into 1-inch cubes

¹/₄ cup rolled oats

2 TB. plant sterol spread, such as Smart Balance

1 clove garlic, sliced

¹/₄ tsp. ground allspice

1 cup onion, sliced

1 lb. green beans, cut into 2-inch pieces

1 can (14.5 oz.) tomatoes, crushed

1. In a blender, add oats and blend into powder. Coat lamb cubes in oat flour.

2. Heat a 10-inch sauté pan on medium-high heat, add sterol spread, and quickly brown lamb for 2 minutes. Add garlic slices and cook for 1 minute more, then put contents of the pan into the slow cooker.

3. Add allspice, onion, green beans, and tomatoes to the slow cooker, cover, and cook on low for 6 to 8 hours.

 Nutri Notes ⎯⎯⎯⎯⎯⎯⎯⎯⎯⎯⎯⎯⎯⎯⎯⎯⎯

> Purchase lamb that is firm and fine-textured and pink in color. Any fat surrounding or marbled throughout the lamb should be white, not yellow.

Lamb Burgers with Pine Nuts

1¹/₂ lbs. ground lamb loin

1 tsp. cumin, whole

³/₄ cup rolled oats

¹/₂ cup onion, diced

¹/₄ cup pine nuts

Nonstick cooking spray

Makes 4 servings
Prep time: 10 minutes
Cook time: 5 minutes
Each serving has:
392.1 calories
43.24 g. protein
22.77 g. carbohydrate
13.86 g. total fat
4.21 g. saturated fat
136.1 mg. cholesterol
78.22 mg. sodium
4.15 g. fiber

1. In a food processor, grind lamb, cumin, and oats. Add onion and pine nuts by hand, and form into burger patties.

2. Spray a countertop grill with high-temperature cooking spray, then heat on high. Grill for 5 minutes.

Smoke Signals _____
Always keep lamb cold, as it is highly perishable. You can freeze ground lamb for four months and chops for up to nine months without affecting the flavor.

Lamb Chops with Sage and Tangerines

2 tsp. ground sage

¹/₂ tsp. tangerine juice

1 tsp. tangerine rind

1 TB. honey mustard

³/₄ lb. lamb rib chops

Serves 2
Prep time: 5 minutes
Cook time: 4 minutes
Each serving has:
274.2 calories
35.43 g. protein
6.53 g. carbohydrate
10.65 g. total fat
4.44 g. saturated fat
129.3 mg. cholesterol
98.54 mg. sodium
0.77 g. fiber

1. Heat a countertop grill on high.

2. Combine sage, tangerine juice, rind, and mustard, and brush over chops. Place on the countertop grill and brown for 4 minutes.

Nutri Notes _____
Tangerine peel contains polymethoxylated flavones, which can lower cholesterol by preventing its ability to stick to the walls of arteries.

Lamb Ragout

Makes 8 servings
Prep time: 10 minutes
Cook time: 45 minutes
Each serving has:
492 calories
31.87 g. protein
74.33 g. carbohydrate
7.63 g. total fat
2.4 g. saturated fat
148.8 mg. cholesterol
128.3 mg. sodium
4.62 g. fiber

1½ lbs. lamb loin, cubed

Nonstick cooking spray

1 cup onion, diced

2 cloves garlic, minced

1 can (14.5 oz.) tomatoes, crushed

1 cup carrots, sliced

⅓ cup champagne vinegar

1 tsp. fresh rosemary

1 bay leaf

½ tsp. fresh thyme

1 tsp. fresh mint leaves

2 cups butternut squash, peeled and cut into 1-inch cubes

1 cup mushrooms, sliced

1½ lbs. egg noodles

1. Spray a Dutch oven with cooking spray, and heat on medium-high heat. Sauté onion and garlic until soft, about 3 minutes. Cook lamb in the pan until browned on all sides. Add tomatoes, carrots, vinegar, rosemary, bay leaf, thyme, and mint. Bring to a boil, reduce the heat, and cover. Simmer for 20 minutes.

2. Add squash and mushrooms and cook for 10 minutes or until soft. Discard bay leaf and keep warm.

3. Bring a large saucepan with 2 quarts of water to a boil, add noodles and cook until tender, about 5 minutes. Drain but do not rinse noodles.

4. Place noodles in serving bowls and top with lamb.

 Food for Thought

Choose winter squash that have a dull skin and are heavy for their size.

Lamb Kabobs

³/₄ lb. lamb loin, cut into 1-inch cubes

1 TB. smoky paprika powder

1 tsp. sumac

1 TB. onion powder

1 tsp. turmeric

1 TB. parsley

¹/₂ cup rolled oats

8 wood skewers, soaked in water

Makes 4 servings
Prep time: 5 minutes
Cook time: 5 minutes
Each serving has:
199 calories
21.67 g. protein
15.51 g. carbohydrate
5.29 g. total fat
1.88 g. saturated fat
68.04 mg. cholesterol
41.64 mg. sodium
2.62 g. fiber

1. In a food processor, place lamb, paprika, sumac, onion powder, turmeric, parsley, and oats. Process into a coarse grind.

2. Heat a countertop grill on high heat. With your fingers, shape lamb mixture around the wooden skewers into long, flat fingers. Place on the countertop grill, close, and cook for 5 minutes or until moderately crisp. Remove and serve with Cucumber Garlic Dill sauce (see Chapter 17).

Lamb Stew with Paprika

¹/₄ cup rolled oats

¹/₂ tsp. smoky paprika powder

¹/₄ tsp. cinnamon, ground

¹/₂ tsp. whole or ground allspice

1¹/₂ lbs. lamb leg, boneless, cut into cubes

1 TB. plant sterol spread, such as Benecol

1 cup onion, diced

7 oz. canned tomatoes, crushed

2 TB. red wine vinegar

Makes 6 servings
Prep time: 10 minutes
Cook time: 45 minutes
Each serving has:
209.3 calories
25.16 g. protein
9.51 g. carbohydrate
6.88 g. total fat
2.64 g. saturated fat
72.57 mg. cholesterol
136.8 mg. sodium
1.88 g. fiber

1. In a blender, combine oats, paprika, cinnamon, and allspice, and grind into blend. Coat lamb with mixture.

2. Heat a 10-inch sauté pan on medium-high heat, and add sterol spread. Brown lamb on all sides, about 2 minutes per side. Add onion and cook until soft, about 2 minutes. Add tomatoes and vinegar, reduce the heat to low, cover, and cook for 30 minutes or until lamb is tender.

Lamb Stir Fry with Black Beans, Melon, and Peppers

Makes 4 servings
Prep time: 10 minutes
Cook time: 15 minutes
Each serving has:
219.6 calories
28.01 g. protein
14.16 g. carbohydrate
5.59 g. total fat
2.27 g. saturated fat
90.91 mg. cholesterol
67.35 mg. sodium
3.67 g. fiber

Nonstick cooking spray

2 medium green bell peppers, sliced

1 lb. lamb loin, cut into strips

1 clove garlic, minced

1 TB. fresh ginger, minced

¹/₂ cup green onions, coarsely chopped

¹/₂ cup black beans, drained

1 cup cantaloupe, cubed

¹/₃ cup reduced-sodium fat-free chicken broth

1. Spray a wok or 10-inch skillet with cooking spray, and heat on medium-high heat. Add peppers and stir for 4 minutes or until they brown and soften. Transfer to a bowl.

2. Add lamb and stir until cooked, about 4 minutes. Transfer to the bowl with peppers.

3. Add garlic and ginger, and stir for 1 minute. Add lamb and pepper mixture with liquid and stir to mix. Add green onions, beans, cantaloupe, and chicken broth, and stir to heat through.

Lamb with Chana Dal and Tomatoes

1 lb. boneless lamb leg, cubed

Nonstick cooking spray

$^1/_2$ cup onion, diced

3 cloves garlic, minced

$^3/_4$ cup chana dal lentils

2 TB. balsamic vinegar

2 tsp. Dijon mustard

$^1/_4$ cup tomatoes, diced

1 cup water

Makes 4 servings
Prep time: 10 minutes
Cook time: 30 minutes
Each serving has:
311 calories
35.19 g. protein
25.41 g. carbohydrate
7.81 g. total fat
2.38 g. saturated fat
72.57 mg. cholesterol
137.1 mg. sodium
5.7 g. fiber

1. Spray a 10-inch skillet with cooking spray, and heat on high. Quickly brown lamb, about 4 minutes. Remove from the skillet and keep warm.

2. Add onion and garlic and cook until soft, about 2 minutes. Add chana dal, vinegar, mustard, tomatoes, and water, return the lamb to the skillet, cover, and lower the heat. Simmer for 20 minutes or until chana dal is softened. Add more water if needed.

Food for Thought

Use garlic fresh or in frozen form to gain the most health benefits. Peeled garlic in a jar can oxidize and lose its potency, giving off a sulfuric odor and bitter taste when cooked.

Oh So Garlic Leg of Lamb

Makes 6 servings
Prep time: 20 minutes
Cook time: 1 hour
Each serving has:
216 calories
31.44 g. protein
2.71 g. carbohydrate
7.98 g. total fat
3.17 g. saturated fat
96.77 mg. cholesterol
128.5 mg. sodium
0.44 g. fiber

2 lbs. boneless lamb leg
12 cloves garlic
2 tsp. fresh rosemary

1 TB. black pepper
1 TB. salt substitute

1. Preheat oven to 325°F.

2. Lay out lamb, and place rosemary sprigs and six whole garlic cloves down center. Season with salt and pepper. Roll up lamb, and tie with kitchen string to keep its shape.

3. Cut slits into lamb, and stuff garlic cloves into slits. Season with more pepper, and place in an ovenproof baking dish. Roast for 1 hour or until internal temperature is about 150 degrees. Remove and let rest for 10 minutes, loosely covered with foil. Slice and serve.

Food for Thought

Garlic can stick to your hands and leave you with a potent odor. To remove it, squeeze some toothpaste into your hands, and wash them. The odor will disappear like magic.

Orange Glazed Lamb Chops

$^1/_4$ cup rolled oats

2 TB. plant sterol spread, such as Smart Balance

1$^1/_2$ lbs. boneless lamb chops

1 cup onion, sliced

6 oz. fresh orange juice

Makes 4 servings
Prep time: 10 minutes
Cook time: 7 minutes
Each serving has:
323.4 calories
37.16 g. protein
14.34 g. carbohydrate
10.21 g. total fat
3.97 g. saturated fat
108.9 mg. cholesterol
111.2 mg. sodium
1.84 g. fiber

1. Process oats in a blender into a fine powder. Coat lamb chops in powder.

2. Heat a 10-inch skillet on medium-high heat, and add sterol spread. Brown chops on both sides, about 2 minutes per side. Remove to a plate and keep warm, tented loosely with foil. Add onions and cook until soft, about 1 minute more.

3. Add orange juice, reduce the heat, return the chops to the pan and simmer chops and onions in juice until reduced to a glaze, turning chops once during cooking to glaze both sides. Serve with any remaining juices.

Food for Thought _____

Plant sterol spreads contain no trans fatty acids unlike margarine. These products help to lower cholesterol by blocking its absorption from the small intestine. I often use a blend of plant sterol spread and unsalted butter for the best combination of fatty acids when cooking.

Turkish Lamb with Couscous

Makes 8 servings
Prep time: 15 minutes
Cook time: 55 minutes
Each serving has:
223.8 calories
18.35 g. protein
30.7 g. carbohydrate
3.38 g. total fat
1.27 g. saturated fat
45.8 mg. cholesterol
114.5 mg. sodium
3.55 g. fiber

1 lb. lamb loin, cut into 1-inch cubes

Nonstick cooking spray

1 can (14.5 oz.) tomatoes, crushed

1 cup green bell peppers, diced

1 cup red bell peppers, diced

2 TB. onion, chopped

2 cloves garlic, minced

1 TB. red wine vinegar

1/4 tsp. paprika

1/2 tsp. ground cumin

1 tsp. ground ginger

1/2 tsp. ground coriander

1 1/2 cups reduced-sodium fat-free chicken broth

1/2 tsp. ground allspice

1/2 cup currants

1 cup couscous

1. Spray a 10-inch sauté pan with cooking spray, and heat on medium-high heat. Add lamb and cook until brown on all sides.

2. Add tomatoes, green and red peppers, onion, garlic, vinegar, paprika, cumin, ginger, and coriander. Bring mixture to boil, cover, reduce heat, and simmer for 45 minutes or until lamb is tender.

3. In a saucepan, bring broth to a boil. Add allspice, currants, and couscous. Stir to mix; then cover and turn off the heat. Let rest for 10 minutes. Fluff with a fork before serving. Place portion in a bowl, and top with serving of lamb.

Buffalo Bill Burgers

1 lb. ground buffalo

4 oz. ricotta cheese

2 tsp. McCormick's Salt Free seasoning

8 slices Oroweat low-carb bread

4 slices tomato

4 leaves romaine lettuce

2 tsp. mustard

Makes 4 servings
Prep time: 10 minutes
Cook time: 5 minutes
Each serving has:
278.7 calories
34.79 g. protein
20.82 g. carbohydrate
6.96 g. total fat
1.93 g. saturated fat
60.89 mg. cholesterol
387.2 mg. sodium
6.47 g. fiber

1. Divide buffalo into 4 portions and shape into patties. Place 1 ounce ricotta cheese in middle of each patty, and gently cover with buffalo. Season with seasoning.

2. Heat counter grill on high. Place patties on the grill, cover, and cook for 5 minutes or until crisp on outside but still moist.

3. Toast bread, and spread mustard on slices. Top with one slice of tomato and romaine lettuce.

Food for Thought _____

Buffalo is a very tasty, lean protein source you will find in chains, such as Whole Foods, or online. The flavor is like prime beef but more tender. Buffalo, or bison, is a nutrient-dense protein source with less cholesterol and fat than other meats. Try it in any of my beef recipes for an exciting, nutritional change.

Buffalo Meatballs in Tomato Sauce

Makes 8 servings
Prep time: 15 minutes
Cook time: 8 hours
Each serving has:
141.7 calories
25.13 g. protein
5.14 g. carbohydrate
2.05 g. total fat
0.61 g. saturated fat
52.24 mg. cholesterol
142.7 mg. sodium
1.28 g. fiber

2 lbs. ground buffalo

¼ cup egg substitute

½ cup onion, grated

1 tsp. ground oregano

1 tsp. ground cumin

2 cloves garlic, minced

Nonstick cooking spray

1 can (14.5 oz.) tomatoes, crushed

1 cinnamon stick

1. In a bowl, add ground meat, egg substitute, onion, oregano, cumin, and garlic, and mix well. Make into 16 balls.

2. Spray a medium sauté pan with cooking spray, and heat on medium-high heat. Add meatballs, cooking in batches as needed until brown on all sides.

3. Place meatballs into a 5- to 6-quart slow cooker, add tomatoes and cinnamon stick, cover, and cook on low for 8 hours. Discard cinnamon stick before serving.

Buffalo Tomato Basil Pizza

Makes 8 servings
Prep time: 5 minutes
Cook time: 20 minutes
Each serving has:
98.75 calories
11.57 g. protein
9.87 g. carbohydrate
3.4 g. total fat
1.29 g. saturated fat
20.14 mg. cholesterol
137.4 mg. sodium
5.25 g. fiber

Nonstick cooking spray

½ lb. ground buffalo

4 cloves garlic, sliced

4 La Tortilla Factory low-carb tortillas, 8-inch size

½ lb. tomato, sliced

¾ cup ricotta cheese

¼ cup fresh basil, chopped or torn

1. Spray a 6-inch sauté pan with cooking spray; cook buffalo and garlic until done, about 4 minutes. Drain.

2. Top tortillas with equal portions of buffalo. Place tomato slices on top, dot with ricotta cheese, and sprinkle basil on top.

3. Heat oven to 450°F. Place pizzas on a baking sheet and place in oven. Bake for 12 minutes or until cheese is bubbling. Remove from the oven, let stand for 5 minutes, and cut into slices.

Sloppy Buffalo Joes

1½ lbs. ground buffalo

1 cup onion, diced

1 clove garlic, minced

6 oz. canned tomatoes, crushed

2 TB. sugar substitute, such as Splenda Brown Sugar

1 TB. mustard

2 tsp. chili powder

1 tsp. Worcestershire sauce

¼ cup black beans, drained

Makes 6 servings
Prep time: 5 minutes
Cook time: 6 hours 30 minutes
Each serving has:
181.3 calories
25.78 g. protein
13.7 g. carbohydrate
1.96 g. total fat
0.59 g. saturated fat
52.16 mg. cholesterol
136 mg. sodium
2.92 g. fiber

1. In a large skillet, brown buffalo, onion, and garlic until meat is brown and onion is soft and translucent, about 5 minutes.

2. In a medium bowl, combine tomatoes, sugar, mustard, chili powder, and Worcestershire sauce.

3. In a 5- to 6-quart slow cooker add meat, pour tomato sauce over top, cover, and cook on low for 6 hours. Increase the heat to high, add beans, mix, and warm for 10 minutes more.

Spaghetti with Ground Buffalo

1 lb. ground buffalo

1 cup canned tomatoes, crushed

1 tsp. dried oregano

1 tsp. dried marjoram

1 tsp. black pepper

1 tsp. Worcestershire sauce

1 cup dried mushrooms, chopped

¾ lb. whole-wheat spaghetti

Makes 6 servings
Prep time: 10 minutes
Cook time: 30 minutes
Each serving has:
405.4 calories
27.95 g. protein
76.42 g. carbohydrate
2.6 g. total fat
0.48 g. saturated fat
34.78 mg. cholesterol
110.9 mg. sodium
5.71 g. fiber

1. Heat a 10-inch sauté pan on medium-high heat, and add buffalo. Stir until cooked, about 4 minutes. Add tomatoes, oregano, marjoram, pepper, Worcestershire sauce, and mushrooms, cover. Reduce to simmer and cook for 20 minutes.

2. Bring a 2-quart saucepan with water to a boil. Place pasta into the pot and bring to a boil. Cook until tender, about 5 minutes. Drain but do not rinse.

3. Divide into portions, and top with meat sauce.

Goat Keema with Peas

Makes 4 servings
Prep time: 5 minutes
Cook time: 10 minutes
Each serving has:
182.9 calories
26.66 g. protein
11.05 g. carbohydrate
3.13 g. total fat
0.87 g. saturated fat
64.64 mg. cholesterol
136.8 mg. sodium
3.1 g. fiber

1 lb. ground goat
$^1/_2$ cup onion, diced
2 cloves garlic, minced
1 TB. ground ginger
1 TB. fenugreek leaves
$^1/_2$ tsp. ground cinnamon

$^1/_2$ tsp. ground coriander
$^1/_2$ tsp. ground cumin
$^1/_4$ cup canned garbanzo beans, drained
$^1/_2$ cup tomatoes, quartered
1 cup peas

1. Heat a 10-inch sauté pan on medium-high heat, and cook goat until brown, about 4 minutes.

2. In a spice grinder, combine onion, garlic, ginger, fenugreek, cinnamon, coriander, and cumin, and grind to blend. Add mixture to meat, and cook for 2 minutes more. Add garbanzos, tomatoes, and peas. Stir, cover, turn off the heat, and let blend. Serve with pita bread.

Nutri Notes

Goat meat is eaten by 70 percent of the world's population. It is easy to digest and is lower in fat and calories than most meats. It is also known as chevon or cabrito. You can find it in Hispanic or Asian grocery stores or such chains as Whole Foods.

Goat with Chana Dal

1 cup squash, peeled and cubed

1 cup onion, diced

2 TB. fennugreek leaves

6 TB. coriander, chopped

3 TB. fresh mint leaves, chopped

1 tsp. turmeric

1 tsp. chili powder

1 tsp. sugar substitute, such as Splenda

1 cup chana dal lentils

2 cups water

Nonstick cooking spray

1½ lbs. ground goat

¼ cup white wine vinegar

Makes 4 servings
Prep time: 10 minutes
Cook time: 40 minutes
Each serving has:
406.7 calories
51.02 g. protein
37.26 g. carbohydrate
6.36 g. total fat
1.26 g. saturated fat
96.96 mg. cholesterol
143 mg. sodium
7.68 g. fiber

1. In a large saucepan, add squash, onion, fenugreek, coriander, mint, turmeric, chili powder, sugar, chana dal, and water. Bring to a boil, reduce heat, cover, and simmer for 30 minutes or until lentils are soft.

2. Spray a small sauté pan with cooking spray. Cook goat on medium-high heat until just cooked, about 4 minutes.

3. Add goat and vinegar to vegetable mixture, and simmer for 5 more minutes to blend.

Roast Goat Leg with Thyme

Makes 8 servings
Prep time: 10 minutes
Cook time: 20 minutes
Each serving has:
186.8 calories
35.09 g. protein
35.09 g. carbohydrate
3.93 g. total fat
1.21 g. saturated fat
96.96 mg. cholesterol
139.6 mg. sodium
0.04 g. fiber

3 lbs. goat leg
12 sprigs fresh thyme leaves
2 cloves garlic

1 tsp. lime zest
1 tsp. orange zest

1. Have the butcher trim any fat from goat leg and debone it.

2. In a food processor or blender, process or grind thyme, garlic, and lime and orange zests. Cut slits into meat, and push mixture into slits.

3. Heat a charcoal grill to high heat, place leg on the grill, and roast until charred, turning once, about 20 minutes or until a meat thermometer registers 125°F. Let rest for 5 minutes, loosely covered with foil, slice thinly, and serve.

Country Mustard Rabbit

Makes 4 servings
Prep time: 10 minutes
Cook time: 30 minutes
Each serving has:
208.5 calories
24.75 g. protein
11.41 g. carbohydrate
7.16 g. total fat
2.01 g. saturated fat
64.64 mg. cholesterol
109.5 mg. sodium
1.37 g. fiber

Nonstick cooking spray
1 lb. rabbit, cut into pieces
1/4 cup rolled oats
2 cloves garlic, minced

1 cup apple cider
1 cup water
2 tsp. black pepper
1 TB. Dijon mustard

1. Spray a 10-inch skillet with cooking spray, and heat on high. Sear rabbit pieces in the pan; then remove to a dish to keep warm.

2. Place oats in a blender and reduce to a fine powder.

3. Lower the heat and add garlic, cooking until soft, about 2 minutes. Add cider and water, and scrape up any bits from the pan. Stir in mustard and oats flour to thicken sauce. Return rabbit to the pan, reduce the heat to simmer, cover, and cook for about 20 minutes or until rabbit is tender and cooked. Serve with sauce over each piece.

Drunken Rabbit

Nonstick cooking spray

2 lbs. rabbit, cut in pieces

1 cup carrots, sliced

1 cup celery, sliced

1 cup onion, diced

12 oz. beer

¼ cup red chili paste

¼ cup barley

Makes 4 servings
Prep time: 10 minutes
Cook time: 50 minutes
Each serving has:
417.8 calories
48.18 g. protein
19.39 g. carbohydrate
13.02 g. total fat
3.85 g. saturated fat
129.3 mg. cholesterol
527.1 mg. sodium
4.35 g. fiber

1. Spray a 10-inch skillet with cooking spray, and heat on high heat. Add rabbit and brown on both sides, about 5 minutes. Remove meat to a plate and keep warm.

2. Add carrots, celery, and onions to the pan and sauté until soft, about 5 minutes. Add beer, chili paste, and barley to the pan, stir to mix, bring to a boil, and then return rabbit to the pan. Cover, lower the heat to simmer, and cook for 20 minutes or until rabbit is tender and done. Serve with sauce.

Food for Thought _____

Beer is a great tenderizer of meats, so choose a dark beer which will be richer in flavor than light varieties. Don't worry about the alcohol content as most is evaporated during the cooking process. A glass of beer has fewer calories than an equivalent amount of milk or apple juice. If you don't want to use beer, then substitute apple cider in this recipe.

Rabbit Stew

Makes 4 servings
Prep time: 5 minutes
Cook time: 40 minutes
Each serving has:
532 calories
50.66 g. protein
32.12 g. carbohydrate
18.13 g. total fat
4.33 g. saturated fat
129.3 mg. cholesterol
107.6 mg. sodium
3.69 g. fiber

Nonstick cooking spray

2 lbs. rabbit, cut into pieces

1 cup onion, diced

4 cloves garlic, sliced

2 cups red burgundy wine

1 TB. red wine vinegar

2 cups tomatoes, diced

1 cinnamon stick

3 cloves, whole

1 bay leaf

2 allspice berries, whole

1/2 cup spaghetti Dreamfields pasta, broken into 3-inch segments

1. Spray a 10-inch skillet with cooking spray, and heat on high. Place rabbit in the pan and brown on both sides, about 10 minutes. Remove meat to a plate and keep warm.

2. Add onion and garlic to the pan, cook until soft, about 3 minutes. Then add wine, vinegar, tomatoes, cinnamon, cloves, bay leaf, allspice, and broken pieces of pasta. Mix, return the rabbit to pan, cover, reduce the heat to simmer, and cook for 30 minutes. Remove whole spices before serving.

Rabbit with Chocolate

¹/₄ cup rolled oats

1¹/₂ lbs. rabbit, cut into pieces

1 TB. plant sterol spread, such as Smart Balance

2 TB. fresh rosemary

4 bay leaves

1 cup onion, diced

¹/₂ cup celery, diced

1 cup fennel, sliced

1 TB. fennel seeds

¹/₄ cup carrots, sliced

3 cloves garlic, whole

¹/₄ cup raisins

1 cup apple cider vinegar

1 TB. sugar substitute, such as Splenda

1 TB. unsweetened dark chocolate powder

Makes 6 servings
Prep time: 10 minutes
Cook time: 40 minutes
Each serving has:
257.7 calories
25.23 g. protein
18.51 g. carbohydrate
9.64 g. total fat
3.63 g. saturated fat
64.64 mg. cholesterol
65.96 mg. sodium
2.42 g. fiber

1. In a blender grind oats to a fine powder. Coat rabbit pieces in oat flour.

2. Heat a 10-inch sauté pan on medium-high heat, and add sterol spread. Brown rabbit pieces on both sides, about 5 minutes per side. Remove from the pan and keep warm, loosely covered with foil.

3. Add onion, celery, fennel, fennel seeds, and carrots, and cook until soft, about 5 minutes. Return rabbit to the pan, and add garlic, raisins, vinegar, sugar, and chocolate powder. Stir to blend, cover, reduce the heat, and simmer for 30 minutes or until thick sauce has developed.

Food for Thought

This dish is a popular Italian version that uses chocolate to highlight the flavor of the rabbit. I'm sure you'll agree any dish with chocolate can't be all bad!

Slow Down Rabbit

Makes 4 servings
Prep time: 5 minutes
Cook time: 6 hours
Each serving has:
282.8 calories
32.1 g. protein
13.85 g. carbohydrate
8.36 g. total fat
2.47 g. saturated fat
66.38 mg. cholesterol
143.5 mg. sodium
2.46 g. fiber

¹/₂ cup celery, sliced
¹/₂ cup carrots, sliced
1 cup onion, diced
1 cup mushrooms, sliced
1 can water chestnuts, sliced

1 TB. tapioca
1 lb. rabbit thighs
3 cups reduced-sodium fat-free chicken broth
¹/₂ cup red burgundy wine

1. Place celery, carrots, onion, mushrooms, and water chestnuts into the bottom of the slow cooker along with tapioca. Then add rabbit and chicken broth. Cover and cook on low heat for 6 hours.

2. Remove rabbit from the slow cooker, and add wine, stirring to mix. Return rabbit to sauce, and let simmer for 10 minutes.

Nutri Notes

Water chestnuts are the roots of an aquatic plant popular in Chinese cuisine. Water chestnuts are a good source of fiber and B vitamins. One cup is only 135 calories and adds a great crunchy taste to any dish.

Venison Chili

2 lbs. ground venison

1 cup onion, sliced

1 medium jalapeño pepper, diced

2 cloves garlic, sliced

1 can (14.5 oz.) tomatoes, crushed

3 TB. red wine vinegar

3 TB. chili powder

2 tsp. ground cumin

2 TB. Worcestershire sauce

1/2 tsp. cayenne

10 oz. pinto beans, drained

Makes 6 servings
Prep time:
Cook time:
Each serving has:
274.6 calories
38.92 g. protein
19.5 g. carbohydrate
4.84 g. total fat
1.66 g. saturated fat
128.5 mg. cholesterol
354.3 mg. sodium
5.99 g. fiber

1. Heat a 10-inch skillet on high heat, and quickly cook venison until done. Place in a slow cooker, and add onion, jalapeño, garlic, tomatoes, vinegar, chili powder, cumin, Worcestershire sauce, cayenne, and pinto beans. Cover and cook on low heat for 8 hours.

Venison Pot Roast

Nonstick cooking spray

2 lbs. venison roast

1 cup onion, sliced

4 cloves garlic, sliced

1/2 cup carrots, sliced

1/2 cup celery, sliced

2 tsp. fresh oregano

1 cup tomatoes, diced

2 cups hot water

Makes 4 servings
Prep time: 10 minutes
Cook time: 6 hours
Each serving has:
320.9 calories
53.6 g. protein
11.1 g. carbohydrate
5.9 g. total fat
2.23 g. saturated fat
192.8 mg. cholesterol
140.9 mg. sodium
2.8 g. fiber

1. Spray a 10-inch skillet with cooking spray, and heat on high. Sear venison in the pan on all sides, about 8 minutes. Remove and place in the slow cooker.

2. Stir onion and garlic in the pan, cook until soft, about 3 minutes, and transfer to the slow cooker. Add carrots, celery, oregano, tomatoes, and water. Cover and cook on low heat for 6 hours.

Venison Steaks with Mushroom Sauce

Makes 4 servings
Prep time: 5 minutes
Cook time: 12 minutes
Each serving has:
470.3 calories
46.8 g. protein
53.88 g. carbohydrate
5.43 g. total fat
1.89 g. saturated fat
144.6 mg. cholesterol
98.98 mg. sodium
8.32 g. fiber

1½ lbs. venison steaks

1 cup onion, diced

3 cloves garlic, minced

8 oz. dried mushroom mixture

1 cup white wine

¼ cup ground rolled oats

1. Heat a pan on high heat, and sear roast steaks until done, about 5 minutes. Remove from the pan and keep warm.

2. Add onion and garlic and cook until soft, about 3 more minutes. Toss mushrooms into the pan, add wine, and scrape up any bits. Bring to a boil, add oat flour, and stir to mix into gravy. Return venison to the pan, and coat with sauce. Serve.

Smoke Signals

Venison contains purines, which can be broken down into uric acid, which may cause kidney stones and gout in susceptible people. Always defrost venison in the refrigerator and not at room temperature to avoid any contamination with bacteria.

Part 5

Side Dishes, Sassy Sauces and Dips, and Dessert Show Stoppers

This part completes your cooking lesson, and what a way to end it. It starts with leading you through a colorful side show of vegetables, pastas, and sauces and ends with desserts—even chocolate ones. Now you seriously didn't think someone who slaved away getting a certificate in pastry work could leave out that one little item when it comes to healthy eating, did you? Not on your life!

Like comfort food, desserts evoke memories of celebration and holiday family gatherings, but my recipes take away the guilt. You'll learn how to prepare what I call "controlled fat versions" of your favorites along with new ways to make fruit sparkle with delicious flavors. I've even included a family recipe for rice pudding that will make you feel like a child again—that is, a very healthy one. So enjoy this part and reward yourself for learning to cook with total nutrition as your guide.

Chapter 15

Side Shows

In This Chapter

- ◆ Mother Nature knows best
- ◆ Crisp and crunchy goodness
- ◆ Colors of the rainbow

Side dishes can be an exciting way to provide your family with the best in total nutrition cooking. Mother Nature certainly knew her stuff when she loaded vegetables with so many healthy benefits—fiber, minerals, vitamins, and taste. What's not to like? Plenty if you don't know how to prepare them. I have memories of mushy foods cooked to grey colors languishing on my plate as a child, but today there is no excuse for cooking the life out of your veggies. And I'm going to show you several secrets to making your sides appealing to everyone.

First, remember that crisp and crunchy are good. I'm not talking raw per se, but still with some snap or bite to them. Avoid boiling veggies as much as possible, as you're really pouring all the health benefits down the drain. Instead, consider steaming, microwaving, and blanching, all techniques I'll share with you in this chapter.

Enjoy the colors of the rainbow when you shop by choosing dark-colored vegetables. Think of your sides as a great painting, and be creative.

Not only will you make a dinner plate look scrumptious, but you'll also be sneaking tons of nutrient-dense foods into your curious family's stomach with fewer calories. Now that's a satisfying feeling!

Artichokes with Garlic Sauce

Makes 4 servings
Prep time: 5 minutes
Cook time: 30 minutes
Each serving has:
182 calories
5.49 g. protein
18.15 g. carbohydrate
4.43 g. total fat
2.14 g. saturated fat
0.31 mg. cholesterol
132.7 mg. sodium
7.15 g. fiber

4 medium artichokes
$^1/_2$ cup water
12 cloves garlic
4 TB. nonfat yogurt

1 TB. lemon juice
1 tsp. dried tarragon
8 TB. plant sterol spread, such as Benecol

1. Remove tips from artichokes using scissors, and slice off tops. Remove stems from bottom so each artichoke stands up.

2. In a microwaveable baking dish, place artichokes in water. Put garlic cloves (in their skins) in a small bag of plastic wrap and place in water. Cover the dish with plastic wrap, and microwave on high for 30 minutes.

3. Remove from the microwave, and allow to rest for 5 minutes before removing the plastic wrap to prevent steam burns. Drain artichokes upside down for a minute to remove any remaining water. Remove garlic cloves, and squeeze out contents into a small bowl.

4. Combine yogurt, lemon juice, tarragon, and spread with garlic to make sauce. Serve alongside each artichoke.

Food for Thought _____

Tarragon is an excellent herb that imparts a licorice flavor to sauces, fish, chicken, or egg dishes. You can rehydrate dry tarragon leaves by placing them in a damp paper towel for a few minutes before chopping and adding to the sauce.

Baby Bok Choy with Coconut Curry Paste and Oyster Mushrooms

Nonstick cooking spray, olive oil flavor

1 TB. red curry paste

$^1/_3$ cup reduced-fat coconut milk

1 TB. chili powder

4 dry shiitake mushrooms

1 lb. bok choy

Makes 6 servings
Prep time: 2 minutes
Cook time: 7 minutes
Each serving has:
34.08 calories
2.09 g. protein
4.69 g. carbohydrate
1.73 g. total fat
0.73 g. saturated fat
0 mg. cholesterol
98.21 mg. sodium
1.45 g. fiber

1. Spray a medium saucepan over medium heat with cooking spray, and add *curry paste*. Gradually stir in milk and chili powder. Cook for 2 minutes.

2. Place mushrooms into milk mixture; then add bok choy on top. Cover and turn off the heat. Allow to steam for 5 minutes. Serve bok choy in a small bowl, pouring over mushroom milk sauce to taste.

Nutri Speak

Curry paste is a combination of chilies, peeled garlic, lemon grass, fresh turmeric, sea salt, and shrimp paste pounded in a mortar with a pestle.

Butternut Squash with Cinnamon Brown Sugar

Makes 4 servings
Prep time: 5 minutes
Cook time: 25 minutes
Each serving has:
157.3 calories
2.65 g. protein
27.93 g. carbohydrate
3.98 g. total fat
0.81 g. saturated fat
0 mg. cholesterol
9.89 mg. sodium
0.97 g. fiber

2 lb. butternut squash

1 cup water

2 TB. plant sterol spread, such as Benecol

2 tsp. cinnamon

2 TB. sugar substitute, such as Splenda Brown Sugar

2 TB. pecan pieces

1. Peel butternut squash, remove seeds, and cut into 4 pieces.

2. In a small microwavable baking dish, add squash, face down. Pour water into the baking dish. Cover with plastic wrap.

3. Microwave on high for 20 minutes.

4. Allow to cool for 5 minutes before removing the plastic wrap to prevent steam burns.

5. Dot each portion with sterol spread. Combine equal amounts of cinnamon and sugar substitute; then sprinkle evenly on top of squash. Sprinkle pecan pieces on top just before serving.

Carrots with Honey Dill

Makes 4 servings
Prep time: 5 minutes
Cook time: 8 minutes
Each serving has:
134.2 calories
1.21 g. protein
20.25 g. carbohydrate
2.3 g. total fat
1.08 g. saturated fat
0 mg. cholesterol
41.32 mg. sodium
3.43 g. fiber

1 lb. carrots

4 TB. plant sterol spread, such as Benecol

2 TB. fresh dill, chopped

2 TB. honey

Salt and pepper to taste

1. Slice carrots into 1-inch slices on an angle.

2. Pile into a steamer, cover, and bring to a boil. Steam for 8 minutes or until just crisp tender. Drain and pour into a serving bowl.

3. Whisk together spread, dill, and honey, and pour over carrots. Season with salt and pepper to taste.

Nutri Notes _____

Dill is a member of the parsley family with a delicate caraway flavor. It goes well with fish, dairy, potatoes, and vegetables. It's a very good source of vitamin A, vitamin C, calcium, and iron.

Eggplant Towers

1½ lbs. unpeeled eggplant

1½ lbs. tomato

¾ tsp. salt substitute, such as Morton's

Nonstick cooking spray

½ tsp. garlic powder

½ tsp. black pepper

2 TB. goat cheese

1 tsp. dried basil

1 TB. reduced-sodium Parmesan cheese

Makes 8 servings
Prep time: 30 minutes
Cook time: 30 minutes
Each serving has:
54.4 calories
2.61 g. protein
9.49 g. carbohydrate
1.54 g. total fat
0.73 g. saturated fat
2.2 mg. cholesterol
25.22 mg. sodium
3.19 g. fiber

1. Slice eggplant into 8 slices. Slice tomatoes into 8 slices. Place eggplant on paper towels, sprinkle with salt substitute, and let drain for 30 minutes.

2. Preheat oven to 400°F.

3. Arrange eggplant pieces on a baking sheet lightly sprayed with cooking spray and spray each piece in addition. Bake at 400°F for 12 minutes; then turn over and sprinkle with garlic powder and pepper. Bake for 12 minutes more or until tender. Remove from the oven.

4. Preheat broiler.

5. Top each eggplant piece with tomato slice. Combine goat cheese, basil, and Parmesan, and crumble on top of each tomato slice. Broil 2 minutes. Remove to a serving plate, and top with basil.

Smoke Signals

Eggplant belongs to the deadly nightshade family and can cause bowel pain, arthritis symptoms, bladder irritation, and migraine problems for sensitive people.

Gingered Broccoli, Cauliflower, and Carrots

Makes 4 servings
Prep time: 5 minutes
Cook time: 10 minutes
Each serving has:
139.4 calories
6.32 g. protein
17.57g. carbohydrate
2.89 g. total fat
1.18 g. saturated fat
0 mg. cholesterol
99.42 mg. sodium
8.16 g. fiber

1 lb. broccoli crowns

1 lb. cauliflower

½ lb. frozen carrots, chopped

2 tsp. fresh ginger, grated

4 TB. plant sterol spread, such as Benecol

¼ cup rice wine vinegar

1. Cut broccoli crowns into florets. Cut cauliflower into florets. Open bag of chopped carrots. Pile vegetables into a steamer basket, cover, and bring to a boil. As soon as you can smell a broccoli or cauliflower odor, about 4 minutes, turn off the heat and leave covered for 3 minutes. Broccoli and cauliflower should be crisp-tender, but not soft. You should be able to just pass the tip of a small, sharp knife into stem. Drain and place in a serving bowl.

2. In a small bowl, whisk together spread with ginger and vinegar.

3. Pour ginger mixture over vegetables, and serve immediately.

Green Beans with Mushrooms

Makes 4 servings
Prep time: 3 minutes
Cook time: 10 minutes
Each serving has:
74.15 calories
3.6 g. protein
11.83 g. carbohydrate
2.57 g. total fat
0.41 g. saturated fat
0 mg. cholesterol
10.51 mg. sodium
4.89 g. fiber

1 tsp. peanut oil

¼ cup onion, coarsely diced

1 lb. green beans, sliced

1 tsp. toasted sesame oil

8 oz. mushrooms

1. In a medium sauté pan, add peanut oil and onion, and sauté until translucent and tender.

2. Add sliced green beans, and sauté until tender, about 3 minutes.

3. Add sesame oil, then mushrooms. Sauté for one minute. Cover, turn off the heat, and gently steam for 2 minutes; then serve.

Green Beans with Salsa

³/₄ lb. green beans

2 TB. plant sterol spread, such as Benecol

1 small jalapeño pepper, deseeded and diced

1 clove garlic, mashed

¹/₄ cup tomato, finely diced

¹/₄ tsp salt substitute, such as Morton's

2 TB. fresh cilantro, chopped

Makes 4 servings
Prep time: 3 minutes
Cook time: 10 minutes
Each serving has:
57.39 calories
1.75 g. protein
7.02 g. carbohydrate
1.21 g. total fat
0.55 g. saturated fat
0 mg. cholesterol
7.96 mg. sodium
3.15 g. fiber

1. Clean green beans by cutting off any stem portions. Pile in a steamer basket, cover, and bring to a boil. As soon as you can smell a green bean odor, about 4 minutes, turn off the heat and leave covered for 3 minutes. Green beans should be crisp-tender but not soft. Turn out into a serving bowl.

2. In a saucepan over medium heat, add spread, peppers, and garlic. Sauté for 2 minutes, stirring often or until garlic becomes translucent and gives off a nutty fragrance. Remove from the heat and add tomato. Pour into the bean bowl and top with salt and cilantro.

Grilled Fennel with Ginger Orange Glaze

1 lb. fennel bulbs

4 TB. plant sterol spread, such as Benecol

¹/₂ cup orange juice

1 tsp. dried ginger

Makes 4 servings
Prep time: 4 minutes
Cook time: 5 minutes
Each serving has:
101.5 calories
1.63 g. protein
11.59 g. carbohydrate
2.36 g. total fat
1.05 g. saturated fat
0 mg. cholesterol
60.51 mg. sodium
4.84 g. fiber

1. Trim fennel bulbs of any fronds; then cut in half down the middle. Soak in cold water before grilling.

2. Heat a grill on high. Shake each fennel piece, place it over the grill grates and grill until tender, turning once.

3. In a small saucepan, combine spread, orange juice, and ginger. Stir until blended. Brush on grilled fennel bulbs, and serve immediately.

Grilled Leeks

Makes 4 servings
Prep time: 5 minutes
Cook time: 4 minutes
Each serving has:
69.17 calories
1.7 g. protein
16.05 g. carbohydrate
0.34 g. total fat
0.05 g. saturated fat
0 mg. cholesterol
22.68 mg. sodium
2.04 g. fiber

1 lb. leeks   2 cups ice water

1. Cut off sprouted ends of leeks and split in half. Rinse under running water to remove any dirt. Soak in ice water for 5 minutes.

2. Heat a grill on high. When you cannot hold your hand over the grill for a count of 5, pull leeks from ice water and toss them onto the grill. After 2 minutes, change direction of leeks to give a nice cross-hatch mark. Turn over and grill for 2 minutes more. Serve immediately.

Nutri Notes

Leeks are the national emblem of Wales and were worn as a badge. Medieval healers believed they could prevent common colds, foretell the future, prevent being hit by lightning strikes, and if placed under a pillow, cut the pain of childbirth.

Pan Roasted Potatoes de Provence

Makes 4 servings
Prep time: 5 minutes
Cook time: 15 minutes
Each serving has:
86.13 calories
1.38 g. protein
10.99 g. carbohydrate
2.2 g. total fat
0.68 g. saturated fat
0 mg. cholesterol
7.13 mg. sodium
1.13 g. fiber

1 tsp. olive oil

2 TB. plant sterol spread, such as Benecol

¹/₂ lb. red potatoes, quartered

8 cloves garlic

2 tsp. herbs de Provence

1 tsp. salt substitute, such as Morton's

¹/₂ tsp. black pepper

1. In a medium nonstick sauté pan over medium heat, add olive oil and spread. Toss in potato pieces and allow to crisp, turning only a few times, for about 5 minutes.

2. Toss in garlic cloves in their skin and sprinkle with herbs de Provence. Cover, reduce the heat to low, and allow to slow cook for about 10 minutes.

3. Season with salt substitute and pepper to taste. Squeeze garlic out of skins and serve cloves alongside potatoes.

Mustard Greens and Spinach with Bulgur

2 cups boiling water

2 cups ice water

$^1/_2$ lb. mustard greens

$^1/_2$ lb. spinach leaf

Nonstick cooking spray

1 TB. peanut oil

4 cloves garlic

1 small serrano chili

1 tsp. dried ginger

$^1/_2$ cup onion

2 small tomatoes, cut into quarters

1 cup quinoa

Makes 6 servings
Prep time: 5 minutes
Cook time: 10 minutes
Each serving has:
162.4 calories
6.41 g. protein
26.27 g. carbohydrate
4.97 g. total fat
0.62 g. saturated fat
0 mg. cholesterol
48.85 mg. sodium
4.66 g. fiber

1. In a large saucepan, bring water to a boil. Tear stems off greens.

2. *Blanch* greens by dropping batches of greens and spinach into boiling water for 2 minutes, remove to a bowl with ice water to cool, and then drain in a colander.

3. Spray a medium sauté pan with cooking spray. Place over medium heat and add oil. Mash garlic, and gradually add along with diced chili, ginger, and onion. Cook until translucent, about 4 minutes. Add green mixture, cook for 2 minutes more. Top with tomato quarters, and stir to blend.

4. Prepare quinoa according to recipe (see the Quinoa Cooked Cereal with Cherries and Pecans in Chapter 8). Sprinkle on top of greens and stir to absorb any liquid. Turn out into a serving bowl.

Nutri Speak

Blanching is a cooking process in which food is rapidly heated in boiling water, then cooled in ice water to stop the cooking process. This allows the food to firm up and makes both the color and the flavor more pronounced.

Orange Almond Broccoli

Makes 4 servings
Prep time: 4 minutes
Cook time: 10 minutes
Each serving has:
139.7 calories
7.3 g. protein
15.93 g. carbohydrate
3.66 g. total fat
1.23 g. saturated fat
0 mg. cholesterol
62.74 mg. sodium
8.57 g. fiber

2 lbs. broccoli

4 TB. plant sterol spread, such as Benecol, melted

2 TB. orange zest

½ cup orange juice

1 TB. almonds

1. Cut broccoli crowns into florets. Pile into a steamer basket, cover, and bring to a boil. As soon as you can smell a broccoli odor, about 4 minutes, turn off the heat and leave covered for 3 minutes. Broccoli should be crisp-tender, green but not soft. You should be able to just pass the tip of a small, sharp knife into stem. Drain and place in a serving bowl.

2. In a small bowl, whisk spread with orange zest and juice.

3. Pour orange mixture over broccoli, and dust with almond slices.

Food for Thought

When selecting broccoli, look for tight crowns that are firm to the touch and dark green in color. Avoid broccoli that has any yellow color, or hard, dry stems.

Proper Peas and Mint

Makes 6 servings
Prep time: 1 minute
Cook time: 7 minutes
Each serving has:
111.4 calories
3.95 g. protein
10.38 g. carbohydrate
2.36 g. total fat
1.09 g. saturated fat
0 mg. cholesterol
90.51 mg. sodium
3.57 g. fiber

4 cups water

1 lb. frozen peas

6 TB. plant sterol spread, such as Benecol

2 tsp. mint leaves

1. Put water into a large saucepan and bring to a boil. Empty package of frozen peas into water, cover, and turn off the heat. Allow to rest for 5 minutes. Peas should be green and firm in shape.

2. Drain peas and place into a bowl.

3. Melt spread in the microwave on high for 5 seconds; then pour over peas. Sprinkle mint on top, season with pepper to taste, and serve.

Roasted Asparagus

1 lb. asparagus

Nonstick cooking spray

1 tsp. salt substitute, such as Morton's

4 TB. plant sterol spread, such as Benecol

1 TB. lemon juice

Makes 4 servings
Prep time: 4 minutes
Cook time: 7 minutes
Each serving has:
82.02 calories
2.6 g. protein
5.48 g. carbohydrate
3.25 g. total fat
1.09 g. saturated fat
0 mg. cholesterol
5.6 mg. sodium
2.4 g. fiber

1. Trim asparagus spears by bending and snapping them where they give. Discard woody ends.

2. Preheat the oven to 500°F.

3. Spray a cooking sheet with cooking spray; then lay asparagus single file on the tray. Spray with more cooking spray, and sprinkle with salt substitute.

4. Place in the oven for 7 minutes.

5. Combine spread and lemon juice, and whisk to blend. Serve asparagus immediately when done with lemon butter.

Sesame Lemon Broccoli

2 lb. broccoli

4 TB. plant sterol spread, such as Benecol

1 TB. lemon zest

1 TB. lemon juice

2 cloves garlic, mashed

2 tsp. sesame seeds

Makes 4 servings
Prep time: 5 minutes
Cook time: 10 minutes
Each serving has:
128.1 calories
7.12 g. protein
13.3 g. carbohydrate
3.53 g. total fat
1.26 g. saturated fat
0 mg. cholesterol
70.5 mg. sodium
7.23 g. fiber

1. Cut broccoli crowns into florets. Pile into a steamer basket, cover, and bring to a boil. As soon as you can smell a broccoli odor, about 4 minutes, turn off the heat and leave covered for 3 minutes. Broccoli should be crisp-tender, green but not soft. You should be able to just pass the tip of a small, sharp knife into the stem. Drain and place into a serving bowl.

2. In a small bowl, whisk spread with the lemon zest, juice, and garlic.

3. Pour butter mixture over broccoli, and dust with sesame seeds.

Spaghetti Squash with Goat Cheese, Basil, and Tomatoes

Makes 6 servings
Prep time: 5 minutes
Cook time: 20 minutes
Each serving has:
210.1 calories
7.75 g. protein
22.31 g. carbohydrate
12.31 g. total fat
3.78 g. saturated fat
9.07 mg. cholesterol
116.2 mg. sodium
3.44 g. fiber

3 lb. spaghetti squash

$^1/_3$ cup goat cheese

3 small Roma tomatoes, diced

$^1/_2$ cup fresh basil, torn into pieces

$^1/_2$ cup walnuts

1. Pierce skin of squash all over, and place in the microwave on high for 20 minutes. Let rest for 5 minutes before splitting it open and removing seeds. With a fork, scrape out strands of squash and place into a bowl.

2. Add goat cheese, tomatoes, basil, and walnuts, and toss to blend.

Food for Thought _____

Spaghetti squash makes a great substitute for pasta if you must restrict your carbs to control your blood sugar levels. Reheat it simply by pouring boiling water through the strands in a strainer.

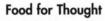

Smashed Cauliflower with Horseradish Cream

1 lb. cauliflower

¹/₂ cup fat-free yogurt

1 TB. prepared horseradish

1 tsp. salt substitute, such as Morton's

4 TB. plant sterol spread, such as Benecol

Makes 4 servings
Prep time: 5 minutes
Cook time: 12 minutes
Each serving has:
95.76 calories
3.54 g. protein
8.7 g. carbohydrate
2.35 g. total fat
1.08 g. saturated fat
0.63 mg. cholesterol
63.71 mg. sodium
2.96 g. fiber

1. Cut cauliflower into florets. Pile into a steamer basket, cover, and bring to a boil. As soon as you can smell a cauliflower odor, about 6 minutes, turn off the heat and leave covered for 3 minutes. Cauliflower should be soft. Drain and place into a serving bowl.

2. Using a mixer, whip cauliflower into a mash, then add yogurt, horseradish, salt substitute, and spread. Serve immediately.

Spinach with Garbanzo Beans and Cumin

1 tsp. olive oil

2 TB. plant sterol spread, such as Benecol

2 cloves garlic, mashed

6 oz. canned garbanzo beans, drained

³/₄ lb. spinach leaves

¹/₂ tsp. dried cumin

Makes 6 servings
Prep time: 2 minutes
Cook time: 5 minutes
Each serving has:
74.53 calories
3.21 g. protein
9.02 g. carbohydrate
2.12 g. total fat
0.52 g. saturated fat
0 mg. cholesterol
131.2 mg. sodium
2.87 g. fiber

1. In medium saucepan over medium heat, add olive oil, spread, and garlic. Sauté until soft, about 2 minutes.

2. Add garbanzo beans, stir to warm, and then top with spinach and cumin. Cover and turn off the heat. Allow to sit for about 3 minutes.

3. Uncover, stir to mix, and serve immediately.

Summer Squash with Tomatoes, Basil, and Bell Peppers

Makes 4 servings
Prep time: 5 minutes
Cook time: 5 minutes
Each serving has:
68 calories
2.82 g. protein
68 g. carbohydrate
2.16 g. total fat
0.5 g. saturated fat
0 mg. cholesterol
15.9 mg. sodium
4.16 g. fiber

³/₄ lb. yellow squash, finely diced

³/₄ lb. zucchini, finely diced

1 small red bell pepper, finely diced

1 cup cherry tomatoes, coarsely chopped

1 tsp. olive oil

1 TB. plant sterol spread, such as Benecol

2 TB. fresh basil (stack leaves, roll them up like a cigar, cut crosswise into ribbons)

1 tsp. salt substitute, such as Morton's

¹/₄ tsp. black pepper

1. In a medium saucepan, add olive oil and heat over medium heat. Add squash, zucchini, pepper, and tomatoes, and sauté for 4 minutes or until just tender.

2. Add spread, and toss gently to mix. Pour into a serving bowl and top with basil. Season to taste with salt substitute and pepper.

Sweet Potatoes with Sage Butter Sauce

Makes 6 servings
Prep time: 2 minutes
Cook time: 24 minutes
Each serving has:
217.3 calories
2.58 g. protein
38.53g. carbohydrate
2.55 g. total fat
1.15 g. saturated fat
0 mg. cholesterol
20.91 mg. sodium
4.66 g. fiber

2 lbs. sweet potatoes

6 TB. plant sterol spread, such as Benecol

1 tsp. dried sage

¹/₂ cup lemon juice

1. Pierce skin of sweet potatoes, and place in the microwave on high for 8 minutes per potato. Allow to rest for 4 minutes before peeling and scooping out flesh.

2. In a bowl, combine potato pulp, spread, and sage, and blend with a whisk. Add lemon juice to taste and to thin the texture as needed.

Chapter 16

Sassy Sauces, Pastas, and Rice

In This Chapter

- ◆ Almost homemade
- ◆ Be subtle
- ◆ Don't cover up

You don't have to spend hours slaving over a stove to bring your family a totally nutritious meal because I'll show you how to make your meals "almost homemade." It's simple. Learn to pick out the best store-bought goods as a base; then dress them up with delicious, nutrient-dense additions, and you'll shine like a Food TV star in your very own home. Nowhere is this easier than adapting sauces, pastas, and rice dishes to a more nutritious cooking style for your family.

The secret is layering, the building-up of tastes as a dish cooks. There's no need to have flavors scream at you from the plate when you can be subtle in developing first an aroma, followed by a mouth texture that puts a happy face on everyone. Think of it as playing dress-up with your food. You're limited only by your imagination.

Don't cover up pasta with tons of sauce, either. Noodles are meant to grab a sauce and display its glistening coating, not drown in it. The easiest way to do this is to place the noodles in a serving bowl and add small quantities of sauce at a time, stirring to mix.

Portion control is essential when serving pastas and rices. I have adjusted the recipes in this section for a complete main course, but consider serving much smaller portions as a side dish, the way Italians do, and you'll never miss pasta in your diet. After all, it's a great source of fiber, especially if you try whole grain, soy, or the new carb-controlled brands.

Almost Homemade Béarnaise Sauce

1 cup reduced-fat mayonnaise	$^1/_4$ tsp. mustard powder
1 TB. fresh lemon juice	$^1/_4$ tsp. paprika
1 tsp. fresh tarragon, finely diced	

Makes 16 servings
Prep time: 3 minutes
Cook time: none
Each serving has:
48.4 calories
0.13 g. protein
1.04 g. carbohydrate
4.82 g. total fat
0.69 g. saturated fat
0 mg. cholesterol
105.8 mg. sodium
0.01 g. fiber

1. In a bowl, combine mayonnaise, lemon juice, tarragon, mustard, and paprika, and whisk to blend. This sauce, stored in a jar in the refrigerator, will keep for one month.

Nutri Notes

Tarragon is an herb that imparts a licorice flavor. It is a member of the daisy family and closely related to wormwood, a bitter herb used in the production of absinthe, a highly alcoholic drink that contained the neurotoxin thujone, responsible for blindness, convulsions, and hallucinations.

Cucumber Garlic Dill Sauce

¹/₄ cup cucumber, peeled, deseeded and diced

¹/₄ cup plain nonfat yogurt

1 clove garlic, minced

¹/₂ tsp. fresh dill, finely chopped

2 TB. fat-free mayonnaise

1 TB. lemon dill mustard

1 tsp. apple cider

Makes 12 servings
Prep time: 2 minutes
Cook time: none
Each serving has:
7.8 calories
0.29 g. protein
1.46 g. carbohydrate
0.87 g. total fat
0.02 g. saturated fat
0.1 mg. cholesterol
47.32 mg. sodium
0.03 g. fiber

1. In a blender, combine cucumber, yogurt, garlic, dill, mayonnaise, mustard, and apple cider, and purée until smooth. Refrigerate for an hour to blend flavors. This sauce works great on fish or vegetables.

Food for Thought

If you can't find lemon dill mustard, just take a Dijon mustard and add some fresh dill and lemon zest to it.

Horseradish Sauce

¹/₂ cup nonfat yogurt

2 tsp. prepared horseradish

1. Combine yogurt and horseradish, and blend until smooth.

Makes 6 servings
Prep time: 2 minutes
Cook time: none
Each serving has:
9.13 calories
0.85 g. protein
1.77 g. carbohydrate
0.01 g. total fat
0 g. saturated fat
0.42 mg. cholesterol
16.48 mg. sodium
0.05 g. fiber

Nutri Notes

Horseradish was bottled in 1860, making it one of the earliest convenience foods. Horseradish was even thought to cure headaches if rubbed on the forehead.

Lemon Ginger Poppy Seed Sauce

Makes 2 servings
Prep time: 3 minutes
Cook time: none
Each serving has:
57.43 calories
5.23 g. protein
10.43 g. carbohydrate
0.38 g. total fat
0.05 g. saturated fat
2.5 mg. cholesterol
68.06 mg. sodium
0.25 g. fiber

1 cup fat-free yogurt

2 tsp. sugar substitute, such as Splenda Granular

$^{1}/_{2}$ tsp. poppy seeds

$^{1}/_{2}$ tsp. fresh lemon juice

$^{1}/_{2}$ tsp. lemon zest

1 tsp. fresh ginger, grated

1. Blend together yogurt, sugar substitute, poppy seeds, lemon juice, lemon peel, and ginger. Let sit for 10 minutes to develop flavors. This is best with fruits or over a salad.

Variation: Eliminate ginger and sugar substitute, replace with mashed garlic and mint, and use over ground lamb.

Food for Thought

Poppy seeds pack a lot of nutritional muscle. One tablespoon provides 10 percent of the daily value for calcium. It takes 900,000 of them to equal one pound. Because of their oil content, store them in the refrigerator for up to 6 months to prevent them from going rancid.

Red Sauce

Nonstick cooking spray

1 cup onion, finely chopped

1 clove garlic, chopped

2 lb. Roma tomatoes, peeled and finely diced

$^{1}/_{3}$ can tomato paste (about 2 oz.)

2 tsp. dried basil

$^{1}/_{2}$ tsp. dried oregano

1 tsp. salt substitute, such as Mrs. Dash

$^{1}/_{4}$ tsp. ground black pepper

1 qt. water

Makes 8 servings
Prep time: 10 minutes
Cook time: 45 minutes
Each serving has:
39.43 calories
1.55 g. protein
8.81 g. carbohydrate
0.6 g. total fat
0.07 g. saturated fat
0 mg. cholesterol
71.86 mg. sodium
2.12 g. fiber

1. Spray a 5-quart Dutch oven with cooking oil spray, place over medium heat, and add onion. Cook until translucent, about 5 minutes. Add garlic and cook for 3 minutes, stirring often to prevent burning. Stir in tomatoes, tomato paste, basil, oregano, salt substitute, and pepper. Add water, and bring to a boil.

2. Reduce the heat, cover and simmer for 30 minutes, stirring occasionally.

Variation: Use marjoram and thyme with oregano for a different flavor, or simply add hot pepper flakes or a small, seeded serrano chili with spearmint leaves for a spicy note.

Smoke Signals _____

Never store leftover tomato paste in the tin. Always remove it to a plastic bag or storage container and place in the refrigerator to prevent mold formation.

Wasabi Ginger Sauce

Makes 12 servings
Prep time: 2 minutes
Cook time: none
Each serving has:
5.79 calories
0.37 g. protein
0.7 g. carbohydrate
0.04 g. total fat
0 g. saturated fat
0 mg. cholesterol
198.1 mg. sodium
0.05 g. fiber

$^1/_2$ cup rice wine vinegar

$^1/_4$ cup reduced-sodium soy sauce

2 TB. sugar substitute, such as Splenda White Sugar blend

2 TB. fresh lemon juice

1 tsp. grated ginger

$^3/_4$ tsp. wasabi paste

1. Combine vinegar, soy sauce, sugar substitute, lemon juice, ginger, and wasabi paste, and stir to blend. Use sauce for dipping grilled fish or chicken, or pour over top of grilled fish.

Food for Thought _____

Check the label on rice wine vinegar. Select only a brand that doesn't contain corn syrup for the best flavor and nutritional content. Wasabi paste is available in a tube or as a powder.

White Sauce

Makes 4 servings
Prep time: 3 minutes
Cook time: 5 minutes
Each serving has:
162.1 calories
10.75 g. protein
19.76 g. carbohydrate
4.27 g. total fat
2.26 g. saturated fat
11.28 mg. cholesterol
116.5 mg. sodium
0.45 g. fiber

1 TB. unsalted butter

1 can (14.5 oz.) reduced-sodium chicken broth

2 cups nonfat milk

2 TB. nonfat dry milk

$^1/_2$ cup flour

$^1/_4$ tsp. paprika

1. In a saucepan, melt butter. Add half the can of chicken broth, stir in nonfat milk and dry milk, and heat to boiling, stirring constantly.

2. In a separate bowl, blend together remaining chicken broth, flour, and paprika until smooth. Stir into boiling sauce, and heat until thickened, about 2 minutes, then reduce heat and stir until fully cooked, about 5 minutes.

Variation: Add roasted soft garlic, chives, parsley, or ham to the last step for a variety of flavors that you can use over fish, eggs, or fowl.

Artichoke Cilantro Pesto

4 oz. canned artichoke hearts, water drained (not in oil)

1 cup fresh cilantro

⅓ cup reduced-sodium Parmesan

1 TB. lemon juice

4 cloves garlic

1 small serrano chili

Makes 16 servings
Prep time: 4 minutes
Cook time: none
Each serving has:
13.05 calories
1.05 g. protein
1.17 g. carbohydrate
0.56 g. total fat
0.34 g. saturated fat
1.33 mg. cholesterol
6.57 mg. sodium
0.46 g. fiber

1. In a food processor, combine artichoke hearts, cilantro, Parmesan, lemon juice, garlic, and serrano chili, and purée until smooth. Serve with fresh vegetables.

Food for Thought _____

Artichoke hearts are available packed in oils or water. Keep several cans in your pantry for topping a salad or making this dip.

Cuban Black Bean Dip

1 cup black beans, mashed

1 cup onion, diced

¼ cup fresh cilantro, chopped

2 clove garlic, minced

½ tsp. ground cumin

1 TB. chili powder

⅓ cup orange juice

Makes 8 servings
Prep time: 3 minutes
Cook time: none
Each serving has:
47.01 calories
2.5 g. protein
8.92 g. carbohydrate
0.46 g. total fat
0.07 g. saturated fat
0 mg. cholesterol
3.28 mg. sodium
2.57 g. fiber

1. In a bowl, combine black beans, onion, cilantro, garlic, cumin, chili powder, and orange juice, and stir to mix well. This sauce is excellent as a dip but is also good over fish, chicken, or pork dishes.

Nutri Notes _____

Black beans are also known as turtle beans or frijoles negros. They have a satiny black skin with a white center. When cooked, their texture is creamy and the flavor is sweet.

Curry Dip

Makes 6 servings
Prep time: 3 minutes
Cook time: none
Each serving has:
110 calories
7.05 g. protein
20.51 g. carbohydrate
2.72 g. total fat
0.14 g. saturated fat
1.09 mg. cholesterol
106.6 mg. sodium
3.23 g. fiber

1 cup nonfat yogurt

2 TB. nonfat dry milk

2 tsp. curry powder

1 tsp. cider vinegar

2 cloves garlic

1½ cups canned cannellini beans, drained

3 TB. 97% fat-free mayonnaise

1. Into a blender, add yogurt, dry milk, curry powder, vinegar, garlic, cannellini beans, and mayonnaise, and purée until smooth. Chill overnight to blend flavors. This sauce adds a great taste to grilled fish, chicken, or vegetables.

Food for Thought _____

Cannellini beans are also called Great Northern white kidney beans. They make an excellent substitute for fat in any recipe by using equal weight amounts in replacement of half the butter amount. For example, you can replace ¹/₂ cup butter with ¹/₂ cup mashed beans in a recipe that calls for 1 cup butter.

Gruyère Apple Spread

3 oz. cream cheese

2 oz. low-fat Gruyère cheese

2 tsp. 2% milk

1 tsp. French mustard

¼ cup apple, diced with skin

1 TB. pecans, chopped

1 tsp. chives, diced

Makes 16 servings
Prep time: 5 minutes
Cook time: none
Each serving has:
38.13 calories
1.54 g. protein
0.58 g. carbohydrate
3.36 g. total fat
1.88 g. saturated fat
9.78 mg. cholesterol
31.49 mg. sodium
0.11 g. fiber

1. In a small bowl, beat cream cheese. Shred Gruyère cheese, and stir into cream cheese with milk and mustard until will blended. Stir in apple, pecans, and chives. Cover and refrigerate 1 hour.

2. Serve on rye or stone-ground whole-wheat crackers, or use as a dip for vegetables.

Food for Thought _____

Leaving the skin on the apple adds more fiber to this dish. You can also substitute low-fat cream cheese for the full-fat version. I prefer natural, non-guar gummed cream cheese. If your store carries fresh cream cheese, try it for an extra-special flavor.

Popeye Pesto

Makes 8 servings
Prep time: 3 minutes
Cook time: none
Each serving has:
46.53 calories
1.61 g. protein
6.59 g. carbohydrate
2.08 g. total fat
0.26 g. saturated fat
0 mg. cholesterol
54.89 mg. sodium
2.55 g. fiber

1 cup spinach leaves

1/2 cup fresh basil

1/2 cup fresh cilantro

1 TB. olive oil

1 clove garlic

1 tsp. salt substitute, such as Morton's

1/4 tsp. hot pepper flakes

1/2 cup canned garbanzo beans, drained

1 TB. lemon juice

1. In a blender, combine spinach, basil, cilantro, olive oil, garlic, salt substitute, pepper flakes, garbanzo beans, and lemon juice, and purée until smooth. This sauce tastes great over chicken, fish, or as a dip for vegetables.

Food for Thought

Garbanzo beans are also known as chickpeas and can help control your blood sugar response to carbohydrates. Toast them for added crunch, or toss some into a salad for a boost in fiber. Their nutty taste is addicting!

Chocolate Cinnamon Yogurt Dip

Makes 6 servings
Prep time: 4 minutes
Cook time: none
Each serving has:
20.25 calories
1.88 g. protein
3.67 g. carbohydrate
0.08 g. total fat
0.05 g. saturated fat
0.83 mg. cholesterol
22.95 mg. sodium
0.28 g. fiber

1/8 tsp. ground cinnamon

1 TB. unsweetened chocolate powder

Hot water as needed

1 cup plain nonfat yogurt

1 tsp. sugar substitute, such as Splenda Granular

3 drops flavors2go honey

1. In a bowl, combine the cinnamon, chocolate powder, and hot water as needed to form a smooth paste.

2. Add yogurt and stir to mix. Add sugar substitute and honey flavoring. Chill and serve with fresh fruit pieces, such as strawberries, pineapple, kiwi, or apples.

Tiered Yogurt Cheese Spread

6 cups yogurt

2 cloves garlic, sliced

2 TB. fresh basil, chopped

1 TB. rosemary, chopped

1 TB. thyme, chopped

1 TB. sage, chopped

1 TB. shallot, minced

3 TB. olive oil

1 tsp. lemon zest

$^1/_2$ tsp. sea salt

$^1/_4$ tsp. pepper flakes

$^1/_2$ cup artichoke hearts, drained and finely diced

$^1/_2$ cup red bell pepper, finely diced

Makes 32 servings
Prep time: 30 minutes
Cook time: none
Each serving has:
43.28 calories
1.79 g. protein
3 g. carbohydrate
2.8 g. total fat
1.15 g. saturated fat
5.83 mg. cholesterol
59.88 mg. sodium
0.34 g. fiber

1. Drain yogurt overnight in the refrigerator in a colander lined with 4 layers of cheesecloth or in a yogurt strainer. Discard liquid, and spoon yogurt cheese into a medium-size bowl. Cover and refrigerate for 3 more hours.

2. Combine garlic, basil, rosemary, thyme, sage, shallot, olive oil, lemon zest, salt, and pepper flakes in a small bowl. Chop artichokes and red bell pepper, and combine in another bowl.

3. Place one quarter yogurt cheese into a glass container; then spread half herbal mixture on top. Repeat with another layer yogurt cheese; then place half artichoke and peppers mixture on top. Repeat with another layer cheese and herbal mixture, ending with a layer red bell peppers and artichokes on top. Cover and refrigerate for 12 hours or up to 1 week. Serve at room temperature with rye krisp crackers or vegetable sticks.

Food for Thought

You can purchase yogurt cheese in a container. It is often labeled Mediterranean yogurt cheese. Quark is another version of a soft cheese commercially available in some specialty stores. Like yogurt cheese, it can be substituted for cottage cheese, ricotta, or sour cream.

Bow Tie Pasta with Green Tomatoes

Makes 4 servings
Prep time: 10 minutes
Cook time: 35 minutes
Each serving has:
238 calories
12.48 g. protein
33.13 g. carbohydrate
7.77 g. total fat
1.15 g. saturated fat
5.22 mg. cholesterol
105.3 mg. sodium
4.82 g. fiber

Nonstick cooking spray, olive oil flavor

1 TB. olive oil

2 TB. Canadian Bacon, diced

1 cup onion, finely diced

2 cloves garlic, chopped

1 TB. fresh basil (stack leaves, roll them up like a cigar, cut crosswise into ribbons)

2 cups green tomatoes, sliced

2 TB. pine nuts

1½ cups canned, reduced-sodium chicken broth

¾ lb. whole-wheat bow tie pasta

1. Spray a cold medium skillet liberally with olive oil spray. Add olive oil and heat over low heat. Add diced *Canadian bacon*, onion, and garlic, and cook until onion becomes translucent, about 5 minutes. Add basil, green tomatoes, nuts, and broth, and cover. Simmer for 30 minutes or until tomatoes are soft.

2. Bring a large pot of water to boil, add pasta, and cook until tender. Drain but do not rinse pasta.

3. Toss pasta and sauce together in a large bowl, and serve immediately.

Nutri Notes _____

Canadian bacon is a very lean eye of loin pork, closer to ham than bacon. It is precooked and comes in cylindrical chunks.

Elbow Macaroni with Pork, Asparagus, and Mushrooms

2 TB. unsalted butter

$\frac{1}{2}$ lb. mushrooms, sliced

$\frac{1}{2}$ cup canned, low-salt chicken broth

2 TB. olive oil

$\frac{1}{2}$ cup onion, minced

3 cloves garlic, minced

$\frac{1}{3}$ lb. ground pork

$\frac{1}{2}$ lb. bite-size asparagus

$\frac{3}{4}$ lb. whole-wheat elbow macaroni

1 tsp. hot pepper flakes

3 TB. parsley, chopped

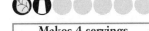

Makes 4 servings
Prep time: 5 minutes
Cook time: 20 minutes
Each serving has:
367 calories
15.59 g. protein
30.82 g. carbohydrate
21.89 g. total fat
7.63 g. saturated fat
43.03 mg. cholesterol
46.21 mg. sodium
5.12 g. fiber

1. Heat butter in a small skillet over medium heat, and add mushrooms. Cook until they release their water, about 5 minutes. Add $\frac{1}{4}$ cup chicken broth, and cook for 3 minutes. Set aside.

2. Heat oil in a medium skillet over medium heat, and add onion and garlic. Cook until translucent, about 5 minutes. Add pork and cook until brown, stirring to prevent scorching. Add remaining broth, and cook until absorbed by pork. Add asparagus pieces and mushrooms, cover, and turn off the heat. Allow to sit for about 10 minutes.

3. Bring a large pot of water to a boil, add macaroni, and boil over high heat until tender. Drain but do not rinse pasta; then put it in a large bowl. Add pork and asparagus mixture, toss, and serve with pepper flakes and parsley.

Fettuccine with Broccoli and Carrots

Makes 4 servings
Prep time: 5 minutes
Cook time: 12 minutes
Each serving has:
305 calories
11.85 g. protein
52.64 g. carbohydrate
5.81 g. total fat
0.8 g. saturated fat
62.09 mg. cholesterol
48.82 mg. sodium
2.45 g. fiber

1 TB. olive oil

2 cloves garlic, minced

1 TB. orange juice

1 tsp. orange zest

1 TB. balsamic vinegar

$^1/_2$ lb. broccoli, cut into small florets

$^1/_4$ cup carrots, finely sliced

$^3/_4$ lb. fresh fettuccine

$^1/_4$ cup parsley, coarsely chopped

1. Heat oil over medium heat in a small skillet. Add garlic, and cook until translucent, about 2 minutes. Stir in orange juice and zest and turn off the heat. Sprinkle with vinegar and set aside.

2. In a large pot, bring water to a boil, and add broccoli and carrots. Cook for about 5 minutes or until barely tender. Add fettuccine and cook until tender, about 4 minutes.

3. Drain but do not rinse pasta and vegetable mixture, and toss into a large bowl. Add garlic and orange mixture, and toss to mix. Serve with chopped parsley on top.

Variation: Cauliflower works equally well in this recipe as a substitute for broccoli. I even mix them together for a more colorful dish.

Linguine with Tomatoes and Pesto

4 cups plum tomato, chopped

½ lb. almonds

3 TB. olive oil

2 TB. fresh basil

2 cloves garlic

¾ pound Dreamfields linguine pasta

1. In a food processor, purée tomatoes, almonds, olive oil, basil, and garlic until blended.

2. Bring a large pot of water to a boil over high heat, and add pasta. Cook until tender. Drain but do not rinse pasta. Toss into a bowl.

3. Top with raw sauce, and mix thoroughly. Serve immediately.

Makes 4 servings
Prep time: 5 minutes
Cook time: 7 minutes
Each serving has:
745 calories
24.37 g. protein
83.76 g. carbohydrate
54.61 g. total fat
5.16 g. saturated fat
0 mg. cholesterol
15.01 mg. sodium
15.35 g. fiber

Food for Thought

The new carb-controlled pastas have insulin added to slow down the absorption of starch. Some people may find this causes gas problems. Always measure the pasta dry to prevent cooking more than the appropriate amount of servings.

Pasta with Fresh Spring Vegetables

Makes 4 servings
Prep time: 5 minutes
Cook time: 7 minutes
Each serving has:
549.8 calories
16.26 g. protein
95.37 g. carbohydrate
34.44 g. total fat
3.93 g. saturated fat
0 mg. cholesterol
16.68 mg. sodium
11.69 g. fiber

4 TB. olive oil

2 cloves garlic, finely chopped

4 cups fresh plum tomatoes, coarsely chopped

1 lb. asparagus spears, chopped into 2 inch pieces

1/2 pound zucchini, chopped into a medium dice

1 tsp. salt substitute, such as Morton's

1 lb. Dreamfields spaghetti pasta

4 TB. fresh basil, chopped

1 TB. parsley, chopped

1. Heat a 10-inch sauté pan on medium heat and add olive oil. Cook garlic, stirring frequently to prevent burning, until soft. Add tomatoes, asparagus, and zucchini to the pan. Continue to cook, stirring occasionally, until soft but not limp, about 5 minutes. Season to taste with salt substitute.

2. Bring a large pot of water to a boil over high heat. Add spaghetti, and cook until tender. Drain but do not rinse pasta, and toss into a serving bowl.

3. Add the vegetables, mix, and serve immediately, sprinkled with basil and parsley.

Variation: You can dot the hot pasta with some ricotta cheese for added flavor and texture. It will melt right in, adding a creaminess to the raw sauce.

Penne with Beef and Onions

Nonstick cooking spray, olive oil flavor

2 lb. white onions, thinly sliced

1¹/₂ cups canned, reduced-salt beef broth

1 TB. fresh marjoram, chopped

³/₄ lb. 15% fat ground beef

Salt substitute such as Morton's, black pepper to taste

¹/₂ lb. whole-wheat penne pasta

¹/₄ cup parsley, chopped

Makes 4 servings
Prep time: 5 minutes
Cook time: 1 hour
Each serving has:
317.3 calories
24.03 g. protein
35.88 g. carbohydrate
9.54 g. total fat
3.43 g. saturated fat
55.26 mg. cholesterol
242.8 mg. sodium
6.27 g. fiber

1. Spray a cold, deep nonstick pan with olive oil spray; then heat over medium heat. Add onion, reduce the heat to low and cook, covered, for about 30 minutes, stirring occasionally, or until the onions are brown and soft or caramelized.

2. Add broth; cover and cook for another 30 minutes until thick. Add marjoram.

3. Spray another cold pan with olive oil spray, and add ground beef. Brown over medium heat. Add to onion mixture. Adjust seasoning with salt substitute and black pepper as needed.

4. Bring a large pot of water to a boil, and add pasta. Cook until tender. Drain but do not rinse pasta. Add it to onion mixture, toss to combine, and add parsley. Serve immediately.

Nutri Notes _____

To caramelize vegetables, you need those with a high sugar content, such as onions. The trick is to leave them alone in the pan so the heat draws out the natural sugars and turns the onions a dark, golden brown. This enhances the sweet flavor of the onion.

Penne with Shrimp, Asparagus, and Walnuts

Makes 4 servings
Prep time: 5 minutes
Cook time: 20 minutes
Each serving has:
567.7 calories
66.39 g. protein
43.63 g. carbohydrate
21.55 g. total fat
2.5 g. saturated fat
129.3 mg. cholesterol
345.6 mg. sodium
17.35 g. fiber

4 TB. olive oil

1 lb. asparagus

2 cloves garlic, chopped

2 cups canned Italian tomatoes, chopped

1 TB. fresh mint leaves, chopped

1 tsp. hot pepper flakes

³/₄ lb. frozen or fresh, peeled shrimp (medium-size, 24 count per pound)

³/₄ lb. soy penne pasta

1/₄ cup walnuts

1. Heat 2 tablespoons olive oil in a large skillet over medium heat. Cut asparagus into 1¹/₂-inch lengths, discarding tough, fibrous ends. Add asparagus to the pan, and cook until tender. Remove it from the heat with a slotted spoon and keep warm on a plate, loosely tented with foil or place a bowl over top to cover.

2. Add remaining olive oil to the pan and heat over low heat. Add garlic, and sauté for 3 minutes or until soft, stirring often to avoid burning. Add tomatoes, mint, and hot pepper flakes to taste. Cover and cook for 10 minutes over low heat or until tomatoes break up. Add shrimp to mixture and simmer for 5 minutes or until just pink.

3. In a large pot, bring water to boil over high heat. Add pasta, and cook until al dente. Drain but do not rinse pasta, and add it to sauce in the skillet. Add asparagus, and mix together.

Nutri Notes

Walnuts are an excellent source of omega-3 fatty acids, a protective fat your body cannot manufacture. They also contain ellagic acid, which has several anti-cancer properties. Walnuts easily become rancid, so boil them in water for a few minutes, and then dry or toast in the oven for 5 minutes. They will keep in the refrigerator in a plastic bag for 6 months.

Penne with Peas and Chicken

3 TB. olive oil

2 medium onions, finely chopped

2 cups canned tomatoes

1 cup frozen peas

2 cups canned chicken

³/₄ lb. whole-wheat penne pasta

2 TB. Italian parsley, finely chopped

Makes 4 servings
Prep time: 5 minutes
Cook time: 10 minutes
Each serving has:
500.1 calories
18.72 g. protein
87.83 g. carbohydrate
12.63 g. total fat
1.46 g. saturated fat
0 mg. cholesterol
252.6 mg. sodium
8.09 g. fiber

1. Heat oil in a large skillet over medium heat. Add onions and cook until soft and translucent. Add tomatoes, cover, and simmer over low heat until tomatoes break up. Add peas and chicken, cover, and simmer for 5 minutes.

2. Bring a large pot of water to boil over high heat, and add penne pasta. Cook until tender. Drain pasta (do not rinse) and toss into sauce. Add parsley and serve.

Variation: This recipe works equally well with tuna, turkey, or shrimp.

Rigatoni with Cabbage

4 TB. olive oil

1 cup onion, thinly sliced

1¹/₂ lb. savoy cabbage, shredded

³/₄ lb. soy rigatoni pasta

¹/₂ tsp. black pepper

Makes 4 servings
Prep time: 5 minutes
Cook time: 20 minutes
Each serving has:
427.5 calories
46.57 g. protein
42.2 g. carbohydrate
15.3 g. total fat
1.87 g. saturated fat
0 mg. cholesterol
110.3 mg. sodium
18.57 g. fiber

1. Heat olive oil in a large skillet over medium heat. Add onion and cook until translucent.

2. Add cabbage, reduce the heat and cover, continuing to cook for about 15 minutes or until cabbage is just tender.

3. Bring a large pot of water to a boil; then cook pasta until tender. Reserve 1 cup cooking liquid before draining pasta.

4. Add ¹/₄ cup pasta liquid to cabbage mixture as needed to moisturize; then add to pasta in a bowl. Top with freshly cracked pepper.

Rigatoni with Cauliflower and Turkey

Makes 4 servings
Prep time: 5 minutes
Cook time: 45 minutes
Each serving has:
544.8 calories
30.13 g. protein
83.88 g. carbohydrate
14.37 g. total fat
2.46 g. saturated fat
45.23 mg. cholesterol
155.3 mg. sodium
7.99 g. fiber

6 tsp. olive oil

1 cup onion, finely diced

4 cloves garlic, minced

1/2 lb. ground turkey

3/4 cup canned, reduced-sodium chicken broth

4 oz. Portobello mushrooms coarsely chopped

2 TB. parsley, chopped

2 TB. fresh basil, chopped

3/4 lb. whole-wheat rigatoni

2 lb. cauliflower florets

1. Heat oil in a large skillet over medium heat. Add onions and garlic, and cook until translucent, about 5 minutes, stirring often to prevent burning. Add turkey and cook until brown, about 10 minutes.

2. Add broth, mushrooms, parsley, and basil, and cook over low heat for about 30 minutes or until sauce becomes thick.

3. Bring a large pot of water to a boil, and add *rigatoni*. Cook for 5 minutes, add cauliflower, and continue boiling for another 5 minutes. Drain pasta and cauliflower, but do not rinse.

4. Toss sauce with pasta and cauliflower in a large bowl, and serve immediately.

Variation: Substitute lean ground beef, lamb, goat, or buffalo for the turkey. Honest! Each meat will give the dish a special exotic twist.

Nutri Speak

Rigatoni is Italian for "large groove." Pasta made in a rigatoni style has ridges, so it can grab onto sauce better than a smooth noodle.

Spaghetti with Clams and Mussels

4 TB. olive oil

4 cloves garlic, sliced

1 TB. fresh basil (stack leaves, roll them up like a cigar, cut crosswise into ribbons)

1 TB. fresh oregano

1¹/₂ cups fish stock

1 lb. fresh mussels

1 cup water (or more as needed)

³/₄ pound Dreamfields spaghetti pasta

³/₄ cup canned clams drained

Makes 4 servings
Prep time: 4 minutes
Cook time: 10 minutes
Each serving has:
557.3 calories
31.08 g. protein
71.12 g. carbohydrate
32.11 g. total fat
4.04 g. saturated fat
43.88 mg. cholesterol
671.1 mg. sodium
7.08 g. fiber

1. In a large, shallow pan, add olive oil, garlic, basil, and oregano, and cook over medium heat until garlic is translucent, stirring often to prevent burning.

2. Add fish stock and mussels and cover. Raise the heat to high for about 5 minutes or until mussels open. Remove mussels from the pan. Discard any mussels that have not opened.

3. After adding additional water as needed, bring to a boil, then add the spaghetti, and turn down the heat to a low boil. Stir pasta often as it cooks until just tender. Add clams and mussels to the pan, and toss before serving.

Smoke Signals

Always check that your mussels are fresh by tapping the shells to see if they close. As an extra precaution, put them in the freezer for no more than 5 minutes. If any are still open, discard them immediately. Live mussels will contract their shells to protect themselves against the cold. Mussels that are not fresh can carry salmonella and neurotoxic poisons.

Spaghettini with Shrimp

Makes 4 servings
Prep time: 4 minutes
Cook time: 10 minutes
Each serving has:
478.4 calories
79.33 g. protein
21.93 g. carbohydrate
10.64 g. total fat
2.42 g. saturated fat
349.3 mg. cholesterol
405.7 mg. sodium
8.27 g. fiber

1 TB. olive oil

3 cloves garlic, minced

2 lb. raw, peeled shrimp (medium-size, 24 count per pound)

1 cup canned, reduced-sodium chicken broth

1/2 lb. soy spaghettini

1 tsp. hot pepper flakes

1/4 cup reduced-sodium Parmesan cheese, grated

1. In a skillet, heat olive oil over medium heat, and add garlic. Cook until tender and translucent.

2. Add shrimp, and cook for about 3 minutes or until just pink. Add broth, bring to a gentle simmer, cover, and then turn off the heat.

3. In a large pot, bring water to a boil, and add pasta. Cook until tender. Drain but do not rinse pasta. Pour into a bowl, and add shrimp with broth; stir, mixing well. Sprinkle with pepper flakes and parmesan, and serve immediately.

Food for Thought

Spaghettini is the same as angel hair pasta. It is very thin and cooks almost immediately. It is also ideal to simply break into small segments and put on top of a hot, simmering sauce without precooking. The moisture from a sauce will cook it al dente.

Spaghettini with Tilapia and Zucchini

2 TB. olive oil

4 cloves garlic, coarsely chopped

1 lb. zucchini, coarsely chopped

¹/₂ cup canned, reduced-sodium chicken broth

1 TB. parsley, chopped

1 TB. fresh basil (stack leaves, roll them up like a cigar, cut crosswise into ribbons)

1 tsp. hot pepper flakes

³/₄ lb. whole-wheat spaghettini

¹/₂ lb. tilapia fish fillets

Makes 4 servings
Prep time: 5 minutes
Cook time: 15 minutes
Each serving has:
466.6 calories
26.08 g. protein
69.63 g. carbohydrate
8.87 g. total fat
1.28 g. saturated fat
28.29 mg. cholesterol
55.03 mg. sodium
4.38 g. fiber

1. Heat olive oil in a deep saucepan, and add garlic. Cook until softened, stirring often to prevent burning, about 2 minutes. Add zucchini, broth, parsley, basil, and pepper flakes, and simmer, covered, over moderate heat for about 10 minutes.

2. Break pasta up into small pieces, and mix into sauce. Place fish on top and cover. Turn off the heat. Check in 5 minutes for flaky fish. If pasta has not cooked enough, remove fish, and stir sauce over low heat for a few minutes more.

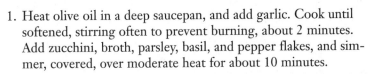

Lemon Pecan Wild Rice

2 cups wild rice

1 TB. lemon zest

1 cup canned, low-salt chicken broth

¹/₂ cup pecan pieces

Makes 6 servings
Prep time: 5 minutes
Cook time: 30 minutes
Each serving has:
271.6 calories
10.53 g. protein
41.78 g. carbohydrate
8.13 g. total fat
0.82 g. saturated fat
0.39 mg. cholesterol
21.01 mg. sodium
4.36 g. fiber

1. In a rice cooker, add rice, lemon zest, chicken broth, and pecan nuts. Cover and set the cooker. Rice should be done in about 30 minutes. Allow to rest for 5 minutes, and fluff before serving.

Food for Thought

This is one of the first dishes I ever tasted with wild rice, and I've made it for years. The nuts enhance the flavor of the natural grass rice, which has additional crunch if it's not overcooked.

Spinach Linguine with Crab

Makes 4 servings
Prep time: 5 minutes
Cook time: 10 minutes
Each serving has:
412.5 calories
19.77 g. protein
64.61 g. carbohydrate
9.65 g. total fat
1.5 g. saturated fat
89.88 mg. cholesterol
368.6 mg. sodium
4.83 g. fiber

2 TB. olive oil

1 cup red bell pepper, minced

3 cloves garlic, minced

1 tsp. hot pepper flakes

3 cups canned tomatoes, chopped

4 TB. parsley, chopped

1 tsp. fresh basil (stack leaves, roll them up like a cigar, cut crosswise into ribbons)

1 can (6^1/$_2$ oz.) crab

^{3}/$_4$ lb. fresh spinach linguine

1. Heat oil in a large skillet over medium heat. Add red bell pepper, garlic, and pepper flakes, and cook until garlic is soft, stirring often to prevent burning, about 4 minutes. Add tomatoes, parsley, basil, and crab. Cover and bring to a boil; simmer for 15 minutes or until tomatoes break down.

2. Bring a large pot of water to a boil, and add spinach pasta. Cook until tender, about 5 minutes. Drain but do not rinse pasta, and add to sauce in a large bowl. Toss and serve immediately.

Food for Thought _____

Spinach linguine makes a great, colorful pasta dish that you can serve in small quantities. Since it is fresh, it will cook quickly. Watch for the noodles to float to the top, then test immediately for doneness.

Pasha's Tabouli

3 cups water

1½ cup bulgur

1 TB. lemon juice

1 cup fresh parsley, finely chopped

15 oz. canned chickpeas

1 TB. olive oil

¼ cup fresh mint leaves, finely chopped

½ cup tomatoes, diced

½ cup green onions, finely chopped

Makes 6 servings
Prep time: 5 minutes
Cook time: 10 minutes
Each serving has:
240 calories
8.9 g. protein
45.8 g. carbohydrate
3.83 g. total fat
0.5 g. saturated fat
0 mg. cholesterol
240 mg. sodium
11.04 g. fiber

1. Bring water to a boil, pour over the bulgar and let sit for 20 minutes, cool, and refrigerate.

2. In a large bowl, combine bulgur, lemon juice, parsley, chickpeas, olive oil, mint, tomatoes, and green onions. Mix well. Refrigerate until ready to serve.

Food for Thought

I never liked this dish until I ate it in Turkey. The secret? Always use the best tomatoes, fresh lemon juice, and fresh mint leaves. It keeps well in the refrigerator and makes a great high-fiber side dish with a high fullness factor as well.

Rice with Fennel and Ricotta

Makes 4 servings
Prep time: 5 minutes
Cook time: 35 minutes
Each serving has:
367.6 calories
19.63 g. protein
44.1 g. carbohydrate
12.35 g. total fat
7.21 g. saturated fat
40.26 mg. cholesterol
164.1 mg. sodium
2.42 g. fiber

2 cups water

1 cup fennel, cored and thinly sliced

1 cup brown rice, uncooked

1 lb. ricotta cheese

1 TB. parsley, chopped

$^1/_4$ tsp. nutmeg

$^1/_3$ cup Parmesan

1. Bring water to a boil on high heat in a medium pot. Add fennel slices and boil for about 10 minutes or until tender. Remove fennel from water with a slotted spoon and reserve water.

2. Add rice to fennel water. Bring to a boil over medium-high heat, cover, reduce the heat to low, and simmer until all liquid is absorbed, about 15 minutes.

3. Heat the broiler.

4. In a bowl, combine fennel, rice, ricotta, parsley, and nutmeg. Pour into a 9-inch ovenproof dish. Sprinkle Parmesan cheese on top, and place rice under the broiler for about 5 minutes or until cheese melts.

Rice with Shrimp

1 TB. olive oil

1 cup onion, finely chopped

4 cloves garlic, finely chopped

2 cups canned, reduced-sodium chicken broth

1 cup brown rice, uncooked

1 TB. olive oil

½ lb. asparagus, 1-inch lengths

¾ cup green onions, finely chopped

½ lb. raw, peeled shrimp (medium-size, 24 count per pound)

3 TB. mint leaves (stack leaves, roll them up like a cigar, cut crosswise into ribbons)

2 TB. fresh lemon juice

Makes 4 servings
Prep time: 4 minutes
Cook time: 45 minutes
Each serving has:
368.8 calories
22.71 g. protein
46.39 g. carbohydrate
10.49 g. total fat
1.77 g. saturated fat
87.35 mg. cholesterol
144.2 mg. sodium
4.25 g. fiber

1. Heat 1 tablespoon olive oil in a medium pan over medium heat, and add onion and 2 cloves garlic. Cook until translucent, stirring often to prevent burning, about 5 minutes.

2. Add broth and rice, cover, and bring to a boil. Reduce the heat to simmer, and cook for about 30 minutes or until rice has absorbed all liquid. Turn off the heat but keep rice covered for about 15 minutes. Alternatively, you can use a rice cooker for this entire step, adding garlic and onion mixture to the cooker when they are translucent.

3. In a medium skillet, heat remaining olive oil over medium heat and add asparagus pieces. Cover and cook for about 5 minutes; then add remaining cloves of garlic and onions, and cook until tender. Add shrimp, 1 TB mint, and lemon juice, and cook until shrimp turn pink, about 2 minutes.

4. To serve, put rice in individual bowls, top with shrimp mixture, and sprinkle remaining mint leaves on top.

Variation: Take out the mint, green onions, and asparagus, and use green bell peppers, red onion slices, and a favorite Cajun spice mix for a New Orleans touch. You can even add hot sausage to the mix for more BAM!

Food for Thought

This dish reheats well in the microwave on defrost for 5 minutes. You can add a small amount of tomato juice to it when reheating to improve the moisture content.

Risotto with Mushrooms and Sea Scallops

Makes 4 servings
Prep time: 5 minutes
Cook time: 20 minutes
Each serving has:
294.2 calories
16.42 g. protein
47.12 g. carbohydrate
5.08 g. total fat
0.68 g. saturated fat
19.15 mg. cholesterol
115.4 mg. sodium
2.61 g. fiber

Nutri Speak

Arborio rice is an Italian short grain rice which releases starch as it cooks. This makes the rice very creamy. It is traditionally used in the making of risotto.

1 TB. olive oil

1 cup onion, chopped

³/₄ cup canned, reduced-sodium chicken broth

1 cup *arborio rice*

1 tsp. fresh thyme

1 cup white mushrooms, chopped

¹/₂ lb. scallops

1. In a tall pot, heat olive oil over moderate heat, and add onion. Cook until soft and translucent, about 5 minutes.

2. Heat broth in a separate pan. Add rice to the pan. Add ¹/₄ cup hot broth to the pan with onion and rice. Allow to simmer until rice has absorbed about half the broth, stirring occasionally.

3. In a skillet over medium heat, add mushrooms, thyme, and ¹/₄ cup broth. Cook until mushrooms are just soft. Remove from the pan.

4. In the same skillet, add scallops and quickly sauté until just turning lightly brown. Do not overcook or scallops will be tough and dry.

5. Add remaining broth to rice, and stir until it is all absorbed. When rice is tender and no more liquid can be absorbed, about 15 minutes, remove to serving plates. Top with scallops and serve.

St. Patrick's Day Rice

2 TB. olive oil

2 cups leeks, finely chopped

2 cups canned, reduced-sodium chicken broth

2 medium carrots, finely chopped

1 TB. fresh parsley, chopped

¹/₂ cup basmati rice, uncooked

¹/₂ lb. spinach leaf

Makes 4 servings
Prep time: 5 minutes
Cook time: 30 minutes
Each serving has:
248.4 calories
9.89 g. protein
35.44 g. carbohydrate
8.4 g. total fat
1.34 g. saturated fat
1.16 mg. cholesterol
117.5 mg. sodium
3.35 g. fiber

1. In a medium skillet, heat olive oil over medium heat. Add leeks, cover, and cook until soft, stirring occasionally, about 5 minutes. Add 1 cup broth, carrots, and parsley. Cover and cook over low heat for about 20 minutes or until soft.

2. In a rice cooker, add remaining broth, rice, spinach, carrots, leeks, and parsley mixture, and cook until tender.

3. Blend together before serving.

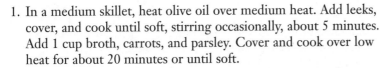

Wild Rice with Tangerine and Pine Nuts

Makes 6 servings

Prep time: 4 minutes

Cook time: 30 minutes

Each serving has:

262.8 calories

5.29 g. protein

47.62 g. carbohydrate

5.56 g. total fat

0.96 g. saturated fat

0 mg. cholesterol

2.12 mg. sodium

3.43 g. fiber

1½ cup brown rice, uncooked

½ cup brown basmati rice uncooked

2½ cups water

¼ cup tangerine juice

1 TB. tangerine zest

2 TB. pine nuts

1 TB. olive oil

2 TB. rice wine vinegar

1. Combine brown rice and basmati rice in a pressure cooker with water. Seal and bring to full pressure. Reduce heat and cook for 20 minutes.

2. In a small saucepan, heat tangerine juice and zest just to warm.

3. In a small pan, toast pine nuts on top of the stove over medium heat until fragrant.

4. When rice is cooked, remove the pan from the heat and allow the pressure to reduce. Open the lid and stir in tangerine zest, juice, olive oil, and vinegar. Add pine nuts just before serving.

Variation: You can substitute orange juice and zest if tangerines are not available. Tangerines have less acidity, which goes nicely with the milder rice wine vinegar.

Chapter 17

Devilish Delight

In This Chapter

- ◆ Natural sugars
- ◆ Chocolate dreams
- ◆ Eat your cake

If you think cooking with total nutrition in mind means eliminating desserts, think again. Sugars naturally abound in fresh fruit and vegetables, and are often combined with blood sugar–controlling fiber. Dazzling colors and aromas that bring back childhood memories all contribute to learning to eat with your senses before your mouth. So dig right into these recipes, and share the pleasure of a sinfully delicious, healthy dessert.

Chocolate was never a bad food as nature designed it. It's rich in fiber when added as a powder and contains flavanoids which can protect you from a heart attack by lowering your blood pressure. You can make any dessert a chocolate one by simply adding unsweetened cocoa powder and a heat-tolerant sugar substitute without adding tons of calories. So play around with your favorite recipes using the tips you'll find in this chapter.

Eating cake can be healthy on a diet if you keep in mind the tips I'm going to share with you. You can substitute at least one third of any flour with whole-wheat flour without noticing a flavor or texture difference.

Don't forget the value of using cannellini beans for half the weight of butter, and you'll not only cut the calories but also slow down the rise in your blood sugar response when indulging in a sweet treat. So feel the joy here, and keep healthful cookies, candy, fruit, and cake desserts in your total nutrition cooking repertoire.

> **Food for Thought** _____
>
> Many of the recipes in this chapter call for "powdered sugar substitute, made with Splenda Granular." It's easy to make your own powdered sugar substitute. Simply put ³/₄ cup Splenda Granular (this is not the type blended with sugar) in a blender with 2 tablespoons of cornstarch. Blend until it turns into a fine powder.

Bugs's Carrot Cake

Makes 12 servings
Prep time: 10 minutes
Cook time: 45 minutes
Each serving has:
322.5 calories
5.6 g. protein
53.07 g. carbohydrate
7.43 g. total fat
0.82 g. saturated fat
17.81 mg. cholesterol
140.7 mg. sodium
3.01 g. fiber

Nonstick cooking spray, butter and flour flavor

1¹/₂ cups flour

¹/₂ cup whole-wheat flour

¹/₄ tsp. baking soda

2 tsp. baking powder

1 tsp. salt substitute, such as Morton's

2 tsp. ground cinnamon

1³/₄ cups sugar substitute, such as Splenda White Sugar Blend

1 cup applesauce

1 large egg

2 large egg whites

1 tsp. vanilla extract

2 cups carrots, shredded

1 cup walnuts, chopped

1 can (8 oz.) pineapple, drained

¹/₄ cup fat-free yogurt

1. Preheat oven to 375°F. Spray a 9×13-inch cake pan with butter and flour cooking spray.

2. In a mixing bowl, add flours, baking soda, baking powder, salt, and cinnamon, and make a well in the center. Add sugar substitute, applesauce, eggs, and vanilla extract. Mix with a wooden spoon until blended.

3. Stir in carrots, walnuts, pineapple, and yogurt and mix well. Pour into the cake pan and bake for 45 minutes. Place cake on a rack to cook.

4. Allow to cool; then ice with Pumpkin Honey Cream Cheese icing (see next recipe).

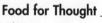

Food for Thought

This is a very easy cake to make and cut into perfect portion-controlled pieces. It easily makes 16 servings instead of 12 if you want to cut the calories down even further.

Pumpkin Honey Cheese Frosting

1 lb. nonfat cream cheese

2 cups powdered sugar substitute, made with Splenda Granular

$\frac{1}{2}$ cup pumpkin puree

$\frac{1}{4}$ cup honey

$\frac{1}{8}$ tsp. allspice

2 TB. cold water

1 tsp. gelatin

5 oz. very cold evaporated nonfat milk

2 TB. sugar substitute, such as Splenda White Sugar Blend

Makes 16 servings
Prep time: 15 minutes
Cook time: none
Each serving has:
58.3 calories
4.31 g. protein
8.39 g. carbohydrate
0.39 g. total fat
0.24 g. saturated fat
2.32 mg. cholesterol
147.1 mg. sodium
0.21 g. fiber

1. On medium speed in a mixer, beat cream cheese, sugar, pumpkin, honey, and allspice until fluffy.

2. Into a separate bowl, put cold water and gelatin, but do not stir. Allow gelatin to bloom or soak up water. You can also place this bowl into another bowl with hot water to help with this process.

3. In a medium bowl, beat cold milk until stiff peaks form; then add sugar and gelatin. Continue beating until stiff peaks form. Set in the freezer for 10 minutes.

4. Fold whipped cream mixture into pumpkin mixture in 2 batches. Refrigerate any unused portions. This will keep 3 days covered.

Variation: Honey comes in many flavors, and each will alter the taste of this recipe. I prefer orange clover honey against the pumpkin purée, but feel free to use your favorite flavor.

Heavenly Chocolate Cake

Makes 18 servings
Prep time: 18 minutes
Cook time: 35 minutes
Each serving has:
22.53 calories
4.25 g. protein
34.73 g. carbohydrate
4.72 g. total fat
2.52 g. saturated fat
10.48 mg. cholesterol
80.29 mg. sodium
1.24 g. fiber

Food for Thought

Baking requires a certain amount of real sugar to result in an acceptable crumb or texture. The new half mixtures of sugar substitute and real sugar give us the best of both worlds. Be sure to select a brand labeled for baking, as some sugar substitutes break down under heating.

Nonstick cooking spray, butter and flour flavor

2 cups sugar substitute, such as Splenda White Sugar Blend

$^1/_4$ cup butter

$^1/_4$ cup canned cannellini beans, drained and mashed

$^3/_4$ cup egg substitute

2 cups flour

$^1/_2$ cup cocoa powder

$^3/_4$ tsp. baking soda

$^1/_4$ tsp. salt substitute, such as Morton's

$^3/_4$ cup reduced-fat sour cream

$^3/_4$ cup boiling water

1 tsp. vanilla extract

1. Preheat oven to 350°F. Spray the bottoms only of two 8-inch round cake pans. Place a circle of wax paper on top, then spray with butter and flour cooking spray.

2. In a mixer, beat sugar substitute, butter, and beans at medium speed until well blended. Gradually add egg substitute and beat well.

3. In a bowl, combine flour, cocoa, baking soda, and salt, stirring well with a whisk. Add flour mixture to sugar mixture alternating with sour cream, ending with flour mixture. Stir in boiling water and extract.

4. Pour mixture into the prepared cake pans, dividing evenly. Sharply tap pans on the counter to remove air bubbles. Bake at 350° for 35 minutes or until cake springs back or a toothpick comes out clean. Loosen the edges with a narrow spatula. Place a wire rack inverted over top and turn out cake layers. Remove wax paper and cool.

5. To frost, place 1 cake layer on a plate. Spread $^1/_2$ cup Double Chocolate Cream Cheese Frosting (see next recipe) and top with remaining cake layer. Spread remaining frosting over top and sides of cake. Store loosely covered in the refrigerator.

Double Chocolate Cream Cheese Frosting

¹/₂ cup fat-free cream cheese, softened

3 TB. nonfat milk

1 TB. nonfat dry milk

3 oz. chocolate chips, melted

3 cups powdered sugar substitute, made with Splenda Granular

¹/₄ cup cocoa powder

1 tsp. vanilla extract

1. Beat softened cream cheese, milk, and dry milk at high speed until smooth.

2. Melt chocolate chips in microwave-proof cup on high for 1 minute, and stir. Heat for 10 second intervals until melted. Add melted chocolate; then add powdered sugar substitute, cocoa powder, and extract. Mix well.

Variation: Simply omit cocoa powder and chocolate chips to make this a vanilla cream cheese frosting. Increase nonfat milk to 6 tablespoons for a creamier texture.

Makes 18 servings
Prep time: 4 minutes
Cook time: 1 minute
Each serving has:
44.49 calories
1.61 g. protein
6.06 g. carbohydrate
1.45 g. total fat
0.87 g. saturated fat
0.76 mg. cholesterol
39.18 mg. sodium
0.66 g. fiber

Smoke Signals

It's easy to burn chocolate chips in the microwave because they don't "melt" down but retain much of their shape when heated. The key is to stir the mixture after 1 minute, then add additional 10-second cooking times as needed, stirring after each interval.

Devil's Own Angel Food Cake

Makes 10 servings
Prep time: 10 minutes
Cook time: 30 minutes
Each serving has:
172.7 calories
7.06 g. protein
43.64 g. carbohydrate
0.19 g. total fat
0 g. saturated fat
0 mg. cholesterol
81.17 mg. sodium
0.46 g. fiber

1 cup cake flour

1¼ cups sugar substitute, such as Splenda White Sugar Blend

½ tsp. salt substitute, such as Morton's

1 tsp. black peppercorns, finely fresh-crushed

2 cups egg whites

1½ tsp. cream of tartar

2 tsp. vanilla extract

1 tsp. red food coloring

1. Sift together flour, ¾ cup sugar substitute, and salt. Stir in peppercorns.

2. Beat egg whites until foamy. Beat in cream of tartar. Gradually add remaining ½ cup of sugar substitute, beating only until soft peaks form. Beat in vanilla extract, and tint with red food coloring to desired color.

3. Sprinkle ½ of flour mixture over egg whites, and whisk on low speed until just mixed. Repeat with remaining flour. Spoon into an ungreased 10-inch angel food tube cake pan and spread evenly. Remove air pockets by gently moving a spatula up and down in a circle around the center of batter.

4. Bake at 325°F for 30 minutes or until a toothpick inserted in center comes out clean. Top should be golden.

5. Invert pan or hang tube over a bottle and allow to cool completely. Loosen sides with a knife, and turn cake out onto a serving platter.

Nutri Notes

Angel food cakes require their own special pan, which was invented in the late 1800s. The first tube pans were square rather than round, with the central tube allowing for a quicker bake time. Unlike other cakes, angel food cakes are inverted to keep their volume and height. I use a wine bottle, but many pans have extension tabs to allow you to invert the pan directly onto a counter to cool.

Hansel and Gretel Gingerbread

¹/₂ cup sugar substitute, such as Splenda Brown Sugar Blend

¹/₄ cup butter

¹/₂ cup molasses

2 cups flour

1¹/₂ cups whole-wheat flour

2 tsp. ground ginger

1 tsp. baking soda

¹/₂ tsp. ground cinnamon

¹/₂ tsp. salt substitute, such as Morton's

¹/₄ tsp. ground cloves

¹/₃ cup water

Nonstick cooking spray, butter flavor

Makes 16 servings
Prep time: 10 minutes
Cook time: 20 minutes
Each serving has:
178.7 calories
3.21 g. protein
33.36 g. carbohydrate
3.27 g. total fat
1.86 g. saturated fat
7.76 mg. cholesterol
84.24 mg. sodium
1.86 g. fiber

1. Preheat oven to 350°F.

2. In the large bowl of an electric mixer, on medium speed, beat sugar and butter until well blended. Add molasses and beat until creamy.

3. In another bowl, combine flours, ginger, baking soda, cinnamon, salt, cloves, and water.

4. Add ¹/₃ flour mixture to butter mixture, and beat on low speed until incorporated. Repeat until all flour is blended in. Gather mixture into a ball.

5. Spray the bottoms of two 8- or 9-inch pie pans with butter cooking spray. Divide dough in half, and press into each pan. With a lightly floured knife, cut into 8 wedges each.

6. Bake until top springs back, about 20 minutes. Let cool for 5 minutes in pan; then invert onto a rack to cool completely.

Canadian Maple Frosting

Makes 18 servings
Prep time: 3 minutes
Cook time: none
Each serving has:
24.14 calories
0.01 g. protein
3.19 g. carbohydrate
1.29 g. total fat
0.8 g. saturated fat
3.45 mg. cholesterol
0.54 mg. sodium
0 g. fiber

3 TB. maple syrup

2 TB. butter

$1/2$ tsp. vanilla extract

$1/2$ tsp. maple extract

$1/8$ tsp. salt substitute, such as Morton's

$1^3/4$ cup powdered sugar substitute, made with Splenda Granular

1. Beat maple syrup, butter, vanilla, and maple extract together in a mixer on medium. Gradually add sugar substitute and mix until just blended.

Caramel Nut Frosting

Makes 36 servings
Prep time: 4 minutes
Cook time: 10 minutes
Each serving has:
36.46 calories
0.29 g. protein
3.65 g. carbohydrate
1.88 g. total fat
0.85 g. saturated fat
3.55 mg. cholesterol
3.26 mg. sodium
0.08 g. fiber

$1/4$ cup butter

$1/2$ cup brown sugar substitute, such as Splenda Brown Sugar Blend

6 TB. fat-free evaporated milk

2 tsp. vanilla extract

3 cups powdered sugar substitute, made with Splenda Granular

$1/4$ cup pecan pieces

1. Melt butter in a saucepan over medium heat. Add brown sugar and cook for 3 minutes, whisking constantly. Add milk 1 tablespoon at a time, stirring constantly. Cook for 3 minutes or until slightly thickened. Cool. Stir in vanilla.

2. Combine butter mixture with powdered sugar on high speed in a mixer until well blended and smooth. Fold in nuts.

Chocolate Glaze

2 cups powdered sugar substitute, made with Splenda
Granular

6 TB. cocoa powder

¹/₄ cup nonfat milk

2 TB. butter

1 tsp. vanilla extract

Makes 18 servings
Prep time: 3 minutes
Cook time: 1 minute
Each serving has:
24.54 calories
0.56 g. protein
2.24 g. carbohydrate
1.45 g. total fat
0.9 g. saturated fat
3.51 mg. cholesterol
2.83 mg. sodium
0.52 g. fiber

1. Combine sugar substitute and cocoa in a medium bowl.

2. In a microwave measuring cup, combine milk and butter.
   Microwave on high 1 minute.

3. Add milk mixture and vanilla to sugar mixture, and stir with a
   whisk until blended.

Food for Thought

Nonfat milk has been linked with a decreased risk of colon
cancer. All milks have similar nutrient content with the exception of fat and calories.

Peach White Tea Icing

Makes 18 servings
Prep time: 5 minutes
Cook time: none
Each serving has:
28.64 calories
1.04 g. protein
2.1 g. carbohydrate
1.75 g. total fat
1.13 g. saturated fat
5.58 mg. cholesterol
29.78 mg. sodium
0 g. fiber

2 bags white peach white tea

¹/₂ cup boiling water

³/₄ cup reduced-fat cream cheese

2¹/₂ cups powdered sugar substitute, made with Splenda Granular

2 drops Flavors2Go Peach

1. Pour boiling water over tea bags and steep for several minutes.

2. Place cream cheese in a large bowl, and beat with a mixer at medium speed until fluffy. Gradually add powdered sugar to cream cheese mixture, and add 3 tablespoons of white peach tea brew to cream cheese. Beat until smooth.

3. Enhance peach flavor with drops of Flavors2Go.

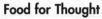

Food for Thought _____

This is a very delicately flavored icing. You can use any white tea flavor for a variation, and simply match up the appropriate Flavors2Go product to increase the aroma without the calories (see www.flavor2go.com).

Puckery Lemon Buttercream Frosting

¹/₂ cup butter

1 lb. powdered sugar substitute, made with Splenda Granular

¹/₂ tsp. lemon zest

3 TB. fresh lemon juice

1 TB. 2% milk

¹/₄ tsp. salt substitute, such as Morton's

Makes 6 servings
Prep time: 5 minutes
Cook time: none
Each serving has:
157.9 calories
0.29 g. protein
5.56 g. carbohydrate
15.39 g. total fat
9.58 g. saturated fat
41.61 mg. cholesterol
4.05 mg. sodium
0.05 g. fiber

1. In a mixer, beat butter until smooth. Then add sugar, lemon zest, juice, milk, and salt.

2. Continue beating until smooth.

Food for Thought

This recipe is not one I would recommend using a fat-free butter substitute in, as it really depends on a mouth feel that only butter can impart. However, if you need to seriously cut your fat intake, substitute nonfat milk and a plant sterol spread for the butter.

Peppermint Candy Fudge

Makes 16 servings

Prep time: 5 minutes

Cook time: 2 minutes

Each serving has:

102.5 calories

2.2 g. protein

16.75 g. carbohydrate

1.62 g. total fat

1.01 g. saturated fat

6.28 mg. cholesterol

80.32 mg. sodium

0.09 g. fiber

8 oz. nonfat cream cheese

1 cup sugar substitute, such as Splenda White Sugar Blend

1 TB. cocoa powder

$^1/_4$ cup heavy cream

$^1/_4$ tsp. peppermint extract

Nonstick cooking spray, butter flavored

12 pieces peppermint candy, crushed

1. Melt cream cheese in microwave oven on high for one minute. Stir. Heat in additional 15-second intervals to prevent burning until smooth and easy to stir.

2. Combine sugar, cocoa, cream, and peppermint extract together and blend. Pour into a butter-sprayed 13×9-inch pan. Top with crushed peppermint pieces, and refrigerate for four hours.

Food for Thought _____

This recipe is a good example of how to control the fat in a recipe. Start with nonfat products; then add back a specific amount of fat, such as the heavy cream to improve both mouth feel and texture. This fudge will be soft in texture but oh … so yummy!

Apple Date Pecan Oat Bars

2 cups apples, unpeeled and chopped

2 TB. sugar substitute, such as Splenda White Sugar Blend

2 TB. lemon juice

2 TB. water

2 cups dates, chopped

$^1/_2$ cup butter

$^1/_2$ cup canned cannellini beans, drained and mashed

1 cup brown sugar substitute, such as Splenda Brown Sugar Blend

1 tsp. salt substitute, such as Morton's

$2^1/_2$ cups rolled oats

$^1/_2$ cup pecan pieces

$1^1/_2$ tsp. ground cinnamon

Nonstick cooking spray

Makes 36 servings
Prep time: 10 minutes
Cook time: 1 hour
Each serving has:
141.7 calories
2.05 g. protein
23.01 g. carbohydrate
4.66 g. total fat
1.72 g. saturated fat
6.9 mg. cholesterol
1.13 mg. sodium
2.43 g. fiber

1. In a heavy saucepan, combine apples, sugar, lemon juice, and water, and simmer mixture, covered, stirring occasionally until apples are tender, about 5 to 10 minutes. Add dates, and simmer mixture, uncovered, stirring it and mashing dates, for 3 to 5 minutes. Mixture should be an almost smooth paste. Let purée cool.

2. In a bowl, combine butter, beans, sugar, salt, oats, pecans, and cinnamon, and blend. Press half mixture evenly into a 13×9-inch baking pan lightly sprayed with cooking spray. Spread purée over it, and crumble remaining oatmeal mixture over purée, pressing it lightly to form an even layer.

3. Bake at 375°F oven for 35 to 40 minutes or until just golden.

4. Cool completely in the pan before cutting.

Nutri Notes

Dates contain 70 percent sugar and are referenced more than 60 times in the Old Testament. California produces 52 million pounds of dates a year, which accounts for 99.5 percent of all dates grown in the United States.

Cranberry Orange Cookies

Makes 24 servings
Prep time: 5 minutes
Cook time: 10 minutes
Each serving has:
68.61 calories
1.36 g. protein
9.19 g. carbohydrate
3.03 g. total fat
0.82 g. saturated fat
10.38 mg. cholesterol
15.93 mg. sodium
0.93 g. fiber

¹/₄ stick butter

1 medium egg

3 TB. orange juice

³/₄ cup whole-wheat flour

¹/₄ cup rolled oats

¹/₃ cup sugar substitute, such as Splenda White Sugar Blend

¹/₄ tsp. baking soda

¹/₈ tsp. cream of tartar

¹/₈ tsp. salt substitute, such as Morton's

1 tsp. orange zest

¹/₂ cup dried cranberries

¹/₂ cup walnuts, chopped

1. Preheat oven to 375°F.

2. In a medium bowl, beat together butter, egg, and orange juice.

3. In a separate bowl, combine flour, oats, sugar, baking soda, cream of tartar, salt, and orange zest. Blend into butter mixture. Add cranberries and walnuts.

4. Drop by teaspoons onto an ungreased cookie sheet lined with parchment. Bake for 10 minutes or until bottoms are lightly browned. Remove to a wire rack to cool.

Almond Chocolate Pudding

Makes 4 servings
Prep time: 5 minutes
Cook time: 7 minutes
Each serving has:
190.3 calories
8.25 g. protein
25.92 g. carbohydrate
6.09 g. total fat
0.8 g. saturated fat
5.68 mg. cholesterol
84.17 mg. sodium
3.56 g. fiber

¹/₂ cup cocoa powder

¹/₃ cup sugar substitute, such as Splenda White Sugar Blend

3 TB. cornstarch

¹/₄ tsp. salt substitute, such as Morton's

2 cups nonfat milk

¹/₄ cup milk chocolate pieces

1 tsp. almond extract

1. Combine cocoa powder, sugar, cornstarch, and salt in a saucepan over medium heat. Add milk and chocolate pieces, and bring to a boil. Lower heat to medium, then stir constantly until mixture is well blended and becomes thickened.

2. Remove from the heat and stir in almond extract. Divide into serving dishes, cover and chill.

Fudge Brownies

$^1/_4$ cup semisweet chocolate chips

$1^1/_2$ cups flour

$^1/_2$ cup cocoa powder

1 tsp. baking powder

$^1/_2$ tsp. salt substitute, such as Morton's

$1^1/_3$ cups sugar substitute, such as Splenda White Sugar Blend

3 TB. butter

3 TB. cannellini beans

$^1/_2$ tsp. bourbon extract

2 large eggs

Nonstick cooking spray

Makes 20 servings
Prep time: 10 minutes
Cook time: 30 minutes
Each serving has:
142.2 calories
2.39 g. protein
23.06 g. carbohydrate
3.16 g. total fat
1.74 g. saturated fat
26.29 mg. cholesterol
32.71 mg. sodium
1.12 g. fiber

1. Preheat oven to 350°F.

2. Melt chocolate chips in the microwave on defrost for 4 minutes. Stir and reheat in 20-second intervals until melted.

3. In a bowl, combine flour, cocoa powder, baking powder, and salt, and stir with a whisk.

4. Combine sugar, butter, and beans in a large mixing bowl. Beat on medium speed until mixed. Add bourbon extract and eggs, one at a time. Add flour mixture to sugar mixture, and beat at low speed until combined.

5. Spray a 9×9-inch baking pan with butter spray, and spread batter evenly in the pan. Bake for 25 to 30 minutes or until a toothpick inserted in middle comes out clean. Cool in pan on a wire rack. Slice when cool.

Food for Thought

Here again is a great recipe adapted to contain less fat and salt than the standard recipe. Portion control is again important, as brownies are really a high-calorie food but well worth it!

Snickering Doodles Cookies

Makes 4 servings
Prep time: 10 minutes
Cook time: 8 minutes
Each serving has:
77.35 calories
1.2 g. protein
11.94 g. carbohydrate
2.23 g. total fat
1.27 g. saturated fat
12.97 mg. cholesterol
29.37 mg. sodium
0.91 g. fiber

$^1/_2$ cup butter

$^1/_2$ cup applesauce

$1^1/_2$ cup sugar substitute, such as Splenda White Sugar Blend

1 tsp. vanilla extract

2 medium eggs

2 3/4 cup whole-wheat flour

2 tsp. cream of tartar

1 tsp. baking soda

$^1/_2$ tsp. salt substitute, such as Morton's

2 TB. Splenda white sugar mix substitute

$1^1/_2$ tsp. ground cinnamon

1. Preheat oven to 400°F.

2. In a large bowl, combine butter, applesauce, sugar, and vanilla extract. Beat in eggs.

3. In another bowl, sift together flour, cream of tartar, baking soda, and salt. Blend into egg mixture in 2 batches. Mix well.

4. Form balls the size of walnut shells, and roll in remaining mixture of sugar substitute and cinnamon. Place on a cookie sheet and bake for 8 minutes or until lightly brown. Cool on wire rack.

Apricot Ravioli with Honey Yogurt

4 cups apricots, chopped

3 TB. honey

$^1/_2$ tsp. ground cinnamon

$^1/_8$ tsp. ground ginger

$1^1/_2$ TB. butter

1 package won ton wrappers, $3^1/_2$-inch square

Nonstick cooking spray, butter flavor

$^1/_2$ cup honey

1 tsp. lemon zest

$^1/_2$ tsp. fresh thyme

Makes 10 servings
Prep time: 15 minutes
Cook time: 45 minutes
Each serving has:
252.2 calories
4.97 g. protein
55.08 g. carbohydrate
1.98 g. total fat
1.09 g. saturated fat
8.66 mg. cholesterol
145.9 mg. sodium
2.45 g. fiber

1. Combine apricots, honey, cinnamon, and ginger in a large saucepan and bring to a boil over medium heat. Reduce heat and simmer for 30 minutes, stirring frequently. Remove from heat and cool. Stir in butter. Cool completely. Recipe can be made ahead to this step.

2. Taking one small individual won ton wrapper, moisten edges with water, and place 1 tablespoon apricot sauce in the middle. Place another won ton wrapper over top, and seal edges. Place on a large baking sheet sprayed with butter cooking spray. Repeat with remaining wrappers and mixture.

3. Bake at 400°F for 15 minutes or until golden.

4. In a small saucepan, warm remaining honey, lemon zest, and thyme. Place 3 ravioli on a plate and drizzle with honey herb mixture. Serve immediately.

Auntie Em's Comforting Rice Pudding

Makes 8 servings
Prep time: 5 minutes
Cook time: 40 minutes
Each serving has:
158.3 calories
7.55 g. protein
31.24 g. carbohydrate
0.75 g. total fat
0.26 g. saturated fat
2.8 mg. cholesterol
95.77 mg. sodium
0.89 g. fiber

$^1/_2$ cup long grain white rice

$^1/_2$ cup water

4 cups nonfat milk

$^1/_3$ cup nonfat dry milk

$^1/_4$ tsp. ground cardamom

1 stick cinnamon

$^1/_2$ cup sugar substitute, such as Splenda White Sugar Blend

1 cup raisins

$^1/_4$ cup egg substitute

$^1/_2$ tsp. almond extract

$^1/_2$ tsp. vanilla extract

1. Combine rice and water in a 4-quart saucepan. Bring to a simmer over medium heat and cover. Cook over low heat until water is absorbed, about 5 minutes.

2. Add milk, dry milk, and cardamom to rice, stirring until blended. Add cinnamon stick, and bring mixture to a boil. Reduce heat to simmer, cover and cook for 20 minutes. Stir in sugar and raisins, and cook for 10 minutes more or until rice is tender and creamy.

3. Remove from the heat. Place 2 tablespoons hot pudding into a small bowl and add egg substitute. Mix this together; then add it back to rice mixture in the pan. Return the pan to low heat, stirring constantly for 2 minutes or until thickened. Remove from the heat, and stir in the extracts. Spoon into a bowl, and let cool to room temperature before chilling.

Chili Coffee Mocha Custard

1 cup nonfat evaporated milk

3 TB. instant coffee powder

$^1/_2$ cup sugar substitute, such as Splenda White Sugar Blend

1 cup nonfat milk

$^3/_4$ cup egg substitute

2 tsp. walnut extract

$^1/_4$ tsp. almond extract

2 TB. cocoa powder

$^1/_2$ tsp. chili powder

Makes 6 servings
Prep time: 5 minutes
Cook time: 20 minutes
Each serving has:
85.54 calories
8.95 g. protein
3.85 g. carbohydrate
1.53 g. total fat
0.37 g. saturated fat
2.72 mg. cholesterol
127 mg. sodium
0.57 g. fiber

1. Heat oven to 325°F.

2. Heat evaporated milk and instant coffee in a small saucepan over medium heat. Stir to dissolve coffee. Add sugar, nonfat milk, egg substitute, extracts, cocoa, and chili powder and stir to blend. Remove from the heat.

3. Divide custard into six 6-ounce baking dishes. Put the baking dishes in a larger baking dish and add water halfway up the sides.

4. Bake until custard is set, about 15 minutes. Remove from water bath and cool. Chill until serving.

Food for Thought

I prefer to use an instant Italian espresso coffee powder for a strong taste in this recipe. The chili powder adds an unexpected kick, but don't overdo it, or you'll miss out on the subtleties of combining chocolate and chili.

Coconut Custard Baked in Acorn Squash

Makes 4 servings
Prep time: 15 minutes
Cook time: 1 hour 30 minutes
Each serving has:
164 calories
5.59 g. protein
25.49 g. carbohydrate
5.76 g. total fat
3.14 g. saturated fat
102 mg. cholesterol
48.78 mg. sodium
3.4 g. fiber

2 lbs. acorn squash (about 4 small)

³/₄ cup canned coconut milk

2 medium eggs

¹/₃ cup brown sugar substitute, such as Splenda Brown Sugar Blend

1 tsp. anise seed

1. Preheat oven to 350°F.

2. Cut ¹/₄ of stem end all around squash or baby pumpkins to make a lid. Scoop out seeds and flesh until squash holds ¹/₃ cup liquid.

3. In a rimmed baking pan, set squash with lids on top next to each other and fill the pan with ¹/₂-inch water. Bake for 15 minutes uncovered.

4. Whisk together coconut milk, eggs, and sugar. Fill squash cups with liquid and set lids back on. Bake until squash is soft and custard filling is firm when jiggled (lift lids off to check), about 1 to 1¹/₂ hours depending on thickness of squash.

5. Sprinkle custard with anise seeds and serve warm.

Variation: Look for pumpkin pie mini pumpkins, or use carnival squash for variety. Be sure to notch the top so you can fit it back on easily in the right direction.

Earl Grey Orange Granita with Mint

2 cups water

1 cup orange juice

¹/₄ cup fresh mint leaves, crushed

3 bags Earl Grey tea blend

¹/₂ cup sugar substitute, such as Splenda White Sugar Blend

Makes 5 servings
Prep time: 5 minutes
Cook time: 5 minutes
Each serving has:
23.22 calories
0.4 g. protein
5.35 g. carbohydrate
0.11 g. total fat
0.02 g. saturated fat
0 mg. cholesterol
3.74 mg. sodium
0.2 g. fiber

1. Bring water to a boil in a saucepan. Add juice, mint leaves, and *Earl Grey tea* bags, and let stand for 5 minutes. Discard tea bags, and strain mint leaves. Add sugar until dissolved. Cool slightly.

2. Pour cooled mixture in an 11×7-inch baking dish. Cover and freeze for 4 hours. Pulse in a food processor until smooth. Return to the freezer for 2 more hours or until firm. Use a fork to scrape up flakes before serving in tall glasses. Garnish with additional mint leaves as desired.

Nutri Speak

Earl Grey tea relies upon bergamot oil for its unique flavoring. Earl Grey tea was named for the second Earl who served as Prime Minister. The family seat is Chillingham Castle in Northumberland, England.

Miami Citrus Soufflé

Makes 4 servings
Prep time: 20 minutes
Cook time: 45 minutes
Each serving has:
164.3 calories
4.22 g. protein
29.28 g. carbohydrate
0.98 g. total fat
0.58 g. saturated fat
3.55 mg. cholesterol
54.81 mg. sodium
0.29 g. fiber

Food for Thought

Get inventive with this recipe, and try some exotic juices, such as guava, pomegranate, or passion fruit. You'll be basking in the tropics without leaving home.

Nonstick cooking spray, butter flavor

1 TB. Splenda white sugar mix substitute

3 TB. flour

3/4 cup 2% milk

1/4 cup sugar substitute, such as Splenda White Sugar Blend

1 tsp. orange zest

1 tsp. lemon zest

1 tsp. lime zest

1 TB. lemon juice

1 TB. orange juice

1/2 tsp. fresh lime juice

5 medium egg whites

1/4 tsp. cream of tartar

1/8 tsp. salt substitute, such as Morton's

2 TB. sugar substitute, such as Splenda White Sugar Blend

1. Preheat oven to 375°F.

2. Coat a 1 1/2-quart soufflé dish with buttered cooking spray. Sprinkle with 1 tablespoon sugar substitute, turning the dish to cover all sides.

3. Place flour in a small saucepan. Gradually add milk, and stir with a whisk until blended. Add 1/4 cup sugar and lemon, orange, and lime zest. Bring to a boil over medium heat, then reduce heat to low. Cook 1 minute or until thick, stirring constantly. Stir in lemon, orange, and lime juices.

4. In a mixer, beat egg whites, cream of tartar, and salt at high speed until stiff peaks form. Gently fold 1/4 of egg white mixture into citrus mixture, and then gently fold in remaining egg white mixture. Spoon into the prepared soufflé dish.

5. Place soufflé dish in a 9-inch square baking pan. Add hot water to the pan to a depth of 1 inch. Bake at 375°F until puffy, about 35 minutes. Serve immediately.

Never Enough Fudge Pops

14 oz. sweetened condensed milk

1 cup sugar substitute, such as Splenda White Sugar Blend

1/2 cup cocoa powder

2 1/2 cups nonfat milk

1 tsp. vanilla extract

12 paper cups

12 popsicle sticks

Makes 12 servings
Prep time: 5 minutes
Cook time: 5 minutes
Each serving has:
218.8 calories
5.21 g. protein
38.37 g. carbohydrate
3.3 g. total fat
2.08 g. saturated fat
12.13 mg. cholesterol
70.08 mg. sodium
1.03 g. fiber

1. In a heavy saucepan, combine milk, 1/2 cup sugar, and cocoa; stir until smooth. Bring to a boil over medium-low heat and stir for 1 minute. Whisk in milk until cocoa and sugar are dissolved. Remove from the heat; stir in remaining sugar and vanilla.

2. Pour into cups. Cover each cup with heavy-duty foil, then insert sticks through the foil. Place in a 13×9-inch pan, and freeze until firm, about 5 hours. Remove the foil and cups before serving.

Food for Thought _____

You can change the sweetness in this dish by decreasing the sugar substitute. Studies show we have adapted our taste buds to a high sugary level which may trick our bodies into failing to count calories properly.

Poached Pears with Blackberry Balsamic Sauce

Makes 4 servings
Prep time: 5 minutes
Cook time: 12 minutes
Each serving has:
98.67 calories
0.88 g. protein
25.2 g. carbohydrate
0.62 g. total fat
0.03 g. saturated fat
0 mg. cholesterol
0.28 mg. sodium
5.85 g. fiber

2 cups frozen blackberries

1 TB. balsamic vinegar

2 tsp. honey

$^1/_4$ tsp. black pepper, finely cracked or ground

2 cups Bartlett pears, peeled

1 TB. lemon juice

1. Place blackberries in a 3-quart dish; cover and microwave on high for 3 minutes or until heated through. Press through a fine sieve over a small bowl, reserving liquid. Discard seeds and solids. Add vinegar, honey, and pepper to reserved liquid.

2. Rub peeled pears with lemon juice, and place in a glass dish. Drizzle with blackberry sauce, and cover with a lid. Microwave on high for 8 minutes or until pears are tender, pouring sauce over pears at 4 minutes.

Sound of Music Blueberry Cream

Makes 4 servings
Prep time: 5 minutes
Cook time: 5 minutes
Each serving has:
97.02 calories
4.78 g. protein
13.32 g. carbohydrate
3.36 g. total fat
0.35 g. saturated fat
1.65 mg. cholesterol
52.96 mg. sodium
2.06 g. fiber

1 TB. unflavored gelatin

2 TB. cold water

$1^1/_2$ cup nonfat milk

$^1/_4$ tsp. salt substitute, such as Morton's

$^1/_4$ cup sugar substitute, such as Splenda White Sugar Blend

$^1/_4$ tsp. mint extract

$^1/_4$ tsp. strawberry extract

$^1/_2$ pint blueberries

$^1/_4$ cup almond slices

1. Sprinkle gelatin over cold water to soften. Bring milk to a low simmer in a small saucepan. Stir in salt and sugar. Add mint and strawberry extract.

2. Pour mixture into a bowl, and chill until slightly thickened. Spoon into stemmed serving glasses, and chill until set. Top with blueberries and almond slices.

Roasted Summer Fruit

$^1/_2$ lb. peaches

$^1/_2$ lb. plums

$^1/_2$ lb. nectarines

2 TB. butter

1 tsp. sugar substitute, such as Splenda White Sugar Blend

1 TB. fresh lime juice

1 TB. mint leaves

Makes 4 servings
Prep time: 10 minutes
Cook time: 20 minutes
Each serving has:
135.3 calories
1.45 g. protein
20.7 g. carbohydrate
6.42 g. total fat
3.64 g. saturated fat
15.53 mg. cholesterol
0.82 mg. sodium
2.91 g. fiber

1. Preheat oven to 400°F.

2. Prick skins of peaches, plums, and nectarines, half them, and remove pits. Cut into quarters. Toss into a roasting pan with butter, sugar, lime juice, and mint. Cook for 20 minutes until fork-tender.

Food for Thought

Grilled fruits, rather than oven baked, work especially well for this recipe. Don't set them directly over the flame, but rather to the side. Turn them at angles to get a nice cross-hatch mark, and enjoy!

Salzburger Nockerl

Makes 6 servings

Prep time: 10 minutes
Cook time: 12 minutes

Each serving has:

54.25 calories

3.13 g. protein

5.4 g. carbohydrate

1.48 g. total fat

0.46 g. saturated fat

62.33 mg. cholesterol

36.32 mg. sodium

0.05 g. fiber

Nonstick cooking spray

2 small eggs

2 egg whites

1 TB. flour

2 TB. sugar substitute, such as Splenda White Sugar Blend

1 tsp. vanilla

$^1/_2$ tsp. lemon zest

2 TB. powdered sugar substitute, made with Splenda Granular

1. Preheat the oven to 400°F. Spray an oval baking dish with cooking spray that will do double duty as your serving dish.

2. In a medium-size mixing bowl, break up egg yolks with a fork, and stir in vanilla and lemon peel. Sprinkle flour over yolk mixture.

3. In another bowl, use an electric mixer to beat egg whites with a pinch of salt until they cling to the beater, a soft peak stage. Add sugar and beat until whites form stiff, unwavering peaks. With a rubber spatula, stir an overflowing tablespoon of whites into yolk-flour mixture; then reverse the process and fold yolk mixture into rest of egg whites, using an over-under cutting motion instead of a mixing motion. Don't overfold.

4. Using the rubber spatula, make three mounds of mixture in the dish.

5. Bake the soufflé in the middle of the oven 10 to 12 minutes or until it is lightly brown on the outside but still soft on the inside. Sprinkle with confectioners' sugar, and serve immediately.

> **Food for Thought**
> This recipe is also known as Heavenly Clouds, and that's how it will look in your serving dish. You can drizzle honey or reduced fruit juice over it for a different flavor.

Appendix A

Glossary

appetizer   The term comes from the French word for "aperitif," a traditional glass of wine or cocktail to whet the appetite.

Arborio rice   An Italian short grain rice that releases starch as it cooks. This makes the rice very creamy. It is traditionally used in the making of risotto.

beard   This is a tuft of strong filaments by which a mussel attaches itself to a surface. To remove it, pull tightly with a small towel holding the mussel.

blanch   A cooking process in which food is rapidly heated, then cooled. This allows the food to firm up and makes both the color and the flavor more pronounced.

Canadian bacon   A very lean eye of loin pork, closer to ham than bacon. It is precooked and comes in cylindrical chunks.

capers   Unopened flower buds from the caper bush. They are often used in Mediterranean cuisine. To achieve their piquant flavor, capers must be pickled or treated with brine, which makes them salty. To reduce the saltiness, rinse before using.

cocoa powder   There are two types of cocoa powder: Regular (American) and Dutch (called European process). The Dutch version has been treated with alkali, such as baking soda, to neutralize its acidity. Both versions of cocoa powder have much less fat and fewer calories than baking chocolate because the cocoa butter has been removed.

cotija cheese A sharp, crumbly Mexican goat cheese known as the "Parmesan of Mexico." You can substitute any sharp, firm feta cheese for it in any recipe.

cottage cheese Also known as pot cheese or farmer's cheese. It comes in small, medium, or large curds. It is drained but not pressed, so some whey remains. Little Miss Muffet ate cottage cheese when sitting on her tuffet.

curry paste A combination of chilies, peeled garlic, lemon grass, fresh turmeric, sea salt, and shrimp paste pounded in a mortar with a pestle.

Earl Grey tea Relies upon bergamot oil for its unique flavoring. Earl Grey tea was named for the second Earl who served as Prime Minister. The family seat is Chillingham Castle in Northumberland, England.

en papillote Means to cook in a paper parcel to retain moisture, flavor, and aroma. Today's cook can also use aluminum foil, but the metal may react with acids to change the taste.

fish sauce An extract of scads, herrings, sardines, mackerels, silversides, and slipmouth fish, fermented in the sun. It is similar to Worcestershire sauce, which is made from anchovies. You can use them interchangeably or substitute soy sauce if fish sauce is unavailable in the Asian food section of your market.

flank steak A triangular-shaped muscle from the underside or flank of beef. It should be cut across the grain, or horizontally, as thick as possible to remain tender.

herbs de Provence A mixture of lavender, basil, fennel seed, sage, rosemary, thyme, marjoram, and summer savory herbs. The mixture is traditionally packed in tiny clay pots. It can be found in grocery stores or ordered from a specialty company.

Milanese Means in the style of Milan. Typically it's a dish dipped in egg and coated with bread crumbs, then fried in butter.

navy beans Also known as Yankee beans, these are white, round beans used by the Navy since the mid-1800s. They are popular in pork and bean recipes.

oat bran A plant food high in soluble fiber. It also goes by Avena farina, common groats, haws, and oatmeal.

Old Bay Seasoning A mixture of celery, bay leaf, mustard seed, red pepper, and ginger, and can be found in the grocery store. It was invented by Gustav Brunn in the 1940s to season crab and shrimp.

panko flakes Japanese bread crumbs, which make a light, crispy coating when cooked in butter or oil. You can find them in the Asian section of your supermarket.

phyllo   Means "leaf" in Greek, but the dough was created in Istanbul, Turkey, during the Ottoman Empire. Today phyllo dough is found in the freezer section of your grocery store. Just remember to defrost it for 24 hours before using or you'll end up with broken sheets.

plate   To arrange one serving of food on a dish.

rigatoni   Italian for "large groove." Pasta made in a rigatoni style has ridges so it can grab on to sauce better than a smooth noodle.

rolled oats   These are also known as steel cut oats. They are sold as Irish oatmeal and contain 50% more protein than bulgur wheat and twice as much as brown rice. Steel cut or rolled oats have a high soluble-fiber content, which can lower cholesterol.

scallopine   In Italian means to form a shell or scallop shape. It occurs when meat is pounded very thin into a rounded shape like a sea scallop shell.

sear   Means to quickly char, burn, or scorch the surface with a hot instrument.

Seviche   Also know as Ceviche, is a fish dish marinated in citrus juice. The acids "cook" the fish to a delicate tenderness, turning the fish opaque. Pompano, snapper, and sole are the fish most often selected for this style of cooking.

skirt steak   A piece of meat cut from the diaphragm of the cow. It freezes well and can be cut horizontally before grilling but should not be overcooked.

tahini   A thick ground paste made from sesame seeds. It is used to flavor mashed beans or hummus. The name is derived from the Turkish word for sesame flour or oil (tahin) and the Arabic word for grind (tahana).

tangerine   A widely cultivated member of the mandarin orange family, having deep orange fruit that is easily separated into segments. It originated in Tangier, Morroco. Today, mandarin oranges and tangerines are different varieties, though they are used interchangeably in cooking.

tortilla   A Mexican unleavened wheat flour or corn masa bread. However, in Spain, tortilla means a potato dish cooked with peppers, olives, and eggs. A whole-wheat tortilla provides 8 grams of fiber, 2 grams of fat, and 11 grams carbohydrates, resulting in a net carb count of 3 grams.

wheat germ   The vitamin-rich seedling plant within the wheat grain. It is removed during processing of cereals, taking the fiber, fats, minerals, and protein with it. It is commonly sold toasted.

whole grains   Contain all the essential parts and naturally occurring nutrients of the entire grain seed. If they are processed, the grain must provide the same rich nutrient balance as found in the whole grain.

Wondra flour   This flour was introduced by General Mills in 1963. It was an all-purpose flour in a revolutionary new granular form. It was made by a process of agglomeration of small flour particles to make a more uniform instantized product. There were no chemical additions in the processing and the baking characteristics of all-purpose flour were not changed. This made it ideal for gravies as lumps were eliminated.

Conversion Tables

U.S. to Metric Conversion Charts

When I lived in England, I had to adapt to the metric system for measuring, so here are some shortcuts to converting American measurements to British standards. It's really not hard.

Converting Oven Temperatures

Fahrenheit	Centigrade	Gas Mark	Heat
225	110	$^1/_4$	Very Cool
250	130	$^1/_2$	
275	140	1	Cool
300	150	2	
325	170	3	Moderate
350	180	4	
375	190	5	Moderately Hot
400	200	6	
425	220	7	Hot
450	230	8	
475	240	9	Very Hot

Converting Baking Pan Sizes

American	Metric
11-inch × 7-inch	28×18×4
13-inch × 9-inch	30×20×3
2-quart	30×20×3
9-inch pie pan	22×4 cm pie pan
7-inch or 8-inch springform	18 or 20 cm springform pan
9-inch × 5-inch × 3-inch loaf pan	23×13×7 cm loaf pan
8-inch round cake pan	20×4 cm cake pan
9-inch round cake pan	23×3.5 cm cake pan
2-quart casserole	2-liter casserole

Converting Lengths

Inches (in)	Millimetres (mm)	Centimetres (cm)
$\frac{1}{8}$ in	3 mm	n/a
$\frac{1}{4}$ in	6.25 mm	n/a
$\frac{1}{2}$ in	12.5 mm	n/a
1 in	25 mm	2.5 cm
2 in	50 mm	5 cm
3 in	75 mm	7.5 cm
4 in	100 mm	10 cm
6 in	150 mm	15 cm
8 in	200 mm	20 cm
10 in	250 mm	25 cm
12 in	300 mm	30 cm

Converting Ounces to Grams

Ounces	Grams
1 oz.	30 g.
2 oz.	60 g.
3 oz.	85 g.
4 oz.	115 g.
5 oz.	140 g.
6 oz.	180 g.
7 oz.	200 g.
8 oz.	225 g.
9 oz.	250 g.
10 oz.	285 g.
11 oz.	300 g.
12 oz.	340 g.
13 oz.	370 g.
14 oz.	400 g.
15 oz.	425 g.
16 oz.	450 g.

Convert U.S. Capacity to Metric

U.S.	METRIC
$1/5$ teaspoon	1 ml
1 teaspoon	5 ml
1 tablespoon	15 ml
1 fluid ounce	30 ml
3.4 fluid ounces	100 ml
1 cup	240 ml
34 fluid ounces	1 liter
4.2 cups	1 liter
2.1 pints	1 liter
1.06 quarts	1 liter
.26 gallons	1 liter

Converting Pounds to Grams and Kilograms

Pounds	Grams; Kilograms
1 lb.	450 g.
1$^1/_2$ lb.	675 g.
2 lb.	900 g.
2$^1/_2$ lb.	1,125 g.; 1$^1/_4$ kg.
3 lb.	1,350 g.
3$^1/_2$ lb.	1,500 g.; 1$^1/_2$ kg.
4 lb.	1,800 g.
4$^1/_2$ lb.	2k g.
5 lb.	2$^1/_4$ kg.
5$^1/_2$ lb.	2$^1/_2$ kg.
6 lb.	2$^3/_4$ kg.
6$^1/_2$ lb.	3 kg.
7 lb.	3$^1/_4$ kg.
7$^1/_2$ lb.	3$^1/_2$ kg.
8 lb.	3$^3/_4$ kg.

Nutritional Health Information Resources

Nutritional Organizations

American Dietetic Association
216 W. Jackson Blvd.
Chicago, IL 60606-6995
312-899-0040
Consumer Nutrition Hotline
1-800-366-1655
www.eatright.org

American Cancer Society
1599 Clifton Rd. NE
Atlanta, GA 30329
1-800-227-2345
www.cancer.org

American Heart Association
National Center
7272 Greenville Ave.
Dallas, TX 75231
1-800-242-8721
www.americanheart.org

American Diabetes Association
Customer Service
1701 N. Beauregard St.
Alexandria, VA 22311
1-800-342-2383
www.diabetes.org

American College of Sports Medicine
P.O. Box 1440
Indianapolis, IN 46206-1440
317-637-9200
www.acsm.org

Vegetarian Resource Group
P.O. Box 1463
Baltimore, MD 21203
410-366-8343
www.vrg.org

Food and Drug Administration Center for Food Safety and Applied Nutrition
5100 Paint Branch Parkway
College Park, MD 20740-3835
1-888-463-5332
www.cfsan.fda.gov

Nutritional Websites

Total Nutrition Cooking
Nutritional advice, products, and recipes
Larrian Gillespie
Healthy Life Publications
264 S. La Cienega Blvd. #1233
Beverly Hills, CA 90211
1-800-554-3335
www.totalnutritioncooking.com

Joy Bauer Nutrition
Individual Nutrition Counseling
116 East 63rd St.
New York, NY 10021
212-759-6999
www.joyofnutrition.com

Gourmet Sleuth
Cooking Conversions Calculator
www.gourmetsleuth.com/cookingconversions.asp

Calorie-Count
Free calorie counters for common foods and exercise
www.calorie-count.com/calories

The Glycemic Index
Database on the Glycemic Index and Glycemic Load of Foods
www.glycemicindex.com

Nutritional Products

Now You're Cooking Nutritional Recipe Software
Loginetics, Inc.
P.O. Box 18274
Knoxville, TN 37928
865-688-8401
www.ffts.com

Flavors2Go
Liquid flavors for cooking
PAES Corporation
1779 North Congress Ave. #345
Boynton Beach, FL 33426
www.flavor2go.com

Kalustyan
Exotic spices
123 Lexington Ave.
New York, NY 10016
212-685-3451
www.kalustyan.com

Sultan's Delight
Fine Mediterranean and Middle Eastern Foods
P.O. Box 090302
Brooklyn, NY 11209
1-800-852-5046
www.sultansdelight.com

La Tienda
Best of Spain food products such as smoky paprika
3601 La Grange Parkway
Toano, VA 23168
888-472-1022
www.tienda.com

The Baker's Catalogue
Great source for sea salts, baking products
58 Billings Farm Road
White River Junction, VT 05001
1-800-343-3002
www.kingarthurflour.com or http://shop.bakerscatalogue.com

Index